THE ARMY OF TRANSYLVANIA 1613-1690

War and military organization from the 'golden age' of the Principality to the Habsburg conquest

Florin Nicolae Ardelean

'This is the Century of the Soldier', Fulvio Testi, Poet, 1641

Helion & Company Limited
Unit 8 Amherst Business Centre
Budbrooke Road
Warwick
CV34 5WE
England
Tel. 01926 499 619
Email: info@helion.co.uk
Website: www.helion.co.uk
Twitter: @helionbooks
Visit our blog http://blog.helion.co.uk/

Published by Helion & Company 2024
Designed and typeset by Mary Woolley, Battlefield Design (www.battlefield-design.co.uk)
Cover designed by Paul Hewitt, Battlefield Design (www.battlefield-design.co.uk)

Text © Florin Nicolae Ardelean 2024
Maps by George Anderson © Helion and Company 2024
Illustrations as individually credited © Helion & Company 2024
Colour artwork drawn by Catalin Draghici © Helion & Company 2024

Every reasonable effort has been made to trace copyright holders and to obtain their permission for the use of copyright material. The author and publisher apologize for any errors or omissions in this work and would be grateful if notified of any corrections that should be incorporated in future reprints or editions of this book.

ISBN 978-1-804513-49-1

British Library Cataloguing-in-Publication Data.
A catalogue record for this book is available from the British Library.

All rights reserved. No part of this publication may be reproduced, stored in a retrieval system, or transmitted, in any form, or by any means, electronic, mechanical, photocopying, recording or otherwise, without the express written consent of Helion & Company Limited.

For details of other military history titles published by Helion & Company Limited contact the above address or visit our website: http://www.helion.co.uk.

We always welcome receiving book proposals from prospective authors.

Contents

Introduction		v
Note on Personal and Place Names		vii
1	The Transylvanian Principality and its Rulers in the Seventeenth Century	9
2	The Organisation of the Transylvanian Army	33
3	Fortifications, Artillery and Garrisons	74
4	Military Campaigns, Battles and Sieges	97
Conclusion		136
Colour Plate Commentaries		139
Bibliography		143

Introduction

The Principality of Transylvania was an ephemeral early modern state, situated in East-Central Europe, in a frontier area that divided the Ottoman Empire from the territories ruled by the Habsburgs. The transition towards an autonomous principality was a gradual process, unfolded in the aftermath of the Ottoman conquest of Buda (1541) which led to the division of the kingdom of Hungary.[1]

In the seventeenth century, Transylvania was already a distinct and well-established entity in East-Central Europe. The prince was officially a vassal of the Ottoman Sultan, but he enjoyed a high degree of autonomy in matters of domestic governance. He was elected by the estates (political factions) and confirmed by the sultan. Although he enjoyed a high degree of authority, the prince shared the burden of leading the country with a Diet (assembly of the estates) and a Council.

Transylvania had a very particular political system based on the three estates: the nobility, the Székley and the Saxons. Nobles represented the social elite of the principality and held the greatest political influence in the Diet. The Székley and Saxons were descendants of settlers brought in by the kings of Hungary in Transylvania to defend its borders. They were able to maintain some of their medieval privileges (especially the Saxons) and were represented as distinct entities within the political framework of the principality. The ethnic composition of Transylvania was much more diverse but most groups, including a very large Romanian community, were not recognised politically and did not take part in the administration of the country.

As in any other early modern states, the army was a fundamental institution in Transylvania. Military organisation was greatly influenced by the particular social structure of the principality. Those who performed military service had varied social backgrounds, from nobles to peasants, and whole communities enjoyed a privileged status because of their military obligations.

---

1 The first seven decades of the Transylvanian Principality, with a special emphasis on its wars and military organisation represented the topic of my previous book: Florin Nicolae Ardelean, *On the Borderlands of Great Empires: Transylvanian Armies (1541–1613)* (Warwick: Helion & Company, 2022).

THE ARMY OF TRANSYLVANIA 1613-1690

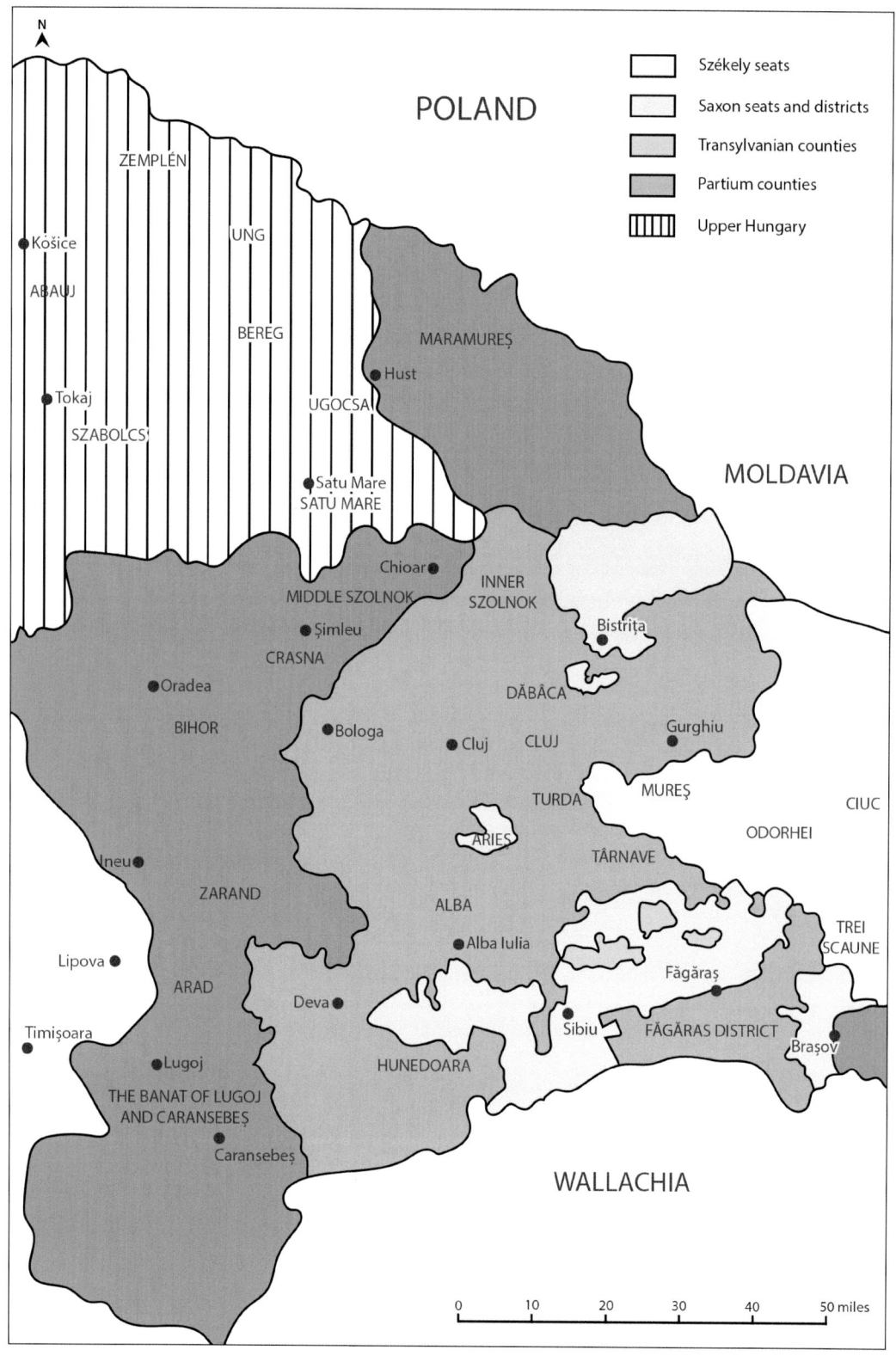

Map 1 Transylvania in the first half of the seventeenth century

Note on Personal and Place Names

Due to the complex ethnic composition of East-Central European regions, places and historical personalities are described in different languages. For the sake of readability and to avoid any confusion I have decided to use the English version for the first names of rulers and other important personalities. Most of the locations (regions, towns, and villages) mentioned in the book are situated at present in various Central and East European states like Romania, Hungary, Ukraine, Slovakia, Poland, Belarus and the Czech Republic. Therefore, I have decided to use their official modern name with one or two alternatives in other languages that were most common in those particular regions during the seventeenth century. However, in the case of locations which are mentioned very often in the text, like important Transylvanian towns and fortresses, I will give an alternate name (usually in Hungarian or German) only the first time it is mentioned and use only the modern, official name in the rest of the text. Some specific concepts and expressions are sometimes followed in brackets by their Hungarian or Latin form, as they appear in contemporary sources.

Both the author and series editor would like to acknowledge and thank Michal Paradowski for his generous help with sourcing many of the illustrations within the book.

1

The Transylvanian Principality and its Rulers in the Seventeenth Century

Gabriel Bethlen (1613–1629)

With the election of Gabriel Bethlen in 1613, Transylvania entered a new phase in its history as an autonomous state. His reign was and is still considered by many historians as the 'golden age' of the Principality of Transylvania. A descendent of an old Hungarian noble family, Bethlen of Iktar, Gabriel was born in 1580 at Ilia (Marosillye), in Hunedoara County (Hunyad vármegye). In 1594, when Transylvania joined the Habsburgs in the Long Turkish War (1591–1606), Bethlen was already a member of the court of Prince Sigismund Báthory. This terrible conflict, especially from a Transylvanian perspective, was his first experience of war. In 1595 he endured the bitter cold of the campaign in Wallachia, which was concluded with the conquest of Giurgiu fortress on the Danube. During the following year he participated in three major sieges on the Ottoman-Transylvanian borderlands: Ineu (Borosjenő), Lipova (Lippa) and Timișoara (Temesvár). He also fought in the most important pitched battles of the war like Mezőkeresztes in 1596 and Șelimbăr (Schellenberg) in 1599, where he was wounded for the first time.[1] This early experience was enough to convince him of the military might of the Turks and throughout his later career he was always careful to be, or to be perceived as, a faithful vassal of the Ottoman sultan.

    Gabriel Bethlen refused the title of prince in 1604, at which time he was exiled in the Ottoman Empire and Transylvania was under Habsburg rule. Such an appointment, in foreign lands, would have been deprived of the significance and authority conferred by the presence of the Transylvanian estates and contrary to the custom of 'free election.' Instead, he chose to support Stephen Bocskay in his anti-Habsburg rebellion and later backed

---

1   Dénes Harai, *Gabriel Bethlen: Prince de Transylvanie et roi élu de Hongrie (1580–1629)*, (Paris: L'Harmattan, 2013), pp.21–28.

THE ARMY OF TRANSYLVANIA 1613-1690

Gabriel Bethlen, Prince of Transylvania 1613–1629, *Trachten-Kabinett von Siebenburgens*, 1729. (The National Museum of Transylvanian History, Cluj-Napoca, Romania).

his claim for the Transylvanian throne. After the death of Bocskay he was held in captivity by his predecessor, Sigismund Rákóczi, during his short rule over Transylvania in 1607. When Gabriel Báthory ascended to the throne, Bethlen was released, and all his lands were returned to him. He served the last prince of the Báthory family as a diplomat and military commander until September 1612 when he was forced to flee to the Ottoman province of Timişoara, because he was suspected of treason.[2] He spent the next year (until October 1613) travelling across the Ottoman Empire. From Timişoara to Buda, Belgrade, Edirne (Adrianople) and Istanbul, Bethlen renewed his contacts with imperial dignitaries, carefully consolidating his position as the favourite candidate for the Transylvanian throne. The sultan accepted his claim and gave him an army of 80,000 men, provided by the Ottoman border commanders, Canibek Ghiray Khan of the Crimean Tatars and the rulers of Moldavia and Wallachia. Such a large army was a terrible burden for Transylvania and the southern parts of the country were devastated by uncontrolled raids and plundering. It is estimated that about 20,000 Transylvanian captives were taken by the Turks and the Tatars on this occasion.[3]

The representatives of the Nobility, Saxons and Székely, the three Transylvanian estates (*Universitas Statuum et Ordinum Trium Nationum Regni Transylvaniae*), were ready to elect their new prince and gathered to convene a Diet in the city of Cluj (Kolozsvár). Before making their choice, they wrote a letter to the Captain General of Upper Hungary, Sigismund Forgács, informing him that they no longer acknowledged Gabriel Báthory as prince and that he should not help him in any attempt to recover the Transylvanian throne.[4] The session of the Diet began on 22 October and lasted until 29 October. The official election took place on the second day and various matters of state were settled in the following days. Bethlen agreed to a set of conditions imposed by the Diet which were meant to preserve the privileges of the Transylvanian estates.[5]

---

2   Tibor Wittman, *Bethlen Gábor* (Budapest: Magyar Történelmi Társulat, 1952), pp.8–15; Harai, *Gabriel Bethlen*, pp.29–48.
3   Harai, *Gabriel Bethlen*, pp.48–53.
4   *Monumenta Comitialia Regni Transylvaniae (MCRT)*, Sándor Szilágyi (ed.), vol. VI (Budapest: Magyar Tudományos Akad. Könyvkiadó Hivatala, 1880), pp.343–346.
5   MCRT, vol. VI, pp.355–363.

The reign of Gabriel Bethlen in Transylvania began under difficult circumstances with a large foreign army in the country, restrictive conditions imposed by both the estates and the Ottoman Empire, and a deposed prince plotting to regain power with the help of the Habsburgs. Nevertheless, the situation changed radically in just a few days after the election. On 27 October 1613, Gabriel Báthory was murdered by his own soldiers in Oradea (Nagyvárad). Thus, a civil war in Transylvania was avoided and the foreign armies had no more reason to remain in the country. It remains unclear if Bethlen played any role in the assassination of his rival, but he benefited greatly from his removal from the scene.[6]

Next on his political agenda was the consolidation of his internal authority. Bethlen needed to establish good relations with all three Transylvanian estates, and among them the Saxons were most affected by the abuses of his predecessor. The representatives of the *Universitas Saxonum* demanded freedom for the Lutheran Church, the restoration of town privileges and the permanent presence of a Saxon representative in the Princely Council. Bethlen agreed to these demands, but the Saxons remained extremely cautious and distrustful of his authority.[7] Mending the relations between the monarch and his German speaking subjects was a lengthy process and some conflict persisted for many years. For example, Bethlen had a long dispute with the town of Brașov (Kronstadt) over the possession of Bran (Törzburg) fortress. In 1625, after more than a decade, the prince backed down and the fortress with its estate were returned to Saxon authority. In exchange, the magistrate of Brașov gave up certain villages which were included in the estate of Făgăraș (Fogaras), the most important fortification in southern Transylvania.[8]

The Székely had been very loyal to Gabriel Báthory, and the new prince had some difficulty in gaining their support. In order to convince them of his good will he issued a law that forbade the transformation of 'free Székely' into serfs. He also ennobled many representatives of the Székely elite, thereby creating strong personal ties with the most influential members of their community.[9]

The nobility was the most powerful political entity and had the most representatives in the Princely Council. At the beginning of Bethlen's reign five councillors were nobles, with important administrative offices in the counties, while the Székely held three positions and the Saxons only one. In the following years Bethlen increased the number of councillors and the nobility maintained a clear majority in this important central institution.

First page from the copy of the letter of Gabriel Bethlen to Polish King Sigismund III, dated 3 January 1614. Bethlen informs the king that he has taken over Transylvanian throne and that he is ready to send envoys to Poland, to discuss matters important for both Poland and Hungary (Kórnik Library)

---

6 Harai, *Gabriel Bethlen*, pp.57–61.
7 Liviu Cîmpeanu, *Universitatea Saxonă din Transilvania și districtele românești aflate sub jurisdicția ei în evul mediu și epoca modernă* (Târgu Mureș: Editura Nico, 2014), pp.152–153.
8 Cîmpeanu, *Universitatea Saxonă*, pp.168–179.
9 Judith Balogh, *A székely nemesség kialakulásának folyamata a 17. század első felében* (Kolozsvár: Az Erdélyi Múzeum-Egyesület Kiadása, 2005), pp.92–101; Harai, *Gabriel Bethlen*, pp.72–73.

The position of councillor was given to leading members of the nobility as a reward and as a means of strengthening their loyalty.[10]

In the first years of his reign, Bethlen was focused on improving relations with the Habsburgs. A first attempt was the treaty of Trnava (Nagyszombat) signed on 15 and 18 May 1615, followed by a second agreement negotiated in the same town in 1617. Mathias II recognised Bethlen as Prince of Transylvania and gave back some of the Transylvanian fortifications and towns that were occupied by Habsburg garrisons during the reign of Gabriel Báthory: Hust (Хуст), Chioar (Kővár), Baia Mare (Nagybánya) and Tășnad (Tasnád). On his part, Bethlen recognised that Transylvania was part of the 'Hungarian Crown' and promised to help Mathias against all enemies, except the Ottomans.[11]

It was not long before the sultan found out about these negotiations. He did not take any punitive measures but insisted that the Transylvanian prince should honour the promise made during his election and surrender the fortresses of Lipova and Ineu. Bethlen was careful to appease his liège lord and began preparations for the restitution of Lipova fortress (May–June 1616) but refused to surrender the fortress of Ineu.[12] Although the prince had sent several orders to evacuate the fortress of Lipova, the garrison refused to obey. Bethlen was forced to mobilise the army and besiege his own border fortress to satisfy the demands of the sultan. While most of the army was concentrated in the southern parts of the western borderland, Transylvania was attacked by George Drugeth of Hommona, a nobleman from Upper Hungary who had the support of the Habsburgs. He was defeated by a smaller Transylvanian force of about 1,500 soldiers led by the captain of Oradea, Francis Rhédey.[13]

Despite these territorial losses and political compromises Bethlen was slowly transforming Transylvania into a regional power. In 1617 he played a significant role in restoring the relations between the Ottoman Empire and Poland, seriously affected by the hostile activities of Cossacks and Tatars on the borderlands of the two states. The Transylvanian prince brought his troops (12,000 soldiers) to Moldavia, joining the army of Skender (Schender) Pasha and Radu Mihnea against a Polish army commanded by Stanisław Żółkiewski. A direct confrontation was avoided and Bethlen played a key role in the peace negotiations culminating in the peace treaty of Busa (Busza), on 23 September 1617. One of the provisions of the treaty regarded Transylvania, namely the fact that none of those present would offer any help

---

10　Ildikó Horn, 'The Princely Council in the Age of Gábor Bethlen,' *Hungarian Historical Review* 2, no.4, (2013), pp.829–847.

11　Teréz Oborni, 'Gábor Bethlen and the Treaty of Nagyszombat (1615)', *Hungarian Historical Review* 2, no. 4, (2013), pp.761–789; Gerald Volkmer, *Siebenbürgen zwischen Habsburgermonarchie und Osmanischem Reich. Völkerrechtliche Stellung und Völkerrechtspraxis eines ostmitteleuropäischen Fürstentums 1541–1699* (München: De Gruyter Oldenburg, 2015), pp.328–332.

12　Harai, *Gabriel Bethlen*, pp.79–86.

13　Andrei Veress, *Documente privitoare la istoria Ardealului, Moldovei și Țării Românești, Acte și scrisori, vol. XI* (București, M.O. Imprimeria Națională, 1937), pp.101–102.

to Drugeth of Hommona who wanted to overthrow and replace Bethlen as prince.[14]

The highlight of Gabriel Bethlen's reign was his participation in the Thirty Years' War (1618–1648). From 1619 to 1626 he organised three campaigns against the Habsburgs, resulting in three very advantageous peace treaties. His intervention was motivated by the need to protect the Protestant population of Hungary, who, like their Bohemian neighbours, were feeling oppressed by the aggressive counter-Reformation promoted by Ferdinand II. During the first expedition (1619–1622) he was elected King of Hungary by a Diet gathered in Banská Bystrica (Besztercebánya) on 25 August 1620. Ferdinand II made peace with his Transylvanian rival after each military campaign, but he never gave up his claim on the title of King of Hungary. On the other hand, Bethlen was more pragmatic and renounced his claim to the throne in exchange for territories in Eastern Hungary.[15] In time, the Principality of Transylvania became a valued member of the Protestant faction. Gabriel Bethlen established direct connections with the most important monarchs of Europe and employed a substantial number of foreign diplomats to achieve his goals. An especially crucial step in this regard was his marriage with Catherine of Brandenburg in 1626.[16]

Although he spent many years away from Transylvania, Gabriel Bethlen proved to be an excellent administrator. He surrounded himself with trustworthy councillors and advisers like his brother Stephen, who implemented his domestic policy with remarkable efficiency. Some historians have characterised Bethlen as a cross between an absolute monarch and a mercantile prince.[17] Instead of pledging sources of important financial income, he chose to administer them directly, through designated officials. In 1615, for example, he assumed direct control over all salt mining operations in Transylvania, thus ensuring a yearly income of 30,000 florins for the treasury. This money was roughly enough to pay the wages of his army for a whole month.

He did the same with the most important commercial tax, 'the thirteenth.' State monopoly was also established over the extraction of metals like mercury and copper. Another important source of income for the prince was his land, the so called 'fiscal estate.' His predecessors had been very generous and donated many villages to maintain the loyalty of the nobility. Bethlen made constant efforts to rebuild the 'crown lands' and annulled all donations made after 1588. The fiscal estate brought no profit to the treasury in 1613

---

14 Valentin Constantinov, *Țara Moldovei în cadrul relațiilor internaționale (1611–1634)* (Iași: Demiurg, 2014), pp.147–156.
15 Cristina Feneșan, 'Transilvania și Războiul de treizeci de ani', *Anuarul Institutului de Istorie și Arheologie, Cluj-Napoca*, no. 26 (1983–1984), pp.119–141.
16 Gábor Kármán, 'Külföldi diplomaták Bethlen Gábor szolgálatában', Gábor Kármán, Kees Teszelszky (eds.), *Bethlen Gábor és Európa* (Budapest: ELTE BTK Középkori és Kora Újkori Magyar Történeti Tanszéke and the Transylvania Emlékeiért Tudományos Egyesület, 2013), pp.145–183.
17 Dominic Kosáry, 'Gabriel Bethlen: Transylvania in the XVIIth century,' *The Slavonic and East European Review*, vol. 17, no. 49 (1938), pp.162–173; Ágnes Várkonyi, 'Historical Personality, Crisis and Progress in 17th Century Hungary', *Etudes Historiques*, Budapest (1970), p.279.

but things began to change gradually and by the end of Bethlen's reign (1629) the income generated by these lands was estimated at 40,000 florins per year.[18] Important revenues were also drawn from the newly acquired lands in Hungary and from the Duchy of Oppeln and Ratibor, which was estimated to generate an income of 300,000 florins per year.[19]

A significant part of state income was used to support the court in Alba Iulia (Gyulafehérvár) and the other princely residencies in Transylvania. In the last years of his reign Gabriel Bethlen spent substantial amounts of money on luxury goods. In 1625 his agents purchased a wide range of precious objects with an estimated value of 464,000 florins, more than the cost of maintaining a field army during a whole campaign (about 400,000 florins).[20]

Teaching institutions across Transylvania and Upper Hungary also benefited from his generosity. Bethlen understood the value of having an efficient administrative apparatus, so he tried to create an educational infrastructure able to provide qualified personnel for all the needs of a modern state. Colleges and academies were endowed with estates and other regular sources of income and a sizeable number of foreign professors were invited to teach there.[21]

In an age when religious violence was a constant threat, Transylvania was a haven for some persecuted minorities. With a system of four official confessions (Calvinist, Unitarian, Catholic and Lutheran) the principality embraced religious diversity unlike any other country in Early Modern Europe. The large Orthodox community was only barely tolerated, but Gabriel Bethlen gave some important privileges to their priesthood, financed their schools, and even encouraged the translation of the Bible into Romanian. His real aim was to convert the Romanian population to Calvinism, a plan which enjoyed little success.

Ornamented saddle, part of the gifts sent, probably in 1625, by Gabriel Bethlen to Swedish King Gustav II Adolf (Livrustkammaren, Stockholm)

Anabaptists from Bohemia and Hungary were also welcomed to Transylvania. The first members of this community (186 persons) settled at Vințul de Jos (Alvinc) in 1621. They were very skilled artisans, and the prince gave them privileges and tax exemptions with the condition of selling their wares to the state at an established (below market level) price. Two years later, in 1623, their community had grown to 735 members. Other groups travelled to Transylvania in the following decades until 1649, raising their numbers to about 1,700 people.[22] A significant Sephardic Jewish group decided to

---

18   Katalin Péter, 'Two Aspects of War and Society in the Age of Prince Gábor Bethlen of Transylvania,' János M. Bak, Béla K. Király (eds.) *From Hunyadi to Rákóczi. War and Society in Late Medieval and Early Modern Hungary* (New York: Columbia University Press, 1982), p.303.
19   Harai, *Gabriel Bethlen*, pp.195–201.
20   Harai, *Gabriel Bethlen*, pp.210–219.
21   Harai, *Gabriel Bethlen*, pp.219–221.
22   Magdalena Bunta, 'Habanii în Transilvania', *Acta Musei Napocensis* VII (1970), pp.201–225.

move from Istanbul to Transylvania when Prince Bethlen guaranteed their freedom. Of course, there was a strong political and financial motivation behind the goodwill of the Transylvanian prince who understood the advantages brought by prosperous communities.

The last years of Bethlen's reign were dedicated to diplomacy. His envoys travelled across Europe to ensure the recognition of Transylvania as a regional power. Matthias Quadt, a German mercenary captain and skilled diplomat, represented Bethlen in England, the United Provinces and Denmark. Another group of Transylvanian nobles accompanied Péter Bethlen, a young nephew of the Transylvanian prince in an educational tour with the purpose of establishing and consolidating contacts around Europe. An important ally for the Transylvanian prince was his brother-in-law the King of Sweden, Gustav Adolph. They shared two common enemies, the Habsburgs and Poland. In 1629 a diplomatic delegation was sent to Istanbul and then to Moscow with the same purpose of gathering allies for a potential confrontation with Poland.[23] Nevertheless, all these plans were abandoned or postponed because of a sudden illness that afflicted the Transylvanian prince in 1629. After several months of suffering, he died in Alba Iulia on 15 November 1629.

Jewel-encrusted mace, used in countries like Transylvania as both weapon and status symbol. Part of the gifts sent, probably in 1625, by Gabriel Bethlen to Swedish King Gustav II Adolf (Livrustkammaren, Stockholm)

During a reign of 16 years Gabriel Bethlen transformed Transylvania into a regional power with an efficient financial system, a respectable army, and a vast network of diplomatic connections. After many difficult decades of war and strife, the principality became a prosperous country where religious freedom was considered a fundament of statehood.

George Rákóczi I (1630–1648)

Transylvania was on the brink of a civil war when Gabriel Bethlen passed away. Princess Catherine converted to Catholicism, gave up her claim on the seven counties in Upper Hungary and was ready to offer Transylvania to the Habsburgs as well. She even managed to gather a strong group of adherents among Transylvanian nobles under the leadership of Stephen Csáky who were ready to follow her plan. The rest of the country was divided between

---

23 Kármán, 'Külföldi diplomaták', pp.145–183; Harai, *Gabriel Bethlen*, pp.181–185.

those who supported Stephen Bethlen, the brother of the deceased prince, and those who preferred George Rákóczi on the Transylvanian throne. After one year of political instability, it was the magnate from Upper Hungary, George Rákóczi, who managed to secure both the election of the estates and the confirmation of his appointment by the Ottoman sultan.[24]

Taking advantage of the tricky situation, the Hungarian Palatine, Miklós Esterházy, moved his troops towards the vicinity of the Western Transylvanian frontier and prepared a strong offensive with the purpose of deposing the newly elected prince. However, the soldiers from the borderlands (mostly *hajdú*), who were loyal to the Transylvanian prince, dealt a decisive blow to the Hungarian army in the battle of Rakamaz, and George Rákóczi took another step towards consolidating his rule and power in the principality.[25]

In 1636 his rule was threatened once again, this time by Stephen Bethlen, brother of the late prince. He convinced the Pasha of Buda, Hussein Nasuh, to support his claim to the Transylvanian throne even without the consent of the Ottoman sultan. Rákóczi organised two armies. One was sent in the north to besiege the fortress of Hust, which was owned by his rival, while the second army was sent in the western borderlands to confront the Ottoman host. The two armies faced each other at Salonta, near the fortress of Oradea, but hesitated to engage in a direct confrontation. A night attack performed by 300 Transylvanian soldiers had a strong negative impact on the morale of the Ottomans who were unsettled and decided to retreat. Several other minor clashes took place in the following days, but the Transylvanians were victorious, and the danger from the Ottomans was averted.[26]

The relations with Moldavia and Wallachia, the neighbouring principalities which were also vassals of the Sublime Porte, was a vital component in the foreign policy of every Transylvanian prince. George Rákóczi I made no exception and took all the necessary measures to ensure the good will of these two rulers. He established strong ties with Matei Basarab, ruler of Wallachia,

George Rákóczi I, Prince of Transylvania 1630–1648, *Trachten-Kabinett von Siebenburgens*, 1729. (The National Museum of Transylvanian History, Cluj-Napoca, Romania)

---

24 Florin Nicolae Ardelean, *Organizarea militară în Principatul Transilvaniei (1541–1691): Comitate și domenii fisclae* (Cluj-Napoca: Editura Academia Română. Centrul de Studii Transilvane, 2019), pp.323–324.
25 Georg Kraus, *Cronica Transilvaniei 1608–1665*, Gheorghe Duzinchevici and Eva Reus-Mârza (ed.), (București: Editura Academiei Republicii Populare Romîne, 1965), pp.72–81.
26 Liviu Borcea, *Cronica de jale a lui Ioan Szalárdi: studiu critic* (Oradea: Arca, 2007), pp.43–71; Kraus, *Cronica Transilvaniei*, pp.95–97.

but he was not so successful with his eastern neighbour, the ambitious Vasile Lupu, voivode of Moldavia. In 1637 he sent one of his commanders, John Kemény, with several thousand Székely troops to help Matei Basarab who was facing an invasion from Moldavia. The Transylvanian intervention was fundamental in maintaining the Wallachian ruler on his throne but the attempt to depose Vasile Lupu ended in failure. Having trustworthy allies on the thrones of the two Romanian Principalities meant security on the southern and eastern borders of Transylvania and created a reliable network of intelligence regarding the changes that were taking place in the Ottoman Empire.[27]

In the meantime, the Thirty Years' War was following its course and the Protestant faction was looking to gain new allies against the Habsburgs and the Catholic League. From the beginning of his reign in Transylvania, George Rákóczi sought to conclude an alliance with Sweden. Negotiations began with Gustav II Adolph in 1630 and, after the latter's death in 1632, continued with the Swedish high chancellor, Axel Oxenstierna. The Transylvanian prince took the initiative and sent envoys to Gustav Adolph while he was on campaign in Bavaria. Paul Strassburg, the Swedish diplomat sent to Istanbul, travelled through Transylvania in 1632 and 1633, and set the foundations for a future treaty between the two monarchs. However, it took 12 years for the two states to reach an agreement and finally sign a treaty at Alba Iulia on 16 November 1643. This treaty was also signed by France, a state which had taken a leading position in the anti-Habsburg coalition.[28]

With the hopes of receiving financial and strategic help from his allies, in February 1644 George Rákóczi I launched the fourth Transylvanian campaign against the Habsburgs in the Thirty Years' War. His main objectives were to conquer territory in Eastern Hungary and to ensure the religious freedom of Protestants. The religious motive behind this campaign cannot be denied as the Transylvanian prince was often described by his contemporaries as a very pious Calvinist. The war did not go as expected because Sweden was caught up in a war with Denmark and the French subsidies did not arrive.

Left on his own, Rákóczi did the best he could against a superior enemy. He tried to avoid major battles and engaged in small scale actions such as raids and skirmishes. Nevertheless, this war proved to be a very costly endeavour, especially for a monarch that was known for his greed. By the end of the first year Transylvania was in control of the seven counties in Upper Hungary which had been previously in the possession of Gabriel Bethlen, and Rákóczi was satisfied that he still had a more or less intact army. In 1645 the Swedes were finally able to focus on attacking the Habsburg territories in Bohemia and Moravia. Transylvanian troops arrived in the area and provided support to the Swedish army, especially with their light cavalry detachments, but they

---

27 Nicolae Stoicescu, *Matei Basarab* (București: Editura Academiei Republicii Socialiste Romania, 1988), pp.150–152.
28 Gábor Kármán, 'The Thorny Path to an Uneasy Alliance: Transylvanian–Swedish Negotiations 1626–1643', Gábor Kármán (ed.), *The Princes of Transylvania in the Thirty Years' War* (Paderborn: Brill Schöningh, 2022), pp.154–199; Zsuzsanna Hámori Nagy, 'Transylvania and France in the Thirty Years' War: The Origins of a Treaty', Gábor Kármán (ed.), *The Princes of Transylvania in the Thirty Years' War* (Paderborn: Brill Schöningh, 2022), pp.199–230.

were unable to achieve significant success against the well-fortified towns held by the Habsburgs. Under these circumstances Rákóczi was looking to reach an advantageous agreement with the enemy.

The peace treaty of Linz was signed in December 1645 and brought the seven counties from Upper Hungary (Abaúj, Bereg, Borsod, Szabolcs, Szatmár, Ugocsa and Zemplén) back into the possession of the Transylvanian crown, with a special provision regarding the counties of Szabolcs and Szatmár which were inherited by the successor of George Rákóczi I and remained a part of the principality until 1659.[29] This was a considerable financial and political gain for the prince. Furthermore, Transylvania was represented in the peace negotiations of Westphalia. The envoy of Prince Rákóczi, Francis Jármi, arrived at Osnabrück in May 1647 but his main task was to obtain some of the subsidies promised by the French court during the war. He was well received by the French envoys who used his presence to exert pressure on the representatives of the Habsburgs. Nevertheless, Transylvania was not among the states who signed the treaty, and the only notable result was the inclusion of Prince Rákóczi's name in the text of the peace treaty.[30]

In terms of domestic policy, George Rákóczi excelled at consolidating central authority through all possible means. One of his most controversial initiatives was the persecution of the Sabbatarians, a dissident religious group within the Unitarian community. Their most notable representative was Simon Péchi, former chancellor during the reign of Gabriel Bethlen. In 1638 Rákóczi gave an ultimatum to all the Sabbatarians who had the option to convert to one of the four official confessions (Catholic, Calvinist, Unitarian or Lutheran) or to forfeit their lives and property. Hundreds of nobles and commoners refused to convert and while the prince eagerly confiscated their possessions, most of them were simply imprisoned for varying lengths of sentences rather than killed.[31]

Unlike Bethlen, who focused on drawing revenues from commercial enterprises, Rákóczi acquired vast estates, especially through confiscations. Treason trials, his favourite stratagem, were a particularly effective way of eliminating real, or potential, political adversaries and gaining new properties. By the end of his reign, he owned over 27,000 peasant households in Hungary and Transylvania, with over 100,000 people living on his estates.[32]

On 20 May 1648, Władysław IV Vasa, King of Poland and Grand Duke of Lithuania died. When the Polish-Lithuanian *sejm* (estates assembly) gathered for a new royal election in Warsaw, George Rákóczi I was regarded as a potential candidate for the throne. It remains uncertain whether the

---

29 Géza Pálffy, 'The Kingdom of Hungary in the Thirty Years' War,' Gábor Kármán (ed.), *The Princes of Transylvania in the Thirty Years' War* (Paderborn: Brill Schöningh, 2022), pp.5–6.
30 Gábor Kármán, *Confession and Politics in the Principality of Transylvania 1644–1657* (Göttingen: Vandenhoek&Ruprecht, 2020), pp.75–85.
31 István Keul, *Early Modern Religious Communities in East-Central Europe: Ethnic Diversity, Denominational Plurality and Corporative Politics in the Principality of Transylvania (1526–1691)* (Leiden, Boston: Brill, 2009), pp.196–201.
32 Péter, Katalin, 'The Golden Age of the Principality (1606–1660)', in László Makkai, Zoltán Szász (eds.), *History of Transylvania, vol. II* (New York: Columbia University Press, 2002), pp.117–118.

Transylvanian prince had any real chances of being elected. He died on 11 October 1648 and the ambition of ascending to the Polish-Lithuanian throne was passed on to his son, George Rákóczi II.[33]

George Rákóczi I successfully continued to enhance the legacy of Gabriel Bethlen and brought the Principality of Transylvania to the apex of its political and military power. One of his most remarkable achievements was the fact that he waged his wars beyond the borders of Transylvania and thus spared his country from all the devastating effects of being fought over.

Signature of George Rákóczi I, Prince of Transylvania 1630–1648, from one of the letters sent in 1644 to Lithuanian Field Hetman Janusz Radziwiłł (AGAD, Warsaw)

George Rákóczi II (1648–1657; 1658–1659; 1659–1660)

Even before the death of his father, George Rákóczi II was acknowledged by the Diet as heir to the Transylvanian throne. In 1648, the Ottoman sultan confirmed his election but demanded an increase of the annual tribute because of the two Hungarian counties (Szatmár and Szabolcs) which remained in the possession of the Transylvanian prince.[34]

George Rákóczi II was never able to attain the level of internal authority held by his father and made some important concessions in favour of the estates. In 1653, he sanctioned a compilation of laws known as the *Approbatae Constitutiones* which was based on the most important provisions previously approved by the Diet.[35] This was a necessary step in securing the support of the Transylvanian elite for his ambitious foreign policy.

The beginning of his reign coincided with the Cossack rebellion of Bohdan Khmelnytsky, which generated a long-term political crisis in the Polish-Lithuanian Commonwealth and provided a favourable context for Transylvanian involvement in the dramatic events that were affecting its northern neighbour.[36] Prince Rákóczi followed with great concern the crisis that was unfolding there and kept close contact with some of the most important political actors such as Bohdan Khmelnytsky or the Lithuanian magnate Janusz Radziwiłł. But before getting involved in the conflict, the ruler of Transylvania knew he had to build strong alliances with his

---

33 Kármán, *Confession and Politics*, pp.87–102.
34 Susana Andea, 'Evoluții politice în secolul al XVII-lea. De la Ștefan Bocskai la Mihail Apafi', in Ioan-Aurel Pop, Thomas Nägler, András Magyari (eds.), *The History of Transylvania*, vol. II (Cluj-Napoca: Center for Transylvanian Studies. Romanian Cultural Institute, 2009), p.133.
35 Alexandru Herlea, Liviu Marcu (eds.), *Constituțiile Aprobate ale Transilvaniei (1653)* (Cluj-Napoca: Editura Dacia, 1997).
36 Victor Ostapchuk, 'Cossack Ukrain in and out of the Ottoman Orbit, 1648–1681', in Gábor Kármán, Lovro Kunčević, (ed.), *The European Tributary States of the Ottoman Empire in the Sixteenth and Seventeenth Centuries* (Leiden and Boston: Brill, 2013), pp.123–152.

George Rákóczi II, Prince of Transylvania 1648–1657; 1658–1659; 1659–1660, Trachten-Kabinett von Siebenburgens, 1729. (The National Museum of Transylvanian History, Cluj-Napoca, Romania)

two Romanian neighbours, the rulers of Wallachia and Moldavia.[37]

Vasile Lupu, the ambitious voivode of Moldavia, was never going to accept a relationship of subordination towards Transylvania, thus the only available option for Rákóczi was to support a new candidate on the Moldavian throne, one who would be willing to follow his lead. Gheorghe Ștefan, a high-ranking boyar, proved to be the best choice available at the time because he enjoyed a significant degree of authority among the political adversaries of Vasile Lupu. In 1653, a Transylvanian army commanded by John Kemény, who had risen to the position of captain general, was sent to Moldavia to offer military assistance to Gheorghe Ștefan, who had already rebelled against Vasile Lupu.[38] A small detachment of soldiers from Wallachia had also joined the Moldavian rebels who now had sufficient strength to overthrow their old ruler.

Aware of the plans set in motion against him, Vasile Lupu decided to leave the country and seek help from his son-in-law, Timuș Khmelnytsky, the son of the Grand Hetman of the Cossacks. Timuș did not hesitate to get involved in this civil war because the Cossacks also needed a strong ally in Moldavia. Leading an army of 8,000–16,000 Cossacks, the son of the Grand Hetman drove off his father-in-law's enemies and restored him to the Moldavian throne. Kemény retreated towards the Transylvanian border and suffered significant loses in the process, including most of his artillery. The Cossack army swept across Moldavia and continued beyond, marching towards Wallachia. Vasile Lupu's plan was to overthrow Matei Basarab and to replace him with Timuș. Although there was a serious risk of being surrounded by hostile neighbours, Rákóczi sent only a few soldiers (about 800 men) to his Wallachain ally. Luckily for him, Matei Basarab was able to deal with the threat on his own and defeated the Cossack army in the battle of Finta (27 May 1653).[39]

After these events, Vasile Lupu sought refuge in the lands of the Crimean Tatars but was imprisoned and sent to Istanbul because his actions had angered the sultan. Gheorghe Ștefan returned to sit on the Moldavian throne,

---

37 Gábor Kármán, 'György Rákóczi II's Attempt to Establish a Local Power Base among the Tributaries of the Ottoman Empire 1653–1657', in ed. Maria Baramova et al. (eds.), *Power and Influence in South-Eastern Europe, 16th–19th Century* (Zürich: Lit, 2013), pp.229–244.

38 Petronel Zahariuc, *Țara Moldovei în vremea lui Gheorghe Ștefan voievod (1653–1658)* (Iași: Editura Universității Al. I. Cuza, 2003), p.123.

39 Stoicescu, *Matei Basarab*, pp.182–205.

once again with the help of Transylvanian troops. The wife of the former voivode, with a significant part of his treasury, took refuge in the fortress of Suceava and refused to surrender. The Transylvanian army, estimated at 10,000 men, laid siege to the fortress but lacked sufficient artillery to breach the walls. In the meantime, Timuș Khmelnytsky, who had survived the battle of Finta, returned with another Cossack army of 12,000 men. The Cossacks outmanoeuvred the Transylvanian army and occupied their camp. Nevertheless, the siege continued as new troops were arriving from Transylvania, Wallachia and Poland. Timuș managed to organise a second line of defence around the fortress, strengthened with trenches, palisades and traps. The besiegers were not willing to risk a direct assault and preferred to starve the defenders of Suceava into submission.

The outcome of the siege was decided by an unusual and unfortunate accident. Timuș Khmelnytsky was killed in his tent while sleeping by a random cannon shot. His unexpected death caused the Cossacks to accept negotiations and surrender.[40] For the next few years, the rule of Gheorghe Ștefan was secured and George Rákóczi II had a reliable ally in Moldavia.

During the long years of his reign in Wallachia, Matei Basarab (1632–1654) proved to be a loyal ally of the Rákóczi family. After his last victory against Vasile Lupu, the Wallachain voivode had to deal with several uprisings of his soldiers and repeatedly requested military assistance from Transylvania. He died on 9 April 1654 because of an old wound inflicted upon him in the battle of Finta.

The new ruler, Constantin Șerban, was also loyal to the Transylvanian prince but his reign was threatened by internal instability. The army of Wallachia had increased considerably during the reign of his predecessor through the recruitment of a large number of foreign mercenaries, known as *seimeni*. Hailing from the Balkans (Serbians, Bulgarians, Bosnians, Greeks and so forth), the *seimeni* were good infantry troops bearing firearms. They remained in the service of the Wallachian ruler for extended periods and were rewarded not only with wages but also with lands.[41] In 1655 their leader, Hrizea, convinced many soldiers to rebel against the voivode and assumed control over most of the country. The Prince of Transylvania's response against the rebels was swift and they won a crushing victory in the battle of Șoplea on 26 June 1655.[42] With order restored in Wallachia, Prince Rákóczi was now able to focus on establishing a military alliance with Sweden and the Cossacks.

Soon after he assumed the Swedish throne, King Charles X Gustav decided to attack the Polish-Lithuanian Commonwealth, taking advantage of its weakness. During 1655, his troops advanced successfully through Greater Poland and Livonia, and then occupied Warsaw in September, followed by

---

40 Miron Costin, *Opere*, edited by Petre P. Panaitescu (București: Editura pentru Literatură, 1965), pp.163–168.
41 Claudiu Neagoe, *Seimenii în Țările Române: Contribuții la istoria organizării militare a românilor în secolele XVII-XVIII* (București: Ars Docendi, 2017), pp.29–64.
42 Claudiu Neagoe, Costin Peligrad, 'Lupta de la Șoplea, pe Teleajen (16/27 Iunie 1655)', *Revista de Istorie Militară*, pp.5–6 (2019), pp.1–16.

Cracow in October. Many Polish and Lithuanian magnates swore allegiance to the Swedish King in the aftermath of this campaign. Rákóczi remained passive although he received some tempting proposals for the Polish throne. For the time he preferred to maintain contact with all the factions involved and to follow the course of the conflict from a safe distance.[43]

Throughout 1656 Polish resistance was consolidated and managed to retake more territory from the Swedish troops. In July they even managed to free Warsaw. Charles X Gustav realised he was not going to keep control over the Commonwealth by himself and was more willing to share the spoils of war with allies. The best candidate for such a position was the Prince of Transylvania. Rákóczi had already agreed upon a defensive alliance with the Cossacks in September and was in an advantageous position to demand a share of Polish-Lithuanian territory. Swedish envoys had arrived in Transylvania during the summer and spent the following months debating the conditions of an alliance between the two monarchs. An agreement was reached by the end of the year and the treaty was finally signed at Iernut (Rádnot) on 6 December 1656. Transylvania was promised a share of captured territory, including Cracow, and Rákóczi was going to assume the title of King of Poland.[44]

Entangled in a complex network of alliances but without the consent of the Ottoman sultan, George Rákóczi II left Transylvania at the head of a large army (allegedly 40,000 men) with the purpose of taking the crown of Poland through military force. At the time the odds seemed to be in his favour, and nobody could have guessed that this was the beginning of the downfall of the Transylvanian Principality. Between March and May 1657, the Transylvanians occupied Cracow and Warsaw, but Sweden was forced to withdraw its troops because of unexpected Danish attacks. On 22 July 1657, the Transylvanian army suffered a crushing defeat at the battle of Trembowla and many nobles and common soldiers were taken into captivity by the Tatars. During the same month, the prince signed a peace treaty with Poland and agreed to pay significant war reparations.[45] The Ottoman sultan was outraged by the daring manoeuvre of his northern vassals and banished George Rákóczi II together with his Romanian allies, Constantin Șerban (Wallachia) and Gheorghe Ștefan (Moldavia). After almost five decades of peace and stability, since the beginning of Gabriel Bethlen's reign, Transylvania was once again ravaged by civil war and foreign attacks.

---

43 Kármán, *Confession and Politics,* pp.199–207.
44 Volkmer, Siebenbürgen, pp.418–428; Kármán, *Confession and Politics,* pp.208–222.
45 Ardelean, *Organizarea militară,* pp.331–339.

Francis Rhédey, Ákos Barcsay and John Kemény (1657–1661)

The sultan made it clear that George Rákóczi II could not remain ruler of Transylvania. Although he refused to take responsibility for the disastrous campaign in Poland, Rákóczi abdicated and temporarily retreated onto his estates in Upper Hungary. Soon after this, the Diet elected Francis Rhédey, cousin of the late Gabriel Bethlen, as prince on 2 November 1657. The new prince had extraordinarily little authority over the estates and the Székely overtly refused to obey his order to mobilise the army. In the meantime, Rákóczi returned to Transylvania with a strong retinue of soldiers, with the declared intent of retaking the Transylvanian throne despite the sultan's wishes to the contrary. Rhédey summoned the Diet in Mediaș to rally the country against the former prince, but he had very little success. Rákóczi's troops besieged the town and convinced the Diet to re-elect him.[46]

Francis Rhédey, Prince of Transylvania 1657–1658, (wikimedia commons)

The Grand Vizier Mehmet Köprülü was angered by Rákóczi's return and prepared a campaign against Transylvania with the purpose of punishing the rebel prince and those who supported him. The aggressive approach on the Transylvanian issue was a sign of the changing policy in the Ottoman Empire brought by the rise of the new Grand Vizier.[47]

Rákóczi refused to wait for the attack and mobilised his troops on the south-western frontier of the principality. Ottoman troops from the borderland gathered in the vicinity of Lipova fortress, ready to face the Transylvanian army. A battle took place in mid June and ended with a victory for the rebel prince. In the aftermath, his troops burnt several settlements and fortifications across the Ottoman border.

In August 1658, an invading army of unprecedented size swept across Transylvania. The Ottomans and their allies divided their troops into two columns. The first column (about 35,000 soldiers) consisted of the main Ottoman detachment,

---

46 Kraus, *Cronica Transilvaniei*, p.253.
47 Özgür Kolçak, 'A Transylvanian Ruler in the Talons of the 'Hawks': György Rákóczi II and Köprülü Mehmet Pasha'in Florentina Nițu et. al. (eds.) Turkey & Romania: *A History of Partnership and Collaboration in the Balkans* (Istanbul: Union of Turkish World Municipalities: Istanbul University, 2016), pp.341–359.

commanded by the Grand Vizier himself and the soldiers from the Hungarian borderlands, commanded by the Pasha of Buda. The second army was the most numerous (about 48,000 soldiers) and included the Tatars of Mehmet Ghirai IV, the troops of the Pasha of Silistra, Wallachians, Moldavians, Cossacks and a smaller Polish contingent.[48] The goal of these armies was to capture George Rákóczi II and in the process, they laid waste to almost the whole country. Smaller settlements were already deserted because their inhabitants had fled to seek refuge in the forests and other secluded places. The prosperous towns of the Saxons paid large ransoms to avoid sieges and the consequent pillaging that would have occurred.

The seat of the principality, Alba Iulia, was left defenceless and suffered the most savage destruction. The princely palace and all other buildings inside the fortified perimeter were razed to the ground. The archives of the court were almost completely destroyed, the only surviving documents being those carried away by the fugitives. Most fortifications surrendered or were taken by force with one notable exception, Făgăraș fortress on the southern border. The garrison was strong enough and well supplied to resist a long siege so by the end of August the besieging army left and decided to try their luck with more vulnerable targets.[49] An unprecedented number of captives were taken during this campaign. Estimations are rather imprecise and range from between 40,000 and 180,000 people. While some of them were ransomed in the following months, most would find themselves transported to the Ottoman and Tatar slave markets.[50]

With no real chance of effectively opposing such a large force, Rákóczi retreated close to the Habsburg border and was ready to flee the country at any moment. Ákos Barcsay, one of the leading members of the Transylvanian nobility, travelled to the Ottoman camp and requested the title of prince for himself. In exchange he promised to increase the yearly tribute, to pay war reparations and gave up his claim to a large territory on the south-western frontier, the Banat of Lugoj and Caransebeș. The Grand Vizier agreed, and a hastily assembled Diet

Ákos Barcsay, Prince of Transylvania 1658–1660, (wikimedia commons)

---

48 Liviu Borcea, 'Contribuții la istoria campaniei militare turco-tătare în Transilvania (August-Octombrie 1658)', *Crisia*, XV (1985), pp.97–105.
49 Kraus, *Cronica Transilvaniei*, pp.270–272; Maria Ursuțiu (ed.) *Rétyi Péter Naplója (1645–1674)* (București: Kriterion Könyvkiadó, 1983), pp.39–41.
50 Borcea, 'Contribuții la istoria campaniei', p.118.

elected Ákos Barcsay as Prince of Transylvania at the beginning of October 1658.[51]

Barcsay was never able to assume complete authority over the country because many nobles, soldiers and even commoners remained loyal to the former prince. In the beginning of 1659 Rákóczi returned to Transylvania at the head of an army, determined to retake the throne. Barcsay had no intention of settling the matter on the battlefield and retreated to Deva, one of the few fortifications that he controlled and waited for Ottoman help. At the end of February, he headed for the town of Bistrița, to attend the Diet and he did so accompanied by his entire army. A contemporary report gives a detailed description of his small and heterogeneous force as they entered the town's gates:

- three banners of the 'field army' (*milites campestris*)
- 16 banners of *curteni* (cavalry) from Moldavia and Wallachia
- two banners of Tatars
- the Royal Judge of Bistrița with a guard of 300 horsemen
- four banners from the princely guard (*militia aulica*)
- a janissary guard (unspecified number)
- two banners of dragoons
- six banners of *seimeni* (infantry) from Wallachia[52]

It was unprecedented for a prince to attend the Diet with such a large retinue (roughly 4,000 men), but Barcsay feared a surprise attack from his enemies. It is also relevant for Barcsay's situation at the time that only 1,000 men were Transylvanian soldiers while the rest of his men (3,000 soldiers) were supplied by the Ottomans and their allies.

During the summer and autumn of 1659, the two factions engaged in skirmishes and small confrontations but Rákóczi gradually lost ground and retreated, once again, towards his estates in Upper Hungary. As winter was approaching, most of the Ottoman troops together with their Wallachian and Moldavian allies left Transylvania, and Barcsay found himself in a vulnerable situation. Throughout these troubling times the Saxon University remained loyal to the Ottomans and agreed to shelter the prince in one of their best fortified towns. Accompanied by 1,000 Janissaries, 900 Ottoman cavalry and 300 Transylvanian horsemen, Barcsay was received by the authorities of Sibiu. Close behind him was George Rákóczi II who laid siege to the main settlement of the Transylvanian Saxons from November 1659 until May 1660. The defenders of Sibiu refused to surrender, hoping for the arrival of a new Ottoman army in spring. Their expectations were fulfilled in April

---

51 MCRT, vol. XII, pp.68–76; Sorin Bulboacă, 'Acațiu Barcsai de Bârcea Mare, ultimul ban al Lugojului și Caransebeșului (24 Decembrie 1644–1614 Septembrie 1658)', *Banatica*, 6 (2011), pp.105–114.
52 MCRT, vol. XII, pp.157–158.

1660 when two Turkish contingents from the European side of the empire marched towards Transylvania.⁵³

The Ottomans headed for the central parts of Transylvania in an attempt to cut off the retreat of the rebel prince who, in previous years, had sought refuge on his estates in Upper Hungary. This time Rákóczi had other plans and was determined to settle the matter in a major confrontation. A pitched battle took place in the vicinity of Cluj on 22 May, resulting in an Ottoman victory. The prince himself led one last desperate cavalry charge against the enemy and was mortally wounded. Some of his loyal soldiers were able to carry him away from the battlefield but he died a few weeks later in Oradea, on 7 June 1660.⁵⁴ Thus ended the life of probably the most ambitious, and most valiant, Prince of Transylvania.

John Kemény, Prince of Transylvania 1661–1662, (wikimedia commons)

Seidi Ahmed, the commander of the Ottoman forces, followed the trail of the wounded prince but when he arrived at Oradea, on the western frontier of Transylvania, George Rákóczi II was already dead. Taking advantage of the political confusion and the weakness of the defending garrison, the Ottomans decided to lay siege to Oradea, the centrepiece of the western defensive system of the principality. The siege began on 14 July and after 44 days of resistance the defenders of the fortress surrendered.⁵⁵ The loss of Oradea was perceived as a major tragedy for Transylvania, crowning the series of unfortunate events that began with the failed campaign in Poland.

While the Transylvanian Diet was meeting in the southern parts of the country, in late October 1660, a new contender to the throne crossed the border into Transylvania. John Kemény had been recently ransomed from Tatar captivity and returned home. He made a deal with the Habsburgs who promised to support his claim to the throne in exchange for some territorial concessions and military help against the Ottomans.

---

53 Nicolae Bethlen, *Descrierea vieții sale de către el însuși* (Cluj-Napoca: Casa Cărții de Știință, 2004), pp.90–91.
54 János B. Szabó, *Erdély Tragédiája 1657–1662* (Budapest: Corvina, 2019), pp.236–243.
55 János B. Szabó, 'Asedierea cetății Oradea de către tătari și turci 1658, 1660', Teréz Oborni, (ed.), *Oradea cum e ocrotită": Lupte pentru Oradea în epoca modernă timpurie. Studii despre istoria Țării Bihorului 7* (Oradea: Fundația Culturală Varadinum, 2020), pp.133–151.

Considering his previous career, Kemény seemed to be an ideal candidate. A descendent of a Transylvanian noble family, he made slow progress climbing the political and military hierarchy of the principality. He began as a servant (page) in the entourage of Prince Gabriel Bethlen and accompanied him on two of his campaigns in the Thirty Years' War. Later he advanced from the position of standard bearer (1626) to captain general of the Transylvanian army (1653). His personal connections with the Transylvanian elite ensured a swift transition of power and a new Diet elected Kemény as prince shortly after he made his claim known. The Ottomans, on the other hand, refused to acknowledge Kemény and maintained their initial option of supporting Barcsay who had little following among the Transylvanian estates.[56]

In 1660 the Habsburgs planned a major offensive against the Ottomans and the Imperial Diet agreed to offer subsides for the war. Troops were mobilised during the following year and placed under the command of General Raimondo Montecuccoli. The elected Prince of Transylvania (Kemény) also prepared for war because most Ottoman troops were heading for his country. Kemény retreated towards the northern frontier of the principality because he was counting on the military help of the Habsburgs, but their field army was still far away from Transylvania. Ali Pasha, the commander of the Ottoman troops, advanced without encountering serious opposition and soon controlled most of the country.

Because Barcsay had been executed by his rival, the elected prince, the Ottomans chose a new candidate for the Transylvanian throne, Michael Apafi. A hastily assembled Diet, consisting of the few remaining nobles (most of them were with Kemény near the Habsburg border) and the representatives of the Saxon University elected Apafi on 14 September 1661. When the Imperial army finally reached Transylvania, it was in no shape to fight. Famine and epidemics had ravaged the ranks of Montecuccoli's troops, and the general decided to retreat, without accomplishing anything noteworthy. John Kemény was left to face the Turkish threat on his own. By the end of the year 1661 Transylvania had two ruling princes, one sustained by the Ottomans and acknowledged by the Saxon University (Michael Apafi), while the Habsburg candidate (John Kemény) relied on the support of the Székely and most of the nobility. This peculiar situation was eventually settled on the battlefield of Sleușul Mare (23 January 1662), where John Kemény was defeated and lost his life during the fight.[57]

Michael Apafi I and the Habsburg Conquest of Transylvania (1661–1690)

Michael Apafi began his rule during a complicated political period for Transylvania. After the death of Prince Kemény, most of the political elite accepted him as ruler but a significant part of the country was still

---

56 Kraus, *Cronica Transilvaniei*, pp.391–399.
57 Kraus, *Cronica Transilvaniei*, pp.440–474.

THE ARMY OF TRANSYLVANIA 1613-1690

Michael Apafi I, Prince of Transylvania 1661–1690, *Trachten-Kabinett von Siebenburgens*, 1729. (The National Museum of Transylvanian History, Cluj-Napoca, Romania)

under Habsburg control. Important towns and fortifications from the central parts of Transylvania, like Cluj and Gherla, were occupied by German garrisons and the emperor was unwilling to recall his soldiers until the Turks agreed to retreat as well.[58]

Prince Apafi was a loyal vassal of the Ottomans and in 1663 he was called to fulfil his military obligations during the siege of Nové Zámky (Ersekujvár). Although he initially mobilised the whole army, he disbanded most of the troops before crossing the frontier and kept only the princely guard and an additional 100 mounted hajdú.[59] The Grand Vizier Ahmed Köprülü did not need the help of the Transylvanian Army to conquer the fortress, which he did after a long siege that lasted more than a month (17 August–26 September 1663), but he wanted to have the Transylvanian prince by his side to win the support of the Protestant population in Hungary.[60]

In 1664 the remaining German garrisons from Transylvania swore allegiance to the Transylvanian prince and thus, after almost three years since his election, Apafi was finally able to exert his rule over the whole country.[61] The Habsburg-Ottoman war ended during the same year and a peace treaty was concluded at Vasvár on 10 August. Some of the most important provisions of the treaty regarded Transylvania. Michael Apafi was acknowledged as the legitimate prince by the Habsburg emperor, the fortress of Oradea (conquered in 1660) and the surrounding region were recognised as Ottoman territory and the Transylvanians were obliged to demolish an important fortress in the western borderland, Săcuieni (Székelyhíd).[62]

The Hungarian nobility was outraged by the Treaty of Vasvár (1664) because they were not consulted during negotiations and lost important territories to the Ottomans. A significant part of the political elite was ready to get rid of the Habsburg monarch and sought to transform Hungary into a vassal state of the Ottoman Empire, similar to the Principality of Transylvania. The members of the so called 'Wesselényi conspiracy' tried to contact the

---

58 Susana Andea, *Transilvania, Țara Românească și Moldova. Legături politice (1656–1688)* (Cluj-Napoca: Presa Universitară Clujeană, 1996), pp.165–167.
59 Kraus, *Cronica Transilvaniei*, pp.526–527.
60 Georg B. Michels, *The Habsburg Empire under siege: Ottoman expansion and Hungarian revolt in the age of Grand Vizier Ahmed Köprülü (1661–1676)* (Montreal: McGill-Queen's University Press, 2021), pp.79–80.
61 Kraus, *Cronica Transilvaniei* pp.573–574.
62 Géza Pálffy, *Hungary between Two Empires (1526–1711)* (Bloomington: Indiana University Press, 2021), p.137.

sultan but their plans were discovered by Habsburg authorities. Vienna orchestrated a swift and ruthless response by executing the ring leaders and by temporarily suspending the privileges of the estates in Hungary.[63] Several decades of tensions and conflicts followed, generating a state of political instability in the whole region.

Officially, Prince Apafi was regarded as a protector of the Hungarian rebels and gave shelter to many nobles and commoners who had fled their lands to escape Habsburg persecution. In 1678 he even joined an alliance with France and the Polish-Lithuanian Commonwealth against the Habsburgs. Prince Apafi promised to raise an army of 9,000 cavalry and 6,000 infantry if his allies would offer financial subsidies. Eventually their help proved to be rather limited, consisting of three companies of Polish infantry (about 300 soldiers), recruited with French money. The so called 'French flags' became a part of the court army and were kept in service for several years.[64] Raids and skirmishes became increasingly frequent in the frontier area between Transylvania, Hungary, and the Ottoman Empire. The principality was willing to organise small scale campaigns in support of the Hungarian rebels but could not fully commit to a war against the Habsburg monarchy. When the Ottoman sultan approved, Apafi mobilised his troops and sent them into Habsburg territory but failed to achieve any significant successes.[65]

Internally, Transylvania was once again divided between the two political options represented by the two neighbouring empires. The councillors of the prince could rarely agree on matters of foreign policy and the problem of the Hungarian rebellion was a constant reason for quarrelling. A very influential nobleman, Mihályi Teleki, was slowly gaining more power in the shadow of the prince. One by one he eliminated his political adversaries and dominated the Princely Council and the Diet through shrewd diplomacy and intimidation. Initially he was a follower of the pro-Ottoman policy and personally led two campaigns to help the Hungarian rebels in 1672 and 1678, but later he changed sides, and he became one of the main supporters of the Habsburgs in Transylvania.[66]

In 1681 the relations between the Ottomans and the Habsburgs had reached a critical point and were soon followed by open war. The sultan decided to take advantage of the Hungarian rebellion and established contacts with its leader, Imre Thököly. The European vassals of the Turks were called to arms and sent towards the Hungarian frontier. The voivode of Moldavia sent 3,000 men, Wallachia contributed with 4,000, while Transylvania mobilised an army of 8,000 soldiers. In addition, the Transylvanians brought five cannons (one 24-pdr, one 18-pdr and three 12-pdrs) and two mortars. The Ottomans mobilised a modest army of 9,000 soldiers from the border regions. The total size of the army was rather impressive (about 24,000 men), but its

---

63 Pálffy, *Hungary between Two Empires*, pp.149–151.
64 Ardelean, *Organizarea militară*, pp.190–212.
65 Florin Nicolae Ardelean, 'War and Social Conflicts in Early Modern Border Areas: Colonel Ludovicus de La Borde and Satu Mare (Szatmár) Frotress (1673–1677)', *Hiperboreea*, vol. 8, no.1 (2021), pp.16–38.
66 Ardelean, *Organizarea militară*, pp.354–357.

performance was affected by lack of cohesion and frequent desertions. The army of Transylvania began marching on 21 August, from a camp situated near the fortress of Gherla. Commanded by the appointed captain general, Mihályi Teleki, the Transylvanians headed west, towards the Ottoman fortress of Oradea and then crossed the frontier into Habsburg controlled territory. They targeted fortifications defended by German garrisons like Böszörmény, Kálló, Ecsed and Satu Mare, but in most cases the defenders were able to hold their ground while the attackers preferred to plunder the countryside. On 21 October, after exactly two months, the Transylvanian army had returned home without achieving anything of note.[67]

In the following year, 1682, the Ottomans organised a new offensive in Upper Hungary and Michael Apafi was summoned again to fulfil his military obligation as vassal of the sultan. In this campaign, the size of the Transylvanian army is estimated at between 5,000 and 8,000 soldiers. The prince decided to command the army personally and set out for the fortress of Fiľakovo (Fülek) in early August. They marched at a slow pace and reached their destination almost one month later, on 2 September. There they joined the army of the Ottomans and the Hungarian rebels who were making preparations for the siege. The defenders of the fortress capitulated on 10 September, and the Pasha of Buda appointed Thököly as ruler of Northern Hungary.[68] With the main objective of the campaign completed, Apafi headed back home, and his troops reached their quarters on 15 October.[69]

In 1683 the Transylvanian army was mobilised for the third consecutive year. This time the Ottomans had set their eyes on the imperial city of Vienna and were preparing to deal a decisive blow against their European archenemy, the Habsburg monarchy. Prince Apafi was not very motivated because he feared that the Turks might replace him with the leader of the Hungarian rebels, Thököly. He was also aware of the fact that a drastic change in the balance of power between the two empires could mean the end of an autonomous Transylvania. Nevertheless, the sultan's orders could not be ignored and on 8 July the army of Transylvania was once again on the march. The court guard, Székely detachments, boyars from Făgăraș, musketeers from Chioar and several contingents of mercenaries (the so called 'field army') made up a modest force of about 6,000 soldiers. The Transylvanians were in no hurry to reach Vienna and their march lasted almost two months. When they finally reached the Ottoman camp, they were assigned tasks of secondary importance, like guarding river crossings and patrolling the countryside. Soon after their arrival, the Ottomans were defeated in the battle of Kahlenberg and were forced to lift the siege. Apafi and his troops began a long a tiring march back home. An epidemic (most probably typhus)

---

67 Sándor Szilágyi, 'Az erdély 1681-ik hadjárat előkeszületéinek történetéhez', *Hadtörténelmi Közlemények*, vol. IV, (1891), pp.415–420; MCRT, vol. XVII, p.338; Bethlen, *Descrierea*, pp.170–172.
68 Pálffy, *Hungary between Two Empires*, p.162.
69 MCRT, vol. XVII, p.339; Bethlen, *Descrierea*, p.174.

ravaged the ranks of the army and only half of those who set out for this campaign returned to their homes.[70]

After the failed Ottoman siege of Vienna in 1683, the Habsburgs began a slow but steady offensive in Hungary, conquering many territories and settlements which were once part of the realm of Saint Stephen. In just a few years, Austrian regiments and diplomats had reached 'the gates' of the Transylvanian Principality. After long negotiations, in 1685 Transylvania signed their first agreement with the Habsburgs and agreed to offer quarters to five Austrian regiments, in the county of Maramureș, for the winter of 1685/1686. The whole country had to pay special contributions for the provisions necessary to sustain them. Aware of the changes taking place in Transylvania, the Ottomans tried to impose a new prince, none other than the rebel leader Imre Thököly, but his troops were defeated by a Transylvanian army commanded by Mihályi Teleki.[71]

A significant part of the Transylvanian political elite was unhappy with the prospect of becoming subjects of the Hapsburg emperor, fearing the loss of privileges and religious freedom. The most notable attempt to oppose the Habsburg occupation took place on the lands of the Saxon University, in the southern parts of the country. Representatives of all the three Transylvanian estates gathered in Sibiu and convinced Prince Apafi to mobilise the army and to appoint a new captain general, Gergely Bethlen. The Saxons provided 2,000 infantry according to their old custom, and the Székely had also answered the summons and together with the court guard they set their main camp in the vicinity of Sibiu. Nevertheless, they were denied the chance to prove their valour in battle one last time. The Habsburgs avoided a major confrontation despite their numerical advantage because they wanted to occupy Transylvania as peacefully as possible.

In the autumn of 1687, Charles V, Duke of Lorraine entered Transylvania at the head of a large army (40,000 men) after having achieved a great victory against the Ottomans at Mohács. It was now clear for Prince Apafi and for all his councillors that the Ottomans were unable to provide any assistance and that entering into negotiations with the Habsburgs was the only viable option. According to the terms of a treaty signed on 27 October 1687, the Transylvanians accepted Austrian garrisons in 12 of the most important fortress and fortified towns. In addition, they also agreed to provide money and massive quantities of victuals for the Austrian field army which had established some of its winter quarters on Transylvanian territory.[72]

The presence of Austrian regiments in Transylvania was overwhelming and the political elite of the country had no other choice but to accept the demands of Viennese authorities. Armed opposition was isolated and without any major successes. In 1688 for example, a large group of disgruntled citizens from Brașov, in the lands of the Saxon University, took control of the town's defences and refused to accept the Austrian garrison inside. General Frederico Veterani, with 3,000 soldiers, was sent to quell

---

70 Ardelean, *Organizarea militară*, p.359.
71 Bethlen, *Descrierea*, pp.185–186; Andea, *Transilvania*, pp.326–329.
72 Volkmer, *Siebenbürgen*, pp.481–484; Ardelean, *Organizarea militară*, pp.362–363.

this minor rebellion. He was joined by Mihályi Teleki, as representative of the Transylvanian prince, who tried to persuade the locals to lay down their weapons and accept the new political situation as the rest of the country had already done. The rebels resisted at first and even tried to obtain help from their southern neighbours in Wallachia. Without help from the outside they eventually surrendered, and the leaders were executed.[73]

Prince Michael Apafi I died on 15 April 1690 and the Transylvanian throne was inherited by his son, Michael Apafi II, who had already been elected as his successor in the summer of 1681. However, his authority was greatly diminished by the Habsburg involvement in all aspects of political and administrative life. The history of the autonomous Principality of Transylvania officially ended on 27 October 1690 with the signing of the Treaty of Blaj (Balázsfalva).[74] In the following years the territories of Transylvania were gradually integrated in the political and administrative framework of the composite Habsburg monarchy. The estates were able to maintain some of their freedoms and privileges but, from here on, all important decisions were taken in Vienna.

---

73 Ioachim Crăciun, 'Răzvrătirea sașilor din Brașov la 1688', *Studii și Materiale de Istorie Medie*, I (1956), pp.199–211.
74 Pálffy, *Hungary between Two Empires*, pp.164–165.

2

The Organisation of the Transylvanian Army

From a military point of view, the seventeenth century was a period of reform and innovation in Transylvania. Some of the main elements in the composition of the army, like the noble levy or the military detachments provided by the other estates (Saxons and Székelyi), were maintained from the previous century, but their importance was gradually diminished. The permanent professional military groups, like the court army and fortress garrisons increased in size and importance. Regular wages became the most common and appreciated way of compensation for military service although land donations, tax exemptions and access to political and administrative offices remained an important incentive for the social elite of the country. Compared to the previous century, Transylvanian rulers relied on a more diversified military structure. Sources indicate the presence of new elements in the military framework of the principality like the field army (mostly local mercenaries) and an increased presence of German mercenaries.

Nobility

The nobility was the most influential of the three Transylvanian political estates and performed military service as a duty derived from its privileged status. The obligation of the nobles to join the army was regularly mentioned during estate assemblies (Diets). The laws and regulations issued by the prince and the Diet are some of the most important historical sources for understanding how Transylvanian nobles fulfilled their military duties. Although a general pattern had been set during the Middle Ages, when Transylvania was a voivodate (province) in the Kingdom of Hungary, the military obligations of the nobility changed over time.

Soon after he gained the throne in 1613, Prince Gabriel Bethlen was eager to reorganise the armed forces of the principality. A Diet summoned in February 1614 reiterated the obligation of all nobles to join the army apart from those who were employed in the service of other nobles or at the princely court. Because in previous years many had used this situation as a pretext to avoid mobilisation, the prince and the Diet decided that those who were unable to join the army personally had the obligation to provide an armed servant as replacement.[1]

In 1616, Sultan Ahmed I called Gabriel Bethlen to fulfil his duty as vassal and send his troops into Moldavia. Soon after the sultan's order had reached Alba Iulia, letters of mobilisation, sometimes accompanied by precise instructions, were sent to all counties. A detailed set of instructions was dispatched to Francis Rhédey, lord lieutenant (*ispán/comes*) of Bihor County, princely councillor and captain of Oradea fortress, on 9 January 1616. Before the document was issued, Bethlen sent commissaries to all counties to verify the number of nobles and the size of their estates. The date of the muster was 25 January, and the place of gathering was Oradea fortress, on the western frontier of Transylvania. The *hajdú* (most of them from Bihor County) and the cavalry from Oradea fortress were also expected to present themselves for inspection. Rhédey was instructed to observe with great care all nobles who came to camp and to check the size of their retinues, according to the records made by the commissaries. A noble who had between 15 and 20 serfs on his estates was expected to bring two well-armed horsemen; those with 32, 35 or 40 serfs were to bring three horsemen; those with 50 or 60 serfs five horsemen; those with 70, 75 or 80 serfs were to bring seven horsemen; those with more than 100 serfs were required to bring at least eight horsemen. Poor nobles were expected to fight as light cavalry and if they could not afford a horse they should come as infantrymen, armed with a handgun, a sabre and at least 100 rounds.[2]

Under certain circumstances, nobles had the opportunity to avoid participating in military campaigns, even if these were fought inside the borders of the country. For example, in 1616, the nobility of Maramureș County, situated in the northern parts of the principality, was exempted from attending the military campaign against the rebel garrison of Lipova. The distance between Maramureș and Lipova was considerable, and Gabriel Bethlen preferred to collect an extraordinary tax of 3,338 florins, roughly enough to pay the wages of 500 cavalry for two months.[3]

The counties mobilised their armed detachments for the campaigns of Gabriel Bethlen against the Habsburgs in the Thirty Years' War (1619–1621, 1623–1624, 1626). The Diet complained often about the long length of these expeditions and tried to limit the number of soldiers provided by the estates.[4] In 1620, for example, the counties mobilised only 1,700 cavalry and 1,200 infantry, although their recruitment potential far exceeded these numbers.[5] However, many Transylvanian nobles saw this war as a good opportunity

---

1 MCRT, vol. VI, p.415.
2 Áron Szilády, Sándor Szilágyi (eds.), *Török-Magyarkori Állam-Okmánytár I. Török-Magyarkori történelmi emlékek. Okmánytár*, III (Pest: Eggenberger, 1868), pp.142–144.
3 Livia Ardelean, 'Gabriel Bethlen și politica economică și militară față de comitatul Maramureș', Veronka Dáné et al. (eds.), *Bethlen Erdélye, Erdély Bethlene: Bethlen Gábor trónra lépésének 400. évfordulóján rendezett konferencia tanulmányai: 24–25 október 2013, Kolozsvár* (Cluj-Napoca: Societatea Muzeului Ardelean, 2014), p.511.
4 Ardelean, *Organizarea militară*, pp.75–76.
5 Szilády, Szilágyi (eds.), *Török-Magyarkori*, III, p.218.

for social and financial gain and joined the princely army as members of the expanded court cavalry or as officers in the field army.

George Rákóczi I ordered a general muster of the nobility in the summer of 1634. The reason was an order from the Ottoman Sultan who was preparing for a campaign against Poland.[6] The Transylvanian nobles and their armed servants gathered in a camp near the town of Sebeş and remained there for nine weeks. The prince took advantage of this opportunity and organised thorough inspections of his troops.[7] The nobility of Cluj County was inspected on 18 August. A muster register, one of the few surviving documents of this type regarding the Transylvanian nobility, was drafted on the occasion. The document contains the names of nobles who had their main residence in Cluj County, followed by small notes referring to the number of armed servants or the reason for exemption. Absent nobles were also mentioned at the end of the register.

The total number of registered nobles was 165 but among them 43 were exempted from military obligations and 30 were absent. Most of them were middle and low-ranking nobles who went to war alone. Those who owned larger estates were expected to bring a certain number of mounted armed servants. The largest retinue, of 16 horsemen, was brought by the lord lieutenant (*fő ispán*) Mihályi Bánffy. It is worth mentioning that at the time two lord lieutenants were appointed for each county. While one was designated to command the county banner in war, the other remained home to deal with administrative and juridical matters. The banner of Cluj County counted a total number of 160 cavalry, both nobles and armed servants.[8]

Unfortunately, we lack similar sources for the other counties, but considering Cluj as an average size administrative unit, we can assume that the seven Transylvanian counties should have been able to provide about 1,000–1,200 cavalry. The counties from the western frontier, the so called *Partium* region, performed military service in a similar manner. Situated in a contested borderland these counties could have provided larger military detachments, but many nobles from these parts served in garrisons of border fortifications such as Oradea, Chioar, and Hust. All in all, we can conclude that in 1634, Prince George Rákóczi I relied on a significant cavalry force of roughly 3,000 men, mustered by the nobility and ready to fight beyond the borders of Transylvania.

In case of necessity the nobility could have provided a significantly higher number of armed men. In 1642 all nobles from the principality were gathered to swear an oath of fealty to the son of George Rákóczi I and heir to Transylvanian throne, George Rákóczi II. According to the sources who mention this event, 2,148 nobles came from inner Transylvania (the seven counties who formed the medieval voivodeship) and 5,140 came from the western counties (the so called *Partium* region). The counties of Bihor and

---

6   Mahmut Halef Cevrioğlu, 'Sultan Murad IV's Polish Campaign (1634)', *Acta Poloniae Historica*, 122 (2020), pp.209–246.
7   MCRT, vol. IX, pp.407–408; Kraus, *Cronica Transilvaniei*, p.91; Kemény, *Memorii*, p.172.
8   Miklós Lázár, 'Kolos-vármegye 1634-iki lustrája', *Magyar Történelmi tár*, 3/1 (1878), pp.198–204.

Maramureș, for example, had between 1,500–2,000 noble families but many of them would have qualified as 'petty nobility', unable to perform military duty on horseback.[9] Many of them were exempted from military service because of age, illness or because they served in other positions, including the court army. Based on this exceptional source we can assume that the Transylvanian nobility would have been able to muster up to 10,000 soldiers, including their armed servants, but according to tradition they were fully mobilised only for defensive wars.

In 1653, the Transylvanian Diet issued a general compilation of laws referring to all aspects of governance and public affairs, known as *Approbatae Constitutiones*. The noble levy was, of course, among the major subjects approached by the authors. In theory all members of the noble class had the obligation to join the army. Those who failed to answer the order of mobilisation had to pay a fine according to their status: 12 florins for low-ranking nobles who owned a single house and land plot; 25 florins for nobles who owned less than one *porta* (a fiscal unit consisting of several families of serfs); 50 florins for nobles who owned more than half a *porta*; 100 florins for nobles who owned one whole *porta* or more. Exemptions were clearly defined because authorities were concerned with maintaining a high number of soldiers in the army. Those who were employed at court and those suffering from illness or disability were not expected to personally join the county banner but had to send an armed servant as replacement. A considerable number of Transylvanian noble families had limited material means and were unable to procure a warhorse and all the necessary weapons and equipment. Nevertheless, they were expected to join the army with infantry equipment.[10]

The noble levy continued to be regarded mainly as a defensive military apparatus. When George Rákóczi II went on his Polish campaign in 1657 many nobles chose to follow him but there is no clear evidence that the county banners were fully mobilised for this expedition. On the contrary, some sources suggest that a significant part of the nobility remained at home. After the prince and his army crossed the frontier into Poland, Hetman Jerzy Lubomirski decided to attack the northern parts of Transylvania. Initially the counties which were directly threatened by this attack (Satu Mare, Maramureș, Szabolcs and Bihor) mobilised their banners and gathered in a camp situated in the vicinity of Satu Mare fortress. Ákos Barcsay, appointed regent in the absence of the prince, proclaimed a general levy to answer the unexpected Polish threat. The estates were outraged because they had already sent their best troops with the prince but nevertheless, they were able to muster a small army of 5,000 men, mostly from the counties and the Saxon seats and districts.[11]

---

9   János B. Szabó, 'The Army of the Principality of Transylvania in the Period of the Thirty Years' War', Gábor Kármán (ed.), *The Princes of Transylvania in the Thirty Years' War* (Paderborn: Brill Schöningh, 2022), p.42.
10 *Constituțiile Aprobate*, pp.119–123.
11 Kraus, *Cronica Transilvaniei*, pp.207–214; MCRT, vol. IX, pp.401–402.

THE ORGANISATION OF THE TRANSYLVANIAN ARMY

In the second half of the seventeenth century the size of the county banners steadily diminished. In 1671 the prince called only 100 cavalry form each county, except for Dăbâca County which provided only 50 horsemen. These small detachments were inspected in camp and those who were up to standard were kept in service for the duration of the campaign and received regular wages.[12]

In the first half of the seventeenth century the weapons and equipment of the noble cavalry were roughly the same as in the previous period. The lance and the sabre remained the most important offensive weapons. In addition, more and more Transylvanian mounted troops, including the nobility, used gunpowder weapons, especially pistols and other types of short-barrelled guns.[13] They were very similar, in terms of appearance, weapons and fighting style, to the Croat cavalry, employed by the Habsburgs or elsewhere in Central and Western Europe.[14]

Pistol-armed Hungarian cavalry clashing with Turks. Transylvanian soldiers had similar equipment, clothing, and weapons. Gáspár Bouttats, 1686 (Rijksmuseum)

The curved Ottoman style sabre (*szablya* in Hungarian or *framea* in Latin sources) was present in the personal arsenal of every Transylvanian nobleman and it was also used by infantry troops. Another type of blade was a cavalry long sword, used for stabbing and piercing chainmail, attached to the horse saddle. These swords appear in sources under different names, *kard, pallos* or *hegyestőr*, with small differences in size and shape. Some of the Transylvanian nobles from the seventeenth century owned impressive collection of such blades. For example, an inventory made in 1629 in one of the houses owned by Francis Miko, chief treasurer of Prince Gabriel Bethlen, mentions no less

---

12 MCRT, XV, pp.202–203.
13 Ödön Olchváry, 'Bethlen Gábor hadseregének szervezete s hadviselési módszere a II. Ferdinánd ellen viselt háborúkban', *Hadtörténelmi Közlemények*, I (1881), p.603.
14 János B. Szabó, 'Bethlen Gábor, az újjászervező. A kora újkori hadügyi fejlődés Kelet-Közép-Európában: az Erdélyi Fejedelemség példája a XVII. század első felében (1.rész)', *Hadtörténelmi Közlemények*, 126/4 (2013), p.976.

than 27 long swords (*pallosok*) and 21 swords (*kardok*).¹⁵ Of course, weapons were important symbols of social status and their presence in large quantities in the personal inventories of various noblemen can be linked to their wealth or political connections. Richly decorated weapons were considered valuable gifts and used as such to consolidate relations between the members of the Transylvanian elite. Nevertheless, weapons were also 'practical tools of war' used in battle. High-ranking nobles needed more weapons because they were expected to join the army with retinues of servants (lower ranking nobles and conscripted peasants) armed at their expense.

The distinctive clothes, weapons and equipment of nobles are thoroughly described in various narrative sources. Foreign travellers, like Pastor Iacob Conrad Hiltebrandt from Szczecin (Stettin) who travelled through Transylvania between 1656 and 1658 as a member of the Swedish embassy, were amazed by the mixture of European and Ottoman customs. In Hiltebrandt's opinion the Oriental influence can be seen in the brightly coloured tunics (*mente*), the red and yellow boots, and the silk sash worn instead of a belt. In addition, Transylvanian nobles wore a long overcoat (*dolmány*), trimmed with fox and marten fur. When they went to war, nobles and other mounted soldiers wore a hat adorned with long eagle feathers and a whole wolf fur was carried across one shoulder. Another important accessory was a belt with the cartridge and gunpowder box attached. The most common weapons were a sabre with a 'hook shaped' handle, a long sword used for piercing chainmail, a pistol, and a carbine. Some wore breastplates, helmets, and metal gloves up to the elbow.¹⁶ Although he was a cleric, Hiltebrand was a keen observer of military matters and provided valuable descriptions of other Transylvanian soldiers as we shall see in the following chapters.

Sisak cavalry helmet, seventeenth century (Țării Crișurilor Museum, Oradea, Romania)

One of the most valuable narrative sources on the military customs of Transylvanian nobility in the second half of the seventeenth century is the work of Baron Péter Apor, *Metamorphosis Transylvaniae*. Writing in the beginning of the eighteenth century, after the Habsburg conquest of Transylvania, Baron Apor recalls the days of his youth in the autonomous principality, ruled by Michael Apafi I. His narrative is abundant in details regarding

---

15 Magyar Nemzeti Levéltár Országos Levéltára (MNL OL), Urbaria et Conscriptiones, E 156 – a. - Fasc. 118. - No. 002, f.38–41.
16 *Călători străini despre Țările Române*, vol. V, Maria Holban, Maria Matilda Alexandrescu-Dresca Bulgaru, Paul Cernovodeanu (eds.), (București: Editura Științifică și Enciclopedică, 1973), pp.552–553.

the everyday life of the nobility, including some very important observations regarding clothes, weapons and military equipment in general.

According to Apor, an extremely popular headdress among the nobility, especially during the second half of the seventeenth century, was the so-called Cossack hat (*kozáksüveg*). Even Prince Apafi used to wear such a hat on many occasions. It was a not very tall fur trimmed hat, with velvet lining. The most common type of fur used for this item was pine marten, beech marten, and fox. The hats were often adorned with diverse types of feathers (ostrich, egret, osprey, crane and eagle plumes) attached with jewelled clasps.[17]

There was no clear distinction between everyday clothes and those worn on military campaigns. Nobles wore a coat or tunic called a *mente*, with low hanging sleeves, in the shape of dog ears. This item came in assorted sizes. While some were short, coming to just below the waist others were long enough to cover the knees and most of them were beautifully embroidered. The long *mente* was also called a boyar *mente* (*boér menténak*), being similar to the Ottoman caftans worn by Wallachian and Moldavian boyars. A coloured silk sash was worn around the waist. Another important piece of clothing was the *dolmány*, a long overcoat with gold or silver buttons.[18]

An interesting aspect mentioned by Apor is the habit of wearing whole animal furs over the usual garments or over armour. Towards the end of the seventeenth century high-ranking nobles dressed even their mounted servants in such leopard, tiger, or wolf skins.[19] This habit, probably of Ottoman origin, is also mentioned in earlier narrative sources and was considered a distinctive feature of military fashion in these parts of Europe.[20]

Weapons, with their practical and symbolic value, were present in the everyday life of the social elite. Young nobles used to carry maces decorated with

Two Hungarians or Transylvanians, from the anonymous map dated between 1690 and 1710. Same drawing was used in later map of 'Hungary and Transylvania', published in 1750 (Rijksmuseum)

---

17 Péter Apor of Altorja, *Metamorphosis Transylvaniae* (translated by Bernard Adams), (London and New York: Routledge, 2010), pp.19–20; 27–29.

18 Apor of Altorja, *Metamorphosis*, pp.32–34; Mária Pakucs-Willcocks, 'From "old" fashion to "new" fashion in pre-modern Transylvania', in Constanța Vintilă et al (eds.), *Luxury, Fashion and other Political Bagatelles in Southeastern Europe 16th–19th Century* (București: Humanitas, 2022), pp.357–365.

19 Apor of Altorja, *Metamorphosis*, p.29.

20 Kemény, *Memorii*, pp.258–259; Kraus, *Cronica Transilvaniei*, p.188.

gold, silver, or precious stones, while those hailing from modest families had simple iron maces. Sometimes they also carried small axes, hatchets, or Tatar whips (*nohajka*), decorated in a similar fashion. Boots were usually yellow, or red. Black boots were only worn at funerals and for mourning the passing of a family member. After marriage, men grew beards by custom. Regular shaving was exceptional, but many nobles used to shave their heads.[21] Funerals were also a good opportunity for displaying the symbols of the military profession. The coffin of a deceased noble was usually accompanied by two armour-clad men, mounted on caparisoned horses, and armed with gilded sabres and other richly decorated weapons. One of them carried a black banner while the other held a golden one.[22]

Nobles always carried weapons when they left their estates and were usually accompanied by armed mounted servants. When travelling with a larger retinue, including carriages and pack horses, the nobles' main war horse, with the long sword (*hegyestőr*) attached to the saddle, was always kept at the back of the marching column. A larger broadsword (*pallos*) was strapped in a similar manner on the saddle of another horse. Sabres were always attached to the waist, and some had a sabretache (*szablyatarsoly*) hanging over the sabre. Most nobles and their armed servants wore a bandolier with a small round container for gunpowder and a pouch full of shots. Carbines (*karabély*) were widespread at the time and many nobles possessed several such weapons, some richly decorated. Flints were very rare while the most common gunpowder weapons were a wheel-lock musket called *stuc*, the Teschen musket (*tersényi puska*) with a rifled barrel and another type of wheel-lock musket called *kőszegi pulyhák*, with a smooth barrel, which was very popular among the *Hajdú*. According to their names these weapons were produced in neighbouring regions like Cieszyn (Teschen) in Silesia and Kőszeg in Western Hungary.[23]

Many high-ranking nobles afforded and used pieces of heavy defensive equipment until the end of the seventeenth century. Miklós Bethlen recounts in his autobiography that in his youth he bought an armour set from a famous craftsman in Košice, for the considerable sum of 135 florins.[24] The suit consisted of a helmet, heavy breastplate decorated with gilded tinplate and metal gloves reaching up to the elbow. Among his other personal weapons, he mentions a hunting rifle (rifled barrel gun), a Teschen musket which he used on horseback and a pair of richly decorated pistols.[25]

Seventeenth century nobility performed a fundamental role in the Transylvanian army. Initially, military service was perceived as an obligation deriving from privileged status and thus, all nobles, regardless of their wealth or position, had to obey the 'call to war' of the prince. Their organisation was based on a retinue system, according to which those who owned large

---

21 Apor of Altorja, *Metamorphosis*, pp.31–33.
22 Apor of Altorja, *Metamorphosis*, pp.79–81.
23 Apor of Altorja, *Metamorphosis*, pp.49–50.
24 The value of the armour set was very high considering that at the time a horseman in the court army received a monthly wage of three to five florins.
25 Bethlen, *Descrierea*, pp.58, 95, 107.

estates were expected to join the county banner with a proportional number of armed servants, lesser nobles and conscripted peasants. The lower strata of the nobility, very numerous in the principality, went to war alone, mounted or on foot. With the passing of time the size of county banners decreased. Many nobles preferred to join the court army, the field army or the permanent garrisons of border fortifications in exchange for regular wages and other social and material benefits.

A precise assessment of the size of noble levies is difficult because of insufficient muster registers. Nevertheless, according to existing sources, both official and narrative, we can conclude that the Transylvanian nobility, together with their armed servants, should have been able to muster up to 10,000 soldiers in case of a defensive war and about 2,000–3,000 men for foreign campaigns.

Sources referring to the weapons and equipment of the nobility indicate that they provided a wide variety of cavalry soldiers, armed with both close combat and ranged weapons: semi-heavy shock cavalry armed with lances, long swords and other weapons for close combat; light cavalry with the lance as main offensive weapon; mounted troops armed with gunpowder weapons similar to dragoons; and also, light infantry armed with muskets.

County Militia

The custom of conscripting peasants for military service had a long tradition in the Kingdom of Hungary and was inherited by the Principality of Transylvania after 1541. It was essentially a proportional recruitment of soldiers from the non-privileged strata of society, meant to supply the royal and later princely army with an increased number of combatants in the face of the increasing Ottoman threat. The issue was often discussed during Diet sessions when aspects such as the rate of conscription (for example one soldier for every 10 serfs) or weapon requirements were established. The conscription rate varied from one year to another as well as the recruitment criteria which were sometimes the number of serfs, land plots or fiscal units called *porta*, consisting of 10 serf households. Sometimes, the direct recruitment of peasants was replaced by the payment of a war tax used for the wages of mercenary units.[26]

The rulers of the Transylvanian Principality continued to demand the mobilisation of county militias, especially during the first half of the seventeenth century. The direct recruitment of peasant soldiers was sometimes replaced by the payment of a tax. In 1614, the Diet imposed a special war tax of three florins per every fiscal unit (*porta*), representing the monthly wage of a mercenary soldier.[27] Two years later, Prince Gabriel

---

26 András Borosy, 'The Militia Portalis in Hungary before 1526', in János M. Bak, Béla K. Király (eds.), *From Hunyadi to Rakoczi. War and Society in Late Medieval and Early Modern Hungary* (New York: Columbia University Press, 1982), pp.63–80; Ardelean, *On the Borderland*, pp.34–37.
27 MCRT, vol. VII, p.181.

Bethlen decided to return to direct recruitment of soldiers because he lacked manpower for his infantry. Thus, every fiscal unit (*porta*) was expected to provide one soldier armed with a gunpowder weapon.²⁸ This conscription rate was considered remarkably high and during the same year, in the second session of the Diet, it was reduced to one soldier for every two *portae*. In addition, the provision mentioned the obligation of soldiers to bring enough supplies for the duration of the muster and to refrain from plundering the countryside on their way to the military camp of the prince.²⁹

Gunpowder container, seventeenth century (Țării Crişurilor Museum, Oradea, Romania)

Matters of military organisation were occasionally discussed and settled during the meetings of the nobility in each county (*generalis congregatio dominorum nobilium comitatus*). Following the requirements set during Diet sessions, each administrative division of the country, in this case the noble counties, were expected to organise their own banners. The county militia was one of the most important subjects. The documents issued on these occasions provide details on the conscription rate, weapon and equipment requirements, and mobilisation procedures. On 7 February 1616, the noble congregation of Turda County decided upon the mobilisation of the county militia with the following provisions: one foot soldier had to be recruited for every single *porta/kapu*. Nobles who owned smaller estates were expected to combine with others and provide one foot soldier in a similar manner. Each soldier was expected to have a good wool coat, a musket, a sabre and a hatchet (*köntöse, puskája, szablyája és szekercéje*).

The responsibility for preparing and arming these infantry soldiers was entrusted to each noble (*patronus*). In addition, they also had to oversee the collection of victuals for these soldiers from their own estates. For each *porta/kapu* they had to provide five litres of wine (about 10 pints), two loaves of bread, four pounds of meat, half a pound of salt, one hen, two bushels of oats, and one cart of hay for every two *portae*. Some of the products could be redeemed by paying a small tax equivalent with their market value.³⁰ The size of the detachment provided by Turda County in 1616 can be estimated with the help of a fiscal conscription muster roll made during the same year. A total number of 2,283 serfs (heads of families), meaning roughly 230 *portae*, were registered at the time.³¹ Considering the military conscription rate of one soldier for every *porta* we can conclude that the militia of Turda County

---

28 MCRT, vol. VII, p.280.
29 MCRT, vol. VII, p.389.
30 Veronka Dáné, (ed.), *Torda vármegye jegyzőkönyvei 1607—1658*, vol. I (Cluj-Napoca: Societatea Muzeului Ardelean, 2009), p.127.
31 Veronka Dáné, „*mennyi jobbágya és mennyi portiója*". *Torda vármegye birtokos társadalma a 17. Század első felében* (Cluj-Napoca: Societatea Muzeului Ardelean, 2016), pp.57–58.

counted about 230 soldiers in 1616. The actual size of the detachment might have been smaller because of exemptions or simply because some of the nobles failed to comply with the demands.

When Bethlen joined the Protestant faction in the Thirty Years' War he once again increased the rate of conscription and demanded both infantry and cavalry troops. In the spring of 1620, the prince expected one horseman and five infantry for every six *portae*.[32] It is unclear if this stipulation was referring only to Transylvanian counties or to all territories which were at the time under Bethlen's control (a significant part of Royal Hungary), but the Transylvanian Diet reacted and requested that all infantry troops should be left at home for defensive reasons.[33]

The documents are not always clear about who were those who joined the county militias. The Diet from Alba Iulia, held between 14 May and 6 June 1623, provides and exceptionally detailed instruction on the process of recruiting and mobilising the conscripted infantry and sheds light on the social background of these soldiers. The document clearly states that each lord who owns a large enough estate should mobilise one infantry soldier for every two *portae* (*kapu* in Hungarian). This soldier should be chosen from among his best suited serfs (*jobbágy*) who was going to be exempted from his other fiscal and work obligations. He would thus become a peasant-guardsman (*drabant*) armed with a good musket, obliged to attend musters organised by county commanders and join the army of the prince when required.[34]

George Rákóczi I was also concerned with organising a reliable militia, but mostly for defensive purposes. The Diet agreed that all nobles should keep prepared one foot soldier and one horseman for every single *porta*, who were expected to mobilise only when the country was menaced by an external threat.[35] As an authoritarian ruler, Prince Rákóczi was free to decide when and if such a threat meant taking the militias beyond the borders of Transylvania. In 1643 while he was preparing his campaign against the Habsburgs, he mustered all troops provided by the estates, including the militias. All counties answered the call and sent their detachments into the designated camp. On this occasion, for example, Maramureș County provided 150 infantry and 50 cavalry.[36]

The organisation of the county militia was also mentioned in the *Approbatae Constitutiones*, in 1653. The conscription rate was established at one horseman for every three *portae*, and one infantryman for every two *portae*. Because a significant part of the Transylvanian nobility owned very small estates, often less than one whole *porta*, the authorities decided that they should also contribute to the recruitment of the county militia by means of association, meaning that 10 lesser nobles, owning a single land

---

32 Szilády, Szilágyi (eds.), *Török-Magyarkori*, vol. III, p.218.
33 MCRT, vol. VII, p.542.
34 MCRT, vol. VIII, p.126.
35 MCRT, vol. IX, pp.273–274
36 Ionuț Costea, *Solam virtutem et nomen bonum: Nobilitate, Etnie, Regionalism în Transilvania Princiară* (Cluj-Napoca: Argonaut, 2005), p.164.

plot, had to club together to jointly provide one mercenary horseman in the county militia.[37]

Conscription rates and war taxes in Transylvanian Counties (1614–1653)[38]

Year	Conscription rate	War tax
1614		Three florins/one *porta*
May 1615	One foot soldier/one *porta*	
October 1615	One foot soldier/two *portae*	
March 1620	Five foot soldiers and one horseman/six *portae*	
April 1620	One foot soldier/one *porta*	
1623	One foot soldier/two *portae*	
1625	One foot soldier/three *portae*	
1626	One foot soldier/three *portae*	
1629		Five florins/one *porta*
1653	One horseman/three *portae*; One foot soldier/two *portae*	

The county militia is rarely mentioned in the second half of the seventeenth century because the focus had shifted to the organisation of small units of mercenary infantry at the court of the prince and around border fortifications. Part of the medieval heritage within the military organisation of the principality, peasant militias were regarded as an auxiliary element. Although officially mobilised in case of defensive wars, the county militia participated occasionally in external campaigns as well. Authorities oscillated between demanding a war tax and a direct recruitment of peasant-soldiers, mostly as infantry but sometimes also as cavalry detachments.

Székely

The Székely were a distinct ethnic group who had migrated together with the Hungarians in the Carpathian Basin and eventually settled in the south-eastern parts of Transylvania. In the Kingdom of Hungary they benefited from a privileged status, as a community, in exchange for military obligations. When Transylvania became a separate state, the social and political status of the Székely community underwent a radical change. In the second half of the sixteenth century, Transylvanian rulers were no longer willing to recognise their collective freedom and their privileges were officially suspended in

---

37 *Constituțiile Aprobate*, pp.122–124.
38 Ardelean, *Organizarea militară*, pp.108–114.

1562. Despite the ongoing strife and resentment against central authority they continued to play a vital role in the military organisation of the principality.[39]

At the beginning of the seventeenth century, Prince Stephen Bocskai made many concessions regarding the Székelys, because he wanted to preserve their military capacity. His strategy was followed, to a certain degree, by all the other Transylvanian rulers from the seventeenth century.[40] Székely society was divided into various groups and with the exception of serfs they all had military obligations. Nobles, leaders (*primipili/lófők*), foot soldiers (*pedites pixidari/gyalogpuskás*) and freemen (*libertini*), were all expected to join the army of the prince under certain circumstances.[41]

The military potential of the Székely Seats according to the 1614 conscription[42]

Seat	Nobility (*Primores*)	Leaders (*primipili/lófők*)	Foot Soldiers (*pedites pixidari/gyalogpuskás*)	Freemen (*libertini*)	Total heads of households	Total population with military obligations
Mureș (*Marosszék*)	43	611	382	491	3,682	1,527 (41.5 percent)
Odorhei (*Udvarhelyszék*)	46	683	558	480	4,477	1,767 (39.5 percent)
Trei Scaune (*Sepsi-, Kézdi- és Orbaiszék*)	63	140	285	270	1,545	758 (49.1 percent)
Cașin, Ciuc, Gheorgheni (*Kászon-, Csík- és Gyergyószék*)	120	693	555	525	2,708	1,893 (69.9 percent)
Total	272	2,127	1,780	1,766	12,412	5,945 (47.9 percent)

Soon after he ascended to the Transylvanian throne, Gabriel Bethlen wanted to know what the military capacity of the Székely was. A conscription

---

39 Balogh, *A székely nemesség*, pp.14–63; János B. Szabó, 'A székelyek katonai szerpe Erdélyben a mohácsi csatától a Habsburg uralom megszilárdulásáig (1526–1709)', in József Nagy (ed.), *A Határvédelem évszázadai Székelyföldön: Csíkszék és a Gyimesek vidéke. Szerkesztette és a jegyzékeket összeállította* (Szépvíz, 2018) pp.101–113.
40 Balogh, *A székely nemesség*, pp.66–68.
41 Ludovic Demény, 'Registrele militare – izvoare de demografie istorică și de cercetare a structurii sociale la secuii din secolul al XVI-lea', *Sub semnul lui Clio. Omagiu Acad.Prof. Ștefan Pascu* (Cluj: Universitatea Babeș-Bolyai, 1974), pp.80–85; Szabó, 'A székelyek katonai szerpe', p.113.
42 Lajos Demény, *Székely oklevéltár. Új sorozat 4. Székely népesség-összeírások, 1575–1627* (Kolozsvár: Az Erdélyi Múzeum-Egyesület Kiadása, 1997), pp.197–562.

order drafted in 1614 (as shown in the table above) offers an overview of Székely society, with its four groups who had to perform military service. Although one of their administrative divisions, the Seat of Arieş (*Aranyosszék*) was overlooked, this source provides an accurate estimation regarding the size of military detachments provided by the Székely estate. Nobles and leaders (*primipili/lófők*) fought as cavalry, while foot soldiers (*pedites pixidari/gyalogpuskás*) and freemen (*libertini*) mustered as infantry. According to this source the size of the cavalry detachment was of 2,399 soldiers and the infantry 3,546. It is noteworthy that a high percentage of the total population (47.9 percent) had to perform military duty but there is no evidence of a full mobilisation during the seventeenth century. On the contrary, documents indicate that the prince preferred to mobilise smaller detachments of selected soldiers as in March 1620 when only 600 Székely cavalry were expected to join the army of Prince Bethlen who was fighting against the Habsburgs in Hungary.[43]

George Rákóczi I had a similar approach to the Székely issue and kept a detailed record of their military capacity. In 1635 he organised musters (*lustratio*) in their seats (administrative divisions) but this time only three groups are recorded as having military obligations: nobles, leaders (*primipili*) and foot soldiers (*pedites pixidari*). Freemen are not mentioned in these documents because they were no longer expected to perform military service or, most probably, because they were merged with the foot soldiers.

Another interesting development can be observed in the case of the Székely nobles who are recorded together with a certain number of mounted retainers, just like their peers from the counties. In Trei Scaune (Sepsi-, Kézdi- és Orbaiszék) Seat, for example, 69 noble families are listed, a few more compared to the 63 mentioned in the 1614 conscription. However, the total number of mounted soldiers they were expected to provide was 175. With a few exceptions, Székely nobles went to war accompanied by at least one mounted servant while some had larger retinues of up to 12 men (as was the case of Beldi family). The largest retinue of 24 horsemen was brought by the captain general of the Seat (*Capitaneus Supremus*).[44] The overall size of the military contingents had increased considerably from the times of Gabriel Bethlen. Mureş Seat (Marosszék) mustered a total number of 3,916 soldiers (1,316 cavalry and 2,600 infantry) compared to the 1,527 recorded in 1614.[45]

The number of Székely soldiers was maintained high throughout the second half of the seventeenth century. They were expected to travel regularly for military musters, sometimes beyond the limits of their administrative divisions. In 1677, for example, the camp was set in Inner Szolnok County.[46]

---

43 Szilády, Szilágyi (eds.), *Török-Magyarkori*, vol. III, p.218.
44 Lajos Demény (ed.), *Székely oklevéltár. Új sorozat 5. Székely népesség-összeírások, 1635* (Kolozsvár: Az Erdélyi Múzeum-Egyesület Kiadása, 1997), pp.13–14.
45 Demény (ed.), *Székely oklevéltár* 5, p.480.
46 MCRT, vol. XVI, pp.374–378.

The number of nobles grew steadily to the detriment of other groups with military obligations.[47]

The Székely Seats had a very high proportion of people with military obligations but not all of them were expected to join the army on every campaign. The captain general of each seat was allowed to exempt a certain number of leaders and guardsmen if they agreed to pay a tax. The commander of Trei Scaune (Háromszék), for example, was allowed to exempt up to 100 men with military obligations from his seat. The other high-ranking officials of the seat had similar prerogatives and exempted people from military service in exchange for money contributions. Of course, the money gathered by means of exemption taxes was also used for the war effort.[48]

In terms of weapons and equipment Székely soldiers were similar to the other troops provided by Transylvanian Estates (the Nobility and the Saxons), although they kept their red clothing as a distinctive feature. The foot soldiers (*pedites pixidari*) were light infantry, armed with a musket, sabre and an axe.[49] According to custom, the Székely community provide light cavalry detachments in the Transylvanian army. Most of them used the lance as main offensive weapon but gunpowder weapons became increasingly common in the seventeenth century. As a consequence, some of the Székely horsemen were organised as dragoon companies in the second half of the seventeenth century.

On 28 June 1656, Prince George Rákóczi II raised 88 Székelys to the rank of dragoons (*equitum sclopetariorum*) in recognition of their military merits during the campaign in Wallachia. According to this document they were expected to have good horses, sabres and long muskets with sufficient gunpowder and shot (…*bonis equis, frameis, sclopetis longis, pulveribus ac globis sufficientibus bene instructi…*). They had to fight on horseback but, if necessary, they would dismount and fight as foot soldiers (…*et si res postulaverit equis descendere, et more peditum fidelem patriae operam navare debeant…*). The document also states that they would enjoy the same freedom and privileges as the leaders (*primipili*).[50] Such Székely dragoon companies were also mentioned one year later (1659) in the army of Prince Ákos Barcsay (*centumque bombardariis equestribus vulgo székely dragonyak nominati*).[51]

During the seventeenth century, the Székely Estate was able to regain some of its traditional privileges by providing a considerable number of troops for the Transylvanian army. Although Székely nobles were not nearly as numerous as those from the counties, they were joined on campaigns by significant detachments of cavalry (*primipili*) and infantry (*pedites pixidari*) from the other privileged groups of their community. Although the Székely seats should have been able to provide between 10,000 and 15,000 soldiers,

---

47 MCRT, vol. XVI, pp.606–607.
48 Apor of Altorja, *Metamorphosis*, p.87.
49 András Sófalvi, *Hadakozás és önvédelem a középkori és fejedelemség kori Udvarhelyszéken* (Kolozsvár, Erdélyi Múzeum-Egyesület, 2017), p.110.
50 Lajos Szádeczky (ed.), *Székely oklevéltár*, vol. VI (Kolozsvár: Magyar Történelmi Társulat Kolozsvári Bizottsága, 1897), pp.204–205.
51 MCRT, XII, p.345.

such a substantial number was never mobilised. Transylvanian rulers relied on smaller detachments of soldiers recruited from this area, between 6,000 and 10,000 men, but occasionally even less.[52] Székely foot soldiers were organised as troops of light infantry armed with muskets and some weapons for close combat as sabres and axes. Cavalry was very versatile and included nobles equipped with helmets and breastplates, light lancers without defensive equipment but also cavalry with firearms.

Saxons

The Saxons lived in the southern and eastern parts of Transylvania and were descendants of Western European (mostly German) colonists brought by the kings of Hungary in the twelfth and thirteenth centuries. Initially, their main task was the defence of the frontier, but during the second half of the sixteenth century their military obligations were increased and diversified.[53]

In the seventeenth century the Saxon community of Transylvania maintained some of its traditional military obligations: the mobilisation of local infantry troops, the production and transport of weapons, and the payment of war taxes.

During the decades that followed the formation of the Transylvanian Principality (1541–1613) the Saxons were able to mobilise between 500 and 3,000 infantry bearing firearms. This type of military obligation survived into the seventeenth century, although the number of Saxon soldiers decreased significantly. In 1614, Prince Gabriel Bethlen requested 500 soldiers from the seats and districts of the Saxon University, in addition to a sum of money sufficient for the recruitment of 500 mercenaries.[54]

Whenever Prince Bethlen mobilised the Transylvanian army for internal or external campaigns the Saxons were also called to arms. In 1616, on the occasion of the expedition against the rebel garrison of Lipova, the Saxons had to dispatch detachments of infantry according to their custom. The prince inspected them himself in a camp situated in the vicinity of Făgăraș fortress. During the campaign, Kelemen Béldi was appointed commander of these infantry troops together with the infantry detachments provided by the county nobility. However, the Saxons marched under their own banners and had their own officers. The soldiers sent by the town and district of Brașov had a black flag with a golden crown in the middle and received their wages from the town magistrate. The captains of a company (*hadnagy*) received monthly wages of 16 to 20 florins, while the wages of common soldiers were paid with three to three and a half florins a month. The town magistrate was also in charge of buying clothes and equipment for the soldiers, providing food provisions and wagons for their transport, tents and all that was necessary for

---

52 Szabó, 'The Army of the Principality', p.43.
53 Ardelean, *On the Borderlands,* pp.39–41; Liviu Cîmpeanu, 'The Transylvanian-Saxon University at War: Trabanten in John Sigismund Szapolyai's Campaigns at the North-Western Borders of Transylvania (1561–1567)', *Acta Musei Napocensis,* 58/II (2021), pp.11–29.
54 Harai, *Gabriel Bethlen,* pp.71–72.

daily life during a campaign. At the end of an expedition, wounded soldiers were given medical treatment and the families of those who had lost their lives were compensated.[55]

During his offensive campaigns against the Habsburgs (1619–1626), Gabriel Bethlen relied mostly on soldiers recruited in the western borderlands of Transylvania and in Upper Hungary. Nevertheless, the Saxons continued to provide small detachments of light infantry in addition to other contributions to the war effort. The town and district of Brașov mobilised between 65 and 96 soldiers for all the campaigns fought by Bethlen in the Thirty Years' War.[56]

George Rákóczi I (1630–1648) also mustered the Saxon infantry on a few occasions. In the first years of his reign, he established their contingent at 800 men, provided by each town, district and seat. While large towns recruited over 100 soldiers (Sibiu–164, Brașov–163, Bistrița–128), lesser settlements were expected to provide fewer men. On 14 January 1644, the prince sent an order of mobilisation to the Saxon University. He demanded 500 infantry with firearms, each with 200 bullets. The soldiers were expected 12 days later (on 26 January) at Alba Iulia with their supply wagons.[57]

All Transylvanian-Saxon towns were fortified and defended by small permanent garrisons. These soldiers received regular wages and were known as town guardsmen (*Stadtdrabanten*). In Brașov, for example, their numbers shifted between 60 and 80 men. Their main purpose was to defend the town, but they also fulfilled the role of a local police force. Sometimes these soldiers were locals who chose to perform military duty for regular wages but in many cases, town guardsmen were outsiders, Hungarians or Székely, employed by the town magistrate as mercenaries.[58]

Saxon towns were some of the most important centres of weapon production in Transylvania. They had fulfilled this role in the Middle Ages up to the sixteenth century and continued to do so in the seventeenth century. The town of Brașov, for example, supplied the army of Gabriel Bethlen with weapons and equipment and transported them to court or wherever the prince requested. Among the largest recorded shipments, we have: 1614 (600 lances *kopja*); 1620 (2,400 lances wrapped in linen and transported to the court in Alba Iulia in two different batches); 1621 (2,000 lances); 1623 (200 lances, 200 wagons, tents and blankets); 1626 (200 lances, 200 pairs of boots and 100 saddles and harnesses). The craftsmen of Brașov provided the army of Gabriel Bethlen with at least 5,400 lances (*kopja*). The cost of a lance varied between 14 and 40 denars. The transport of weapons and artillery

---

55 Zsuzsanna Cziráki, 'Brassói és barcasági katonák Bethlen Gábor hadseregében', *Belvedere Meridionale* XXII, (2010), pp.86–88.
56 Cziráki, 'Brassói és barcasági katonák', pp.90–94.
57 Csaba Izsán, 'Between Soldier and Guard: the Roles of the Town Mercenaries in the Late Sixteenth-Early Seventeenth Century Cluj (Klausenburg/Kolozsvár), Sighișoara (Schässburg/Segesvár) and Brașov (Kronstadt/ Brassó)', Florin Nicolae Ardelean et al. (eds.), *From Medieval Frontiers to Early Modern Borders in Central and South-East Europe* (Berlin: Peter Lang, 2022), pp.200–202.
58 Izsán, 'Between Soldier and Guard', pp.197–199; Cziráki, 'Brassói és barcasági katonák', pp.86–87.

was the duty of the Saxon Church and according to sources they continued to fulfil this obligation during the reign of Gabriel Bethlen.[59] In fact, this rather uncommon military obligation was maintained until 1674 when it was officially abolished by Prince Michael Apafi I.[60]

Information about the mobilisation of Saxon infantry contingents in the second half of the seventeenth century is scarce. During the troubled years following the unsuccessful Polish campaign of George Rákóczi II (1657), the Saxon community maintained a consistent pro-Ottoman policy. When Transylvania was faced with the prospect of the Habsburg conquest, Saxons towns were the most notable centres of resistance. In 1686, when some of the Transylvanians attempted to oppose the Habsburg troops that had entered the country, the Saxons provided 2,000 infantry, according to the old custom of mobilisation.[61]

In the seventeenth century, the military role of the Saxon community had decreased compared to the previous century. The prosperous Saxon towns of Transylvania were focused on self-defence, by maintaining permanent garrisons, and provided the army of the prince with logistic support such as weapons, war materials, artillery and transport. When Saxon contingents were mobilised for campaigns, they consisted of light infantry troops with firearms, between 500 and 2,000 men recruited from all the seats and districts of the Saxon community.

Hajdús

The *hajdús* were a social and military category settled in the borderlands of the Hungarian Kingdom, in the beginning of the sixteenth century. Initially cattle herders and traders, the *hajdús* were transformed into a privileged community with military obligations during the uprising of Stephen Bocskai in 1604–1606. Most of their settlements were situated in Szabolcs County (Royal Hungary) and Bihor County (Transylvania). By the time Gabriel Bethlen was elected prince in 1613, they became one of the most important military elements in the frontier area. During a muster organised at Oradea (Bihor County) in 1616, 1,082 *hajdús* were inspected by the captain of the fortress, Francis Rhédey. Previously they had served mostly as infantry but in the seventeenth century they were organised as mounted troops armed with firearms or lances.[62] According to a regulation issued in 1620 the standard equipment of a *hajdú* soldier included a good horse, helmet, breastplate, a hussar saddle, and a long sword (*hegyestőr* or *pallos*).[63]

There were attempts to abolish the privileges of the *hajdú* settlements in the borderlands, but Transylvanian rulers relied too much on their military services and thus decided to protect their status. An attempt to include the

---

59 Cziráki, 'Brassói és barcasági katonák', p.94
60 Keul, *Early Modern Religious Communities*, p.235.
61 Bethlen, *Descrierea*, p.188.
62 Szabó, 'Bethlen Gábor (1)', pp.980–981.
63 MCRT, vol. VII, p.546; Szabó, 'The Army of the Principality', p.39.

hajdú soldiers in the county banners was made in the early years of Bethlen's reign. In Bihor County they were mustered for inspection together with the nobility, but they maintained a distinct leadership.[64]

Sources indicate that their numbers had increased significantly by the time Prince Bethlen entered the Thirty Years' War. In the winter of 1620–1621, most of the 12,610 cavalry billeted in western Hungary were *hajdú* recruited from the counties of Bihor and Szabolcs.[65] When George Rákóczi I was elected Prince of Transylvania in 1630, he knew he could rely on about 20,000 *hajdú* soldiers.[66] According to the Transylvanian Diet their ranks had been swelled by runaway serfs. This was a very concerning phenomenon, especially for the nobles, who were losing their workforce. In several Diet sessions the estates complained that *hajdú* market towns sheltered runaway serfs who were attracted by the prospects of freedom and financial gain offered by military life.[67]

On the other hand, the prince saw the benefits of having a large military force, positioned on the western frontier of the country and ready to join any campaign inside or outside the country. That is one of the reasons why the privileges of the *hajdú* settlements were recognised by the *Aprobatae Constitutiones*, in 1653. *Hajdú* market towns were kept independent from the jurisdiction of county authorities but only the settlements which had received their privileges from Stephen Bocskai in 1605–1606, were recognised. Their freedom was conditional on military service. The prince and his appointed commanders organised regular inspections and all those found unfit for war would lose their status. Only the prince himself or the captain of Oradea fortress had to authority to pass judgement on issues concerning members of the *hajdú* community. On campaign, all their troops had the obligation to join the princely banner.[68]

The decision of George Rákóczi II to confirm the privileges of the *hajdú* proved to be a wise one, at least from his personal perspective. When he returned home from the failed campaign in Poland and the Ottomans wanted to replace him with an obedient vassal, the *hajdú* remained loyal to him and decided to defend his claim to the Transylvanian throne against the sultan's wishes.[69]

In the second half of the seventeenth century the *hajdú* appear in two roles, as semi-privileged groups on the estates of border fortifications or as armed servants of the nobility. At the same time, men claiming the status of *hajdú* had spread beyond the regions of Bihor and Szabolcs counties. The presence of *hajdú* in Maramureș County is attested in the second half of the seventeenth century but their social status was altered. In 1666, for example they were expected to pay the general tax as did all the other inhabitants of

---

64 MCRT, vol. VII, pp.175–176, 239.
65 István Seres, 'Bethlen Gábor hadainak szállás- és hadrendje 1621-ből: Újabb források az erdélyi hadsereg történetéhez', *Hadtörténelmi Közlemények*, 126/4 (2013), pp.1,050–1,066.
66 István Czigány, 'The 1644-1645 Campaign of György Rákóczi I', Gábor Kármán (ed.), *The Princes of Transylvania in the Thirty Years' War* (Paderborn: Brill Schöningh, 2022), p.87.
67 MCRT, vol. VIII, pp.132–133, 317.
68 *Constituțiile Aprobate*, pp.182–184.
69 MCRT, vol. XII, p.125.

the country.[70] On the other hand, some members of the *hajdú* community managed to acquire charters of ennoblement (*litterae armales/nemeslevél*) and swelled the ranks of the petty nobility.[71]

During the Late Medieval and Early Modern Age, the term *hajdú* had spread in many regions and languages of Central and Eastern Europe. It became a synonym for insurgent, brigand, or irregular soldier.[72] In Hungary and Transylvania, they were initially associated with infantry (in the sixteenth century), but in the seventeenth century they were organised almost entirely as cavalry detachments. The total number of *hajdú* soldiers is hard to assess because they were a very dynamic social group, who welcomed many newcomers (runaway serfs) but also suffered significant casualties in campaigns and as a consequence of the everyday perils of frontier warfare. When the rulers of Transylvania participated in the Thirty Years' War, the *hajdú* provided a significant number of soldiers. Although their highest recruitment capacity reached about 20,000 men, the commanders of the Transylvanian army relied on smaller detachments, undulating between a few thousand and over 10,000 men.

The Guard of the Prince

The Guard of the Prince, also known as the court army, was the most important group of professional soldiers in the Transylvanian army, divided in two branches, cavalry, and infantry. The cavalry of the court was maintained although its numbers were reduced in comparison to the sixteenth century. In the years after the election of Gabriel Bethlen the size of the mounted guard was about 600–700 soldiers. The infantry of the court was considered more important, and their numbers increased accordingly. The so called 'blue guardsmen', first mentioned during the reign of Stephen Báthory in the second half of the sixteenth century, were reorganised in the beginning of the seventeenth century. Five infantry captains served at court under Gabriel Bethlen each with 400–600 men. The size of the infantry guard increased significantly during the involvement of Transylvania in the Thirty Years' War at one point reaching up to 20 companies (about 2,000 soldiers).[73]

The guard was mobilised during foreign campaigns, as in 1616 when Bethlen joined the forces of Radu Mihnea and Skender Pasha in Moldavia to face the Polish Army. On the way back home, the army was divided into smaller detachments and followed different routes. The troops from the court army who received regular wages (*fizetet udvari hadunkal*) crossed the Carpathians into the territories of the Saxon town of Bistrița. The town

---

70   MCRT, vol. XII, p.188.
71   Pálffy, *Hungary between Two Empires*, p.170.
72   Michał Németh, 'Remarks on the etymology of Hung. hajdú 'herdsman' and Tkc. haydamak 'brigand', *Studia Turcologica Cracoviensia*, 10 (2005), pp.297–309.
73   Szabó, 'Bethlen Gábor (1)', p.977.

magistrate was asked to provide lodging and food for the soldiers in one of the neighbouring villages for one week.[74]

The soldiers of the guard were rarely concentrated in a single place. They were usually dispatched in various locations across the country, on princely estates but also in other important strategic locations. According to a list of the infantry guard compiled in 1621, 137 soldiers were with Prince Bethlen in Hungary and 100 soldiers were left at home to ensure the safety of the princess.[75] The accounts of Cluj also contain information about smaller groups of soldiers from the court army (up to 64), who resided in the town almost regularly from 1608 to 1630.[76]

Being a member of the court guard had some undeniable advantages. They were among the few soldiers in the principality who received regular wages in times of war and in times of peace. Nevertheless, their pay rate was not above that of other mercenary soldiers in the Transylvanian army. Common soldiers received monthly wages between one florin and 50 denars (in the case of new recruits) and three florins. The officers had, of course, considerably higher pay: four florins for a corporal (*decurionus*), four florins for a drummer, four florins for the standard bearer and 16 florins for a lieutenant (*hadnagy*). The chance of obtaining a title of nobility, lands and houses were a much stronger incentive. There were several cases of commoners from the court army who were raised among the nobility, with appropriate land donations for their faithful service.[77]

The 'Blue Guardsmen' constituted the core of the court infantry, especially in the first decades of the seventeenth century. The 'Green Riflemen' were a small group of skilled shooters organised by Prince George Rákóczi I (1630–1648) who was a very passionate hunter. They resided on various fiscal estates and 60 of them were always in the retinue of the prince. In times of war their numbers were increased to 200–300 and they sometimes fought on horseback.[78] His son and heir, George Rákóczi II, maintained a respectable number of 'Green Riflemen' who lived on some of the most important fiscal estates (Gherla, Gilău and Alba Iulia). According to a register compiled during his reign there were 145 soldiers belonging to this elite group.[79]

Like most contemporary European monarchs, the Prince of Transylvania was accustomed to travelling around the country and his courtiers followed him. Soldiers were an important presence in these itinerant courts. Transylvanian towns, like Bistriţa, kept detailed records of the expenses made during princely visits and are thus an important source for assessing the size

---

74 Nicolae Iorga (ed.), *Documente privitoare la Istoria Românilor*, (colecţia Hurmuzaki) vol. XV/2 (Bucureşti: Academia Română şi Ministerul Cultelor şi Instrucţiunii Publice, 1913), pp.873–874.
75 Béla Radvánszky, *Udvartartás és számadáskönyvek. I. Bethlen Gábor udvartartása* (Budapest: Atheneum, 1888), pp. 211–216.
76 Annamária Jeney-Tóth, "... *Urunk udvarnépe* ...": *Udvar és társadalma Báthory Gábor és Bethlen Gábor fejedelemsége idején a kolozsvári számadáskönyvek tükrében* (Debrecen: Debreceni Egyetemi Kiadó, 2012), pp.180–181.
77 Jeney-Tóth, "... *Urunk udvarnépe* ...", pp.182–183.
78 Szabó, 'The Army of the Principality', p.41; Costea, *Solam virtutem*, p.73.
79 Serviciul Judeţean al Arhivelor Naţionale, Cluj (SJAN CJ), Colecţia socoteli princiare, 46 Evidenţe nominale de efective militare, f.20–22.

and composition of the court guard. However, we must keep in mind that these soldiers who accompanied the prince during his travels represented only a fraction of the whole court army.

The court guard of Transylvanian princes during their visits to Bistriţa (1636–1655)[80]

Year	Infantry	Cavalry	Total
1636	-	69	69
1638	613	372	985
1647	30	91	121
1649	400	500	900
1655	483	75	558

Among those who served in the cavalry guard we find young nobles who were sent by their families at court, for education and to get accustomed to political life. Here they performed various roles, but they were also organised as a distinct cavalry group. In 1636, 38 young nobles from the princely court (*udvari ifjak*) and their mounted servants, 69 horsemen in total, were given quarters in the district of Bistriţa.[81] They were most probably mobilised with the rest of the Transylvanian army during the confrontation between Prince George Rákóczi I and his rival, Stephen Bethlen.

The princely court was a complex institution with a sizeable number of people assigned to various tasks. A clear distinction between those who had administrative duties and those who performed military service is not always easy to make. Such a case is illustrated by three documents issued in October 1638, when the prince and his courtiers spent almost four weeks in Bistriţa and the surrounding villages. In the list of victuals provided by town authorities we can find many individuals and groups who played a direct or indirect military role like a gunsmith, 13 riflemen, 52 young nobles (cavalry) and 28 cavalrymen from the court army.[82]

The second document specifically mentions 300 Hungarian infantry, 300 German infantry and 197 cavalry under the command of four different captains (Péter Borsai with 44 cavalry; Miklós Gáspár with 49 cavalry; István Bojti, captain from the field army with 48 cavalry; Nagy János with 56 cavalry).[83] In addition, a third list of 95 young nobles and their retinues, quartered in neighbouring villages, was compiled by John Kemény, who was treasurer at the time.[84] All in all these sources indicate a court army of 613 infantry and 372 cavalry.

---

80 András Péter Szabó, 'A besztercei levéltár jegyzékei az erdélyi fejedelmi udvarról (1636–1659)', *Lymbus* (2016), pp.67–122.
81 Szabó, 'A besztercei levéltár', pp.69–70.
82 Szabó, 'A besztercei levéltár', pp.71–76.
83 Szabó, 'A besztercei levéltár', pp.77–85.
84 Szabó, 'A besztercei levéltár', pp.85–87.

THE ORGANISATION OF THE TRANSYLVANIAN ARMY

Similar lists were issued in Bistrița, in October 1647, when George Rákóczi II, heir to the Transylvanian throne, attended a meeting of the estates instead of his father. These documents explicitly state that not all members of the armed retinue were registered because they did not receive victuals from town authorities. However, among those who accompanied the prince in town we find 16 young nobles, 30 court infantry (with firearms) and 75 mounted lancers.[85]

One of the most detailed documents on the composition of the court army who accompanied the prince to Bistrița was issued in 1649. Although the document is rather vague regarding the size and composition of the administrative apparatus, the armed retinue is clearly presented as follows: 100 soldiers from the court army (*Udvari katona*), 200 curteni (*Kurtányok*) cavalry from Wallachia, 100 Moldavians, 100 dragoons (*Dragonyok*), 200 Hungarian infantry and 200 German infantry. The presence of Moldavian and Wallachian soldiers in the princely banner was common and, in this context, can be linked to the policy of George Rákóczi II who was trying to forge a very tight alliance with his Romanian neighbours. While the last two entries in the list clearly refer to infantry troops (400 men) the first four entries most probably indicate mounted soldiers (500 men).[86]

During the reign of George Rákóczi II, the composition of the court army became more divers. Occasionally, troops who served in the garrisons of border fortifications or soldiers from the field army were also brought at court and accompanied the prince during his travels. In a document issued in 1655, the guard of the prince consisted of 59 court infantry, 24 foot soldiers from the fortress of Deva and Captain András Barcsay with 75 soldiers (cavalry). A dragoon detachment and a Hungarian infantry detachment are also mentioned but without any information regarding their numbers.

Another document referring to the same period (October 1655) mentions additional troops from the court guard: Captain Pál Csontos with his infantry soldiers (unspecified number), Captain Tamás Kerekes with 200 infantry, 200 *seimeni* (*Szemények*) infantry from Wallachia, a captain of dragoons (*Dragony kapitány*) with his men and three captains from the court guard with their soldiers (unspecified number).[87] In this particular context the size of the court guard is very hard to estimate because the records relating to many detachments lack information about their size but, nevertheless, 483 infantry and 75 cavalry are accounted for. In reality the armed retinue of the prince was much larger, probably reaching a total of 1,000 men.

During the wars of 1658–1661 the Principality of Transylvania suffered important territorial loses (for example in 1658 the Banat of Caransebeș and Lugoj, and in 1660 the fortress of Oradea) which in turn affected the military potential of the country. Prince Michael Apafi I (1661–1690) had to rely on an overall smaller army but he strived to maintain a strong court guard.

---

85 Szabó, 'A besztercei levéltár', pp.88–97.
86 Szabó, 'A besztercei levéltár', p.100.
87 Szabó, 'A besztercei levéltár', pp.112–114.

The Guard of Prince Michael Apafi I from 1663–1683[88]

	1663	1666	1673	1674	1679	1680	1681	1682	1683	1684
Seimeni (Moldavians, Wallachians, Serbs)	53	28	44	44		79	64		77	68
Germans			102	111		211	279		171	162
Hungarians		47	59	46	129	64	231	663	651	527
Polish (French Banners)					300	291	327		271	279
Total	53	75	205	201	429	645	901	663	1,170	1,036

Four distinct groups of soldiers, based on their ethnic origin, can be distinguished in the guard of Prince Apafi: *Seimeni* (Moldavian, Wallachian and Serbian mercenaries), Germans, Hungarians and Polish mercenaries (the so called 'French Banners').

The *seimeni* were initially mercenaries from the Balkan region (Serbians, Bulgarians, Bosnians, Greeks and Turks) in the service of Moldavian and Wallachian rulers. They were organised as infantry troops with firearms, following the model of Ottoman *seğban* infantry. A considerable number of *seimeni* (sometimes more than 1,000 men) are mentioned by sources in the armies of Wallachia during the first half of the seventeenth century. In time, many locals (Romanians) joined the ranks of the *seimeni*.

The reign of Matei Basarab was the most auspicious period for these soldiers, who played a decisive role in the confrontation with Vasile Lupu, ruler of Moldavia. In the last years of Matei Basarab's reign, they were the protagonists of several rebellions within the Wallachian army. Their discontent culminated with a major uprising in 1655 when a direct intervention of the Transylvanian army was needed to secure the reign of the new voivode, Constantin Șerban. The first Transylvanian prince who hired *seimeni* in his court army was George Rákóczi II, which he did as early as 1654. Narrative and official sources mention such groups of soldiers, coming from Wallachia or Moldavia, in the service of Transylvanian rulers during the wars that ravaged the country between 1658 and 1662.[89] Iacob Conrad Hiltebrandt describes them as very brave but lacking loyalty towards their employers. They were armed with long muskets and sabres and wore baggy pants and red hats. In many aspects they were similar to Ottoman Janissaries.[90]

Prince Michael Apafi I kept a small group of *seimeni* in his court army throughout his reign. Their numbers were fluid, between 28 and 79, and were most of them Romanians from Wallachia and Moldavia. The most

---

88 Ardelean, *Organizarea militară*, p.211.
89 Florin Nicolae Ardelean, 'Seimeni în slujba principilor Transilvaniei în a doua jumătate a secolului XVII', Banatica 22 (2012), pp.119–126.
90 *Călători Străini*, vol. V, p.553.

common names in the preserved muster lists are *Muntean* (Wallachian) and *Moldovan* (Moldavian). In addition, a sizeable number of Slavic names are also mentioned and even a few Hungarian ones. These soldiers, although not very numerous, were considered among the best in the court guard and received the highest monthly wage, five florins.[91]

German mercenaries had been an almost constant presence at the Transylvanian court throughout the seventeenth century. During the reign of Michael Apafi I, the Germans were organised in two banners or companies, with a total strength of between 102 and 279 men. Their units had a complex structure, including many officers and auxiliary staff. According to a muster list drafted in 1680 they included:

A captain – 50 florins per month
A flag bearer (*signifer*) – 25 florins per month
Sergeants – 12 florins per month
Corporals – six to seven florins per month
A *fourrier* (company clerk) – 10 florins per month
A notary (*scriba*) – seven florins per month
A surgeon (*Feltscher*) – eight florins per month
A translator – six florins per month
Drummers – five florins per month
Common soldiers (*gregari*) – four florins per month[92]

Local soldiers, or maybe even exiles from Habsburg Hungary, were organised in distinct companies within the court army. A small Hungarian infantry detachment is first mentioned in a muster roll drafted in 1666. Placed under the command of a lieutenant (*hadnagy*), their numbers fluctuated between 47 and 64 soldiers and officers. In addition, the vast majority of mounted soldiers at court were also Hungarians.[93]

Polish mercenaries were one of the most numerous groups of soldiers at the Transylvanian court in the last decades of the seventeenth century. However, in muster rolls they often appear under the name of French companies or banners. This peculiar situation was determined by a specific context generated by the French-Polish-Transylvanian alliance, concluded in 1677–1678 with the aim of opposing the Habsburgs in Central and Eastern Europe. The French and Polish side promised Prince Apafi to provide subsidies and soldiers for his campaigns against the Habsburgs in Hungary.

In 1677, the Marquis de Béthune travelled to Poland and recruited soldiers on behalf of the Transylvanian prince, with subsidies from the French court. The money was enough for the recruitment process and for paying the wages of these soldiers during the first year. From 1679 onwards their wages were paid from the Transylvanian treasury, at the same rate of pay as the other mercenaries from the court guard. They were infantry troops, organised in

---

91 Ardelean, 'Seimeni în slujba principilor', pp.126–134.
92 SJAN CJ, Colecția socoteli princiare, 46 Evidențe nominale de efective militare, f.44–47.
93 Florin Nicolae Ardelean, 'Steaguri de mercenari străini la curtea lui Mihail Apafi (1663–1684)', *Anuarul Institutului de Istorie «George Barițiu» din Cluj-Napoca*, LI (2012), p.74.

three companies (sometimes called banners) under three distinct captains, Henric von Offen, Ioannes Podlesky and Cristoph Crakovsky. Each captain received monthly wages of 38 florins, other officers between four and 20 florins a month and common soldiers were rewarded with three florins monthly. The total size of their detachments varied between 271 and 327 soldiers and officers.[94]

Cavalry banners are also recorded in the accounts of the princely court but not as often as the infantry ones. According to the muster rolls issued in 1682 there were 13 banners of Hungarian mounted soldiers (from Transylvania and possible from Royal Hungary). Most of them were lancers (11 banners) while one of the banners was armed with carbines (*karabélyosok*) and the last one consisted of dragoons. The lancer banners included a total number of 588 men, the carbine cavalry banner consisted of 75 men while the number of dragoons is unspecified.[95]

Although the army of Transylvania had been reduced in size during the second half of the seventeenth century, Prince Michael Apafi I managed to maintain a strong court army of over 1,000 soldiers at its height (1,170 in 1683). The official accounts of the court preserved the muster rolls issued when the monthly wages of the soldiers were paid. According to these sources Apafi relied on seven infantry companies and 13 cavalry banners of professional soldiers, with a considerable proportion of foreigners among them.

Throughout the seventeenth century, the main task of the guard was, of course, to protect the prince and the other members of his family. The officers were carefully selected from noble families which had close ties to the ruling prince. The commander of the infantry guard (*capitaneum peditum praetorianorum/ udvari gyalog kapitány*) was particularly close to the ruler and was often rewarded with possessions or titles of nobility if he was of common origin. The foot guard of the Transylvanian prince consisted of light infantry detachments, bearing firearms.

Cavalry detachments continued to play a key role in the overall military organisation of Transylvania and in the court guard as well. Mounted troops who served in the retinue of the prince were often recruited from the social elite of the country. A significant part of the armed horsemen can be described as 'shock cavalry', bearing the lance as main offensive weapon. Cavalry with firearms, like dragoons and mounted carabineers gained an

Transylvanian cavalry in Poland during the campaign in 1657. Etching based on the drawings by Erik Dahlbergh from Samuel Pufendorf's De rebus a Carolo Gustavo Sveciae rege Gestis Commentatorium Libri septem…, 1696 (National Library, Warsaw)

---

94 Ardelean, 'Steaguri de mercenari', pp.75–77.
95 Ardelean, 'Steaguri de mercenari', pp.77–78.

increasingly prominent position especially towards the last decades of the seventeenth century.

The extended court army, which is sometimes called the 'princely banner', included more groups of soldiers who were stationed in various parts of the country such as the German regiment from Vințul de Jos, the garrisons of border fortifications, and the field army. All of these groups will be analysed separately in the following chapters.

German Mercenaries in the Service of the Transylvanian Prince

Gabriel Bethlen was the first Transylvanian prince who hired large numbers of German mercenaries during his campaigns in the Thirty Years' War. He knew his native light infantry (from Transylvania and Hungary) was no match for the German footmen armed with heavy muskets and drilled in the tactics of volley fire. In 1621, Bethlen already had about 900 German soldiers in his army.[96] Another large German infantry unit was hired during the second campaign against the Habsburgs (August 1623–May 1624), when Lieutenant-Colonel Johann von Wangler surrendered with his 700 musketeers in the city of Trnava. When the campaign ended, the prince settled his new subjects on the estate of Vințul de Jos, close to the capital of the Principality, Alba Iulia. According to some sources the size of the German regiment was even larger, reaching up to 1,200 men.[97]

In 1626, during his wedding with Catherine of Brandenburg celebrated in Košice, Gabriel Bethlen was accompanied by 600 German infantry, all dressed in red clothing. The new princess of Transylvania kept a guard of 50–100 mercenaries from her native province, Brandenburg. Some of them were settled on the estate of Făgăraș fortress in southern Transylvania.[98] The German soldiers of Făgăraș were sometimes referred to as 'Moser' in the accounts of Brașov's magistrate, who in 1625 had to pay 1,996 florins for their maintenance.[99] In 1625 Gabriel Bethlen sent one of his German commanders, Farensbach, with 400 German soldiers to Wallachia with the purpose of enforcing their defence against a Tatar incursion. Farsenbach abandoned his mission and returned to the service of the Habsburgs.[100]

The presence of German mercenaries in Transylvania was observed with great concern by the Diet. The representatives of the estates feared the presence of large detachments of foreign troops and often complained about their abusive behaviour.[101] While most German mercenaries in the Transylvanian army were infantry troops, sources also refer to smaller detachments of dragoons. John Kemény mentions such troops in the army

---

96 Szilády, Szilágyi (eds.), *Török-Magyarkori*, III, p.300.
97 Kemény, *Memorii*, pp.49–50; Kraus, *Cronica Transilvaniei*, p.57.
98 Szabó, 'Bethlen Gábor (1)', pp.982–983; Szabó, 'The Army of the Principality', pp.53–55.
99 Cziráki, 'Brassói és barcasági katonák', p.93.
100 Harai, *Gabriel Bethlen*, p.245.
101 MCRT, vol. VIII, p.426; MCRT, vol. X, p.221.

of Gabriel Bethlen, during the Thirty Years' War, observing that they were especially useful during sieges.[102] George Rákóczi II had German dragoons during his campaign in Poland (1657), but most of them died or were taken into Tatar captivity.[103] One year later, during the Ottoman invasion of Transylvania, Prince Rákóczi employed new detachments of German dragoons and sent them to block the mountain passes into Transylvania, but they were unable to stop the advance of the Ottomans and their allies.[104]

Captains of German troops, although some of them did not have German origins themselves, are sometimes mentioned in contemporary sources as notable members of the court, entrusted with both military and diplomatic missions. Heinrich Matthias von Thurn, famous leader of the Bohemian rebellion against the Habsburgs, entered the service of Gabriel Bethlen, after the crushing defeat suffered in the battle of White Mountain (8 November 1620). He spent the year 1621 serving in the army of the Transylvanian prince, together with other Czech exiles. After Bethlen concluded a temporary peace agreement with the Habsburgs in December 1621, von Thurn accompanied him to Transylvania. In August 1622 he was sent on a diplomatic mission in the capital of the Ottoman Empire, on behalf of the Transylvanian prince. Given his expertise in military matters, we can assume that during the time spent in the entourage of Prince Bethlen, von Thurn served as a military adviser. Even after he left Transylvania and entered Venetian service as a *condotierre*, he kept close contact with other mercenary captains at the Transylvanian court, like Matthias Quadt. He also served Gabriel Bethlen as an officer and a diplomat and was entrusted with important missions to Sweden and Prussia.[105]

Joannes Gluchovski de Benckvitz was one of the most important captains of the German troops during the reign of Gabriel Bethlen and in 1631 he made an oath of fealty to the newly elected Prince George Rákóczi I.[106] Another captain of the German mercenaries in Transylvania was Andrew Gawdy (András Gaudi). A soldier of Scottish origin, he is first found in the service of Prince George Rákóczi I, in 1640, when he was conducting commercial transactions on his behalf in Gdańsk (Danzig). According to a letter signed by Prince Rákóczi himself on 25 January 1640, Gaudi and a Transylvanian nobleman, Ladislaus Ujlaki, were sent in Gdańsk to buy weapons for the Transylvanian army. They were expected to bring 3,000 muskets with all the required tools, at a maximum price of six florins and 76 denars per musket, 600 armours (breastplates) and helmets, each of them proof tested with a shot from close range, at a maximum price of 16 florins, and 359 sets of full armour at 32 florins each. In exchange they were bringing ox leathers and sulphuric acid (vitriol) to trade on Polish markets. They were

---

102 Kemény, *Memorii*, p.58.
103 István Enyedi, 'II Rákóczi György veszedelméről 1657–1660', in *Erdély történelmi adatok*, IV (Kolozsvár: nyomatott az ev. ref. főtanoda betüivel, 1862), p.244.
104 Kraus, *Cronica Transilvaniei*, pp.308–309.
105 Florin Nicolae Ardelean, Florina Ciure, 'Guerra e diplomazia nella Transilvania dell'anno 1625. Da un documento dell'Archivio di Stato di Venezia', *Studia Historica Adriatica ac Danubiana*, X, 1–2 (2017), pp.68–93.
106 MCRT, vol. IX, pp.161–163, 272.

also asked to hire a skilled stonemason and a few gunsmiths who would be willing to work in Transylvania.[107]

Later, in 1644, when the prince initiated his campaign against the Habsburgs, Gaudi was entrusted with the command of a German mercenary detachment. When Transylvania signed a peace treaty with the Habsburgs in 1645, Gaudi joined the Swedish army and continued to fight in the Thirty Years' War, reaching the rank lieutenant-colonel. After spending some years in Prussia, he returned to Transylvania in 1654 to serve in the army of Prince George Rákóczi II.[108] In 1655 he commanded the German infantry of the Transylvanian army, in the campaign against the rebels from Wallachia. In the battle of Șoplea (26 June 1655), Gaudi and his men formed the vanguard of the Transylvanian army and played a key role in securing the victory for Prince Rákóczi. In the aftermath of the battle, Gaudi and 500 of his German mercenaries were left in Wallachia to protect Constantin Șerban, the appointed ruler of the country and trusted ally of the Transylvanian prince.[109] During the Ottoman campaigns directed against Transylvania in 1658, Andrew Gawdy was entrusted with the defence of Oradea, the most important fortification on the western frontier of Transylvania. His troops were able to defend the fortress and, to a certain extent, the neighbouring town, from the incursions of the Tatars.[110]

One thing that set the German infantry apart from the local soldiers was their use of volley fire tactics. The Moldavian chronicler, Miron Costin, makes two separate mentions regarding this tactic employed by the German mercenaries of the Transylvanian prince, one referring to the battle of Șoplea (1655)[111] and the second referring to the battle of Florești in 1660.[112] While in the first battle (1655) the German infantry was placed in the vanguard and played a decisive role in securing the victory for Transylvania, in the second battle (1660) they were decimated during a counterattack of the Ottoman and Wallachian light infantry.

The various groups of German mercenaries were officially part of the 'princely banner'. Some of them were stationed at court in Alba Iulia or in neighbouring estates like Vințul de Jos. Also, most border fortifications were reinforced with small detachments of German infantry in addition to local soldiers. During the seventeenth century, they represented the most common group of foreign mercenaries in the Transylvanian army. Most of them served as infantry, skilled in the use of heavy muskets, but also as we have seen, as dragoons.

---

107 MCRT, vol. X, pp.263–264.
108 Szabó, 'Asedierea cetății Oradea', pp.133–134
109 Kraus, *Cronica Transilvaniei*, pp.181–185.
110 Szabó, 'Asedierea cetății Oradea', pp.133–137.
111 Costin, *Opere*, p.172.
112 Costin, *Opere*, pp.198–199.

The 'Field Army'

In the seventeenth century, the field army (*mezei katonaság/exercitus campestris*) became an extension of the court guard, and it initially included any mercenary units mobilised for the duration of a single campaign. In time, some companies were kept in service even between campaigns and were given permanent quarters in various parts of the country. Some of them were settled in villages situated on the fiscal estate (territories under the direct authority of the ruling prince) and were exempted from taxes and work obligations in exchange for military service. Such was the case of 128 soldiers from the field army who received lands from Prince Gabriel Báthory in 1610, in a village situated near Şimleu (*Somlyó*), an important fortification on the north-western frontier of the country.[113]

In some narrative sources the expression 'free mercenary troops' is used to designate the soldiers from the 'field army'. This element of the Transylvanian army gained and increased importance during Gabriel Bethlen's campaigns against the Habsburgs (1619–1626). They were mostly local troops, from Transylvanian and Hungarian counties, who received regular wages. Most of the *hajdú* soldiers from the borderlands were also integrated in this part of the army during the Thirty Years' War. Nobles and commoners also joined these units on a voluntary basis. The leading officers were usually members of the high nobility, holding other important political administrative or military positions.

In 1625, during the battle of Nové Zámky, the field army was commanded by István Horváth, who was also captain of Ecsed fortress.[114] David Zólyomi, a rich and influential nobleman from Bihor County, held the supreme command of the field army during the first years of George Rákóczi I's reign. Before reaching this eminent position, he held other major military offices such as the captain general of the Székely, captain of the court army and captain of Chioar fortress. In 1631 he was one of the Transylvanian commanders who defeated the troops of the Hungarian Palatine at Rakamaz and secured the reign of Rákóczi in Transylvania. Despite his services the prince suspected Zólyomi of treason and had him arrested in 1633. The former commander of the field army spent the rest of his days imprisoned, until his death in 1649.[115] Another important personality who was appointed general of the field army (*exercitum nostrum campestrium generali*) in 1653 was John Kemény, who later became Prince of Transylvania.[116]

George Rákóczi I kept a substantial number of soldiers in the field army until he was able to consolidate his position on the Transylvanian throne. It is estimated that about 2,000 cavalry were kept in service during the first years of his reign.[117] In times of peace these troops were given quarters on the

---

113 MNL OL, F.7 Armales, no.29.
114 Kemény, *Memorii*, pp.81–82.
115 Florin Nicolae Ardelean, 'Evoluţia funcţiei de căpitan general în Transilvania la sfârşitul secolului al XVI-lea şi începutul secolului al XVII-lea', *Banatica*, 28 (2018), pp.573–575.
116 MCRT, vol. XI, p.172.
117 Szabó, 'Bethlen Gábor (1)', pp.981–982; Szabó, 'The Army of the Principality', pp.50–51.

estates of the prince and occasionally on the lands of the Saxons. In 1634, for example, Prince Rákóczi asked the magistrate of Sibiu to offer lodging to 400 mounted soldiers and to provide fodder for their horses. The soldiers were expected to buy food from their own wages.[118] In 1644, when he launched his campaign against the Habsburgs, Rákóczi relied on a significant number of soldiers in his field army. At the battle of Drégelpalánk (1644) they were positioned in the centre of the battle line, together with the Székely cavalry.[119]

Transylvanian cavalry in Poland during the campaign in 1657. Soldiers appear to be unarmoured, armed with sabres, firearms, and bows, with some troops in the background carrying lances. Etching based on the drawings by Erik Dahlbergh from Samuel Pufendorf's De rebus a Carolo Gustavo Sveciae rege Gestis Commentatorium Libri septem…, 1696 (National Library, Warsaw)

In the second half of the seventeenth century the field army was reduced in size. It consisted of local mercenary troops organised into cavalry detachments. Most historical sources mention these soldiers during the campaigns organised by Prince Michael Apafi I in Habsburg Hungary or during his participation at the siege of Vienna (1683). Their muster rolls were usually issued at the same time as those of the court guard infantry and they appear thus to be part of the same structure, that is, the court army. A register issued at the end of 1684 explicitly mentions that the cavalry banners at court were part of the field army. A total number of 484 mounted soldiers and officers, organised in 10 distinct banners, were on the payroll at the time.

---

118 Ioan Lupaș, *Documente istorice transilvane, 1599–1699* (Cluj: Tipografia „Cartea Românească", 1940), pp.187–188.
119 Kemény, *Memorii*, pp.203–204.

The Field Army in 1684

Nr.	Type of cavalry	Name of the captain/lieutenant (*hadnagy*)	Size of the unit	Total monthly wages
1	Mounted carbineers (*karabélyosok*)	Boldogfalvi János	61	468 florins
2	Mounted lancers	Rácz János	78	279 florins
3	Mounted lancers	Székely Samuel	54	319 florins
4	Mounted lancers	Vajo András	35	192 florins
5	Mounted lancers	Szekeres János	36	241 florins
6	Mounted lancers	Szilágyi Miklós	48	282 florins
7	Mounted lancers	Vasadi György	40	244 florins
8	Mounted lancers	Tolnai András	38	200 florins
9	Mounted lancers	Arany János	55	331 florins
10	Mounted lancers	Sandre Pál	39	234 florins

The size and wages of the cavalry banners varied greatly on criteria which are not specifically mentioned in the document. We can assume that these differences were generated by the length of time spent in service, the total size of the banner and the type of weapons used. For example, the highest wages were given to a cavalry detachment armed with carbines.

On the battlefield the soldiers from the field army were expected to perform the first assault.[120] They were the best cavalry troops in the army of the Transylvanian Principality, kept in service for successive years with wages paid during times of war and peace. Nevertheless, the size of the field army varied greatly from one reign to another. Gabriel Bethlen hired between 8,000–10,000 mercenary cavalry during his campaigns in the Thirty Years' War (1619–1626). His successor, George Rákóczi I, maintained at least 2,000 troops in the field army but their numbers were increased during the anti-Habsburg campaign of 1644–1645. Towards the end of seventeenth century the number of mounted soldiers in the field army decreased to about 500 men, in line with the overall size of the Transylvanian army.

Regulations and Military Justice

Discipline and military justice became important aspects of military organisation in the Early Modern Age. The Principality of Transylvania made no exception, and a substantial number of military regulations were issued during the seventeenth century. These documents are valuable historical sources which reveal details about the daily life of soldiers, their

---

120 Bethlen, *Descrierea*, pp.171–172.

moral standards, the crimes they committed and the prescribed subsequent punishments.

Gabriel Bethlen was the first Transylvanian prince who issued several sets of rules at the beginning of major campaigns.[121] An acclaimed military reformer, Bethlen showed great interest in the efficient organisation of his armed forces. On the eve of his first major military expedition, the siege of the rebel fortress Lipova in 1616, the prince issued his first military regulation while his troops were gathered in camp near the fortress of Deva (*ex castris nostris ad arcem nostrum Devensem positis*). This is a complex and valuable document consisting of 24 articles, meant to establish and enforce discipline in the Transylvanian army.

The military regulation issued on the occasion of the siege of Lipova in 1616

Article No.	General topic	Article content
1	Crime and punishment/ Military hierarchy/Judicial procedure	- Severe punishment for murder, fornication, stealing, bloodshed and other abominations. - Captains (*kapitányok*), vice-captains (*vicekapitányok*), lieutenants (*hadnagyok*) and corporals (*tizedesek*) were tasked with overseeing the moral standards set by the regulation. - Officers who failed to report the crimes of their soldiers had to pay a fine. - The captain-general (*fő kapitány*) and the military magistrate (*hadi bíránk*) decided upon the application of punishments.
2	Judicial procedure	- The highest judicial authority within the army was conferred to the designated chief military magistrate (*fő hadi bíránk*), Boldisár Kemény. - Peasants or servants suspected of crimes should be detained and imprisoned immediately. - Nobles suspected of crimes had to appear before the judge within three days (*ad tertium diem*).
3	Military hierarchy/ Camp life	- Balás Kamuthi was designated to oversee the organisation of the military camp and camp guards (sentinels).
4	Judicial procedure	– Camp guards (sentinels) who failed to perform their duties were sentenced to death.
5	Camp life	- Camp guards (sentinels) should keep a detailed register with all those who left or entered the perimeter of the camp, soldiers or servants alike.
6	Camp life	- Those that made loud noises and spread panic inside the camp were punishable by death. All threats and dangers should be communicated to superior officers.

---

121 Gábor Hausner, 'Bethlen Gábor erdélyi fejedelem hadi edictuma', *Hadtörténelmi Közlemények*, (2001), pp.469–485.

7	Marching order	- Troops should march in their designated order. Blocking the road, mingling between companies and banners, and overcrowding the narrow passes along the road were strictly forbidden.
8	Provisioning/ Marching order	- The organisation and marching of the baggage train was entrusted to Farkas Szalai. All carts, carriages and other means of transportation should maintain their designated order in the marching column. If one of the carts was damaged on the road, all the others had to stop and repair the broken cart.
9	Camp life	- When setting up camp, each company or banner should keep its carriages at the rear. The camp was expected to have a circular form with the carts and carriages forming a 'defensive wall' around the camp. Two chief quartermasters (*főtábormester*) were designated to oversee this process: Farkas Novák and Gergely Kállai.
10	Provisioning	- Horses could be taken outside camp for grazing during the day. During the night, each soldier should keep his horse inside the camp in designated areas.
11	Infantry/Camp life/ Military hierarchy	- Each nation (estate) should keep a register with all the infantry troops they have mobilised for this campaign. The register of the Székely infantry was entrusted to János Matis, while the infantry provided by the Saxons and the nobility were kept in a common registry, assigned to Menyhárt Besenyei. Both clerks were placed under the authority of Kelemen Béldi, overseer of the whole infantry.
12	Cavalry/Marching order	- The organisation and marching of the cavalry was overseen by the prince himself and his appointed delegates. Cavalry troops were expected to follow orders transmitted through drum signals.
13	Provisioning	- The chief military magistrate (*fő hadi biránk*) organised a market within camp where all merchants were expected to bring their goods for sale. All prices were pre-established to avoid haggling and quarrels.
14	Camp life/ Crime and punishment	- Those that disturbed the peace inside camp after the evening prayer were detained until morning and then received three strikes with a wooden staff.
15	Crime and punishment	- Adultery was punishable by beheading; - Petty theft with a fine of two or three florins or beating with a wooden staff; - Greater thefts (horses, cattle) were punishable by hanging.

16	Crime and punishment	- Threatening someone with a drawn sabre was punishable by beating with the wooden staff; - Those who injured fellow soldiers with a weapon would have their hands cut off; - Those who killed fellow soldiers were sentenced to death; - Foul language, drunkenness and fornication were punished with a death sentence;
17	Crime and punishment	- Acts of violence against the local population were punished severely; - Burning down houses was punished by death;
18	Crime and punishment	- Making loud noises inside camp was strictly forbidden; - Beating the drum without an express order was strictly forbidden;
19	Crime and punishment	- Any kind of news or information regarding the enemy should be communicated only to superior officers; - Spreading rumours inside camp was forbidden;
20	Marching/Camp life	- When marching or in camp, each captain is responsible for maintaining good order among his men; - In case of sudden attack, each company or banner should hold their ground until further orders from the prince or the captain-general;
21	Provisioning/Crime and punishment	- Finding lost cattle should be immediately reported to superior officers. Those who failed to do so were punished by beating with a wooden staff;
22	Crime and punishment	- Desertion was punished harshly: nobles had their estates confiscated while lesser nobles, Székely leaders, guardsmen, conscripted peasants or mercenary guardsmen were sentenced to death;
23	Marching order/Weapons	- Every horseman should carry his own lance. Those who placed their lances in carriages were punished by beating with a wooden staff;
24	Marching order/Weapons	- Every nobleman and his mounted retainers should carry their own lances. Those without a lance will be forced to dismount and march with the infantry. The same rule was applied to Székely leaders.

The articles follow no order and while some of them are extensive and refer to various issues, others are very brief and rather vague. Military hierarchy, judicial procedure, crime and punishment, marching order, camp life, provisioning and weapons are the most important topics covered by this invaluable source. A significant number of articles are concerned with identifying the most common types of crimes committed by soldiers on campaign, like murder, fornication, stealing (with a distinction between petty theft and greater theft), bloodshed, drunkenness, foul language, spreading rumours and panic in camp, disturbing the peace inside camp, arson, desertion and failing to carry one's own weapons.

Punishment was very harsh and many of the above-mentioned misdeeds could lead to a death sentence or in some cases to physical punishment (beating). The regulation is particularly harsh because the expedition was taking place inside the borders of the principality and Gabriel Bethlen was careful not to antagonise the nobility and the local population. Some other interesting details can be found in this document. The circular shape of the camp protected by the carriages and carts of the baggage train, the large number of cattle that accompanied the marching army as a source of food, the large proportion of lancers among mounted troops, the importance of merchants among camp followers and the presence of military clerks who kept detailed registers with names of all the soldiers (which unfortunately have not been preserved).[122]

Nevertheless, the efficiency of such military regulations remains hard to assess. These documents provide an ideal picture of how an army should behave, but we have little information on how these rules were applied and how efficient they actually were. Written sources usually emphasise the bad behaviour of soldiers and their negative impact on local communities, suggesting that military justice was not always applied very strictly. For example, in 1621 Prince Gabriel Bethlen eventually pardoned an infantry officer (*gyalog vajda*) named János Horváth, who was initially sentenced to death on account of mutiny. Several nobles had interceded on his behalf and the prince bowed to their wishes and agreed to change his punishment to a lesser one. Other acts of insubordination, like indiscriminate plunder, were treated harshly because of their political consequences. In 1623 a Stephen Basa was hanged for robing some locals in Upper Hungary during the second Transylvanian campaign in the Thirty Years' War.[123] These few examples indicate the fact that military justice was influenced by the political context of each campaign.

Most Transylvanian military regulations issued during the seventeenth century maintained a similar structure and approached the same general issues. However, some interesting changes occurred through time and are visible especially towards the end of the seventeenth century.[124] An interesting example is provided by an extensive regulation issued by Prince Michael Apafi I before setting off for the siege of Vienna in 1683.[125]

---

122 Sándor Szilágyi, *Bethlen Gábor fejedelem levelezése* (Budapest: Magyar Tudományos Akadémia Kiadása, 1886), pp.55–59.
123 Harai, *Gabriel Bethlen*, pp.202–205.
124 Florin Nicolae Ardelean, 'Military Justice, Regulations and Discipline in Early Modern Transylvanian Armies (XVI-XVII centuries)', *Studia Universitas Cibiniensis, Series Historica* VIII/1 (2011), pp.183–189; Florin Nicolae Ardelean, 'Piety, morality and discipline in the military regulations of the Transylvanian principality (1577–1683)', Ulrich A. Wien (ed.), *Common Man, Society and Religion in the 16th century/Gemeiner Mann, Gesellschaft und Religion im 16. Jahrhundert Piety, morality and discipline in the Carpathian Basin/Frömmigkeit, Moral und Sozialdisziplinierung im Karpatenbogen* (Göttingen: Vandenhoeck & Ruprecht, 2021), pp.263–275.
125 MCRT. vol. XVIII, pp.136–141.

THE ORGANISATION OF THE TRANSYLVANIAN ARMY

The military regulation issued by Michael Apafi I for the Transylvanian Army in 1683

Article No.	General topic	Article content
1	Marching order/ Provisioning	- The carriage drivers should maintain the assigned order of marching and obey the orders of the officers assigned to overseeing the baggage train.
2	Camp life/Crime and punishment	- The position of each company and banner inside the camp is decided by the quartermaster (*tábormester*). Those who failed to obey his orders were punished by flogging.
3	Crime and punishment	- Cursing and blasphemy were punishable by death.
4	Camp life	- Leaving the camp perimeter without permission was strictly forbidden.
5	Camp life/Marching order/ Crime and punishment	- When marching or in camp each soldier should stay together with the rest of his banner/company. - Nobody was allowed to leave camp for plunder forays unless specifically ordered by superior officers. Those who failed to do so were flogged and their horse and weapons were confiscated. They were sentenced to death if they disobeyed this rule a second time.
6	Camp life	- Stragglers were punished by flogging.
7	Camp life	- Nobody was allowed to leave camp, under any circumstances, before the morning prayer.
8	Camp life/ Crime and punishment	- Music, shooting and drinking were forbidden after the evening prayer. - Merchants who sold their wares after the evening prayer were flogged.
9	Provisioning/ Crime and punishment	- Soldiers sent out to forage for food and provisions were forbidden to attack poor people, noble estates, mills, churches and schools. Those who failed to do so were sentenced to death.
10	Marching order/Crime and Punishment	- Every soldier must carry his own weapons, placing weapons and equipment in carriages was strictly forbidden. - Every soldier must march together with the rest of his banner/company. Stragglers were punished by flogging.
11	Provisioning/Crime and Punishment	- Acts of violence against camp followers, especially against those who brought provisions in the army, was punishable by death.
12	Marching order/ Crime and Punishment	- Soldiers were not allowed to march among the carriages of the baggage train. Those who failed to do so were punished by flogging the first time and sentenced to death the second time.
13	Crime and Punishment	- Those who threatened fellow soldiers with a drawn weapon would have their hand cut off. - Those who injured fellow soldiers were sentenced to death.

14	Crime and Punishment	- Acts of violence were punishable by death. - Adultery (first offence) was punishable by flogging under the gallows.
15	Crime and Punishment	- Adultery (second offence) was punishable by death.
16	Crime and Punishment	- Servants who left their masters without consent during the campaign were punished by hanging.
17	Crime and Punishment	- Attacking villages or noble manors was strictly forbidden. - Desecrating graves was punishable by death.
18	Marching Order/ Crime and Punishment	- If the marching column is attacked on the road, all banners/companies should maintain their position and wait for further orders. - Shooting practice inside camp was forbidden. Those who did so were flogged. - Injuring fellow soldiers during shooting practice (outside the camp) was punishable by death.
19	Camp life	- Officers were responsible for settling their troops in the designated area inside the camp. Those who failed to keep order among their troops were demoted.
20	Camp life/Judicial procedure	- Lesser officers (corporals, lieutenants) were responsible for supervising the soldiers under their command and report any kind of misdeeds to their captains and the general.
21	Camp life/Crime and Punishment	- Arson was punishable by death. - Leaving unattended fires inside the camp was punished by flogging.
22	Crime and Punishment	- Any kind of information regarding the enemy must be communicated directly to a superior officer. - Spreading rumours inside camp was punishable by death.
23	Crime and Punishment	- Robbing a fellow soldier or taking his camping place was punishable by death.
24	Crime and Punishment	- Making contact with the enemy was punishable by death.
25	Crime and Punishment	- Enemy captives and letters should be handed directly to superior offices. Those who failed to do so were punishable by death.
26	Crime and Punishment	- Robbing a fellow soldier was punishable by death. - Those who protected thieves were also punished.
27	Crime and Punishment	- Those caught near the gunpowder storage area, especially during the night, were flogged.
28	Military hierarchy	- All soldiers, mercenaries or sent by the estates (nobility, Saxons and Székely), had to obey the orders of the general (*főgenerális*) Mihály Teleki.

THE ORGANISATION OF THE TRANSYLVANIAN ARMY

29	Military hierarchy	- Lieutenants (*hadnagy*) reported to their captains and gave orders to their lesser officers (corporals, flag bearers et cetera). - All officers were responsible for keeping order among their men in camp and during the march.
30	Marching order	- Armed servants should not travel near the carriages of their masters but in the banner/company where they belong.
31	Marching order/Crime and punishment	- If wild animals (game) are spotted near the marching column, only a designated hunter should chase them. - Those who left the marching column without approval were flogged.
32	Marching order/Crime and punishment	- Those who left the marching column to plunder, or steal were punishable by death.
33	Camp life	- The smith and other designated craftsmen were responsible for sharpening swords and sabres. They performed their craft in a specific area inside the camp.
34	Camp life	- Drummers and trumpeters should always wait for the orders of the general. - If sentinels sleep on duty their officers will be punished as well.
35	Military hierarchy/ Artillery	- The master gunner (*artellariae magister*) was in charge with overseeing the artillery and gunpowder stores. He was responsible for the distribution of the ammunition among soldiers.
36	Camp life/Supply	- The camp market was organised by an appointed overseer (*vásárbíró*) who was also in charge with setting the price limitations.
37	Camp life/Military hierarchy	- No soldier was allowed to leave camp without the consent of a captain or a lieutenant.
38	Crime and punishment/ Judicial procedure	- Quarrels between soldiers should be addressed to a military judge (*hadi bíró*). - Those who injured fellow soldiers were punishable by death.
39	Supply/ Crime and punishment	- Foraging parties should never exceed a quarter of the whole army placed under the authority of prudent officers. - The transport of provisions should be equally divided among soldiers and abusive behaviour should be avoided. - Those who broke the rules during plunder forays will be punished as follows: captains will be demoted; lieutenants will receive three whip strikes and common soldiers will be flogged.
40	Piety	- Soldiers should pray for a favourable outcome of the expedition. - Soldiers should keep a decent and pious behaviour throughout the campaign to avoid the wrath of God.

The 1683 regulation is much more detailed compared to the one issued in 1616. It shows some interesting signs of change in terms of setting a more rigid moral standard among troops. The author of the document shows a greater concern in clearly defining the 'vulnerable groups', who needed protection from the potential abusive behaviour of soldiers, essentially poor people, merchants, clergy, women, and children. Enforcing discipline among soldiers was the main objective of this regulation and thus, a substantial number of articles (25 out of 40) deal with matters of crime and punishment. The death penalty is mentioned no less than 18 times and was prescribed for a wide range of offences such as cursing, blasphemy, abusive behaviour against vulnerable groups (poor people, women, and clergy for example), injuring a fellow soldier, adultery (at the second offence), desecrating graves, arson, spreading rumours in camp, stealing from fellow soldiers, making contact with the enemy, leaving the camp or marching column without permission or failing to deliver captives and letters to superior officers. A few articles deal with the military hierarchy by establishing the chain of command in the army and the responsibilities of each type of officers.

Military regulations, such as the two examples analysed in this chapter, offer a detailed image of how the seventeenth century Transylvanian army was expected to behave on campaign. These documents were issued on the eve of major expeditions and were communicated to the whole army before departure. The death sentence and severe physical punishments such as beating or flogging are commonly mentioned but were clearly not applied equally across the whole army. High ranking officers, most of them of noble origin, were usually demoted for offences while common soldiers were punished harshly for similar mistakes.

Military Hierarchy in the Transylvanian Army

The prince held the highest position in the military hierarchy as supreme leader of the army and he often commanded his troops personally, inside or outside the country. The second most senior position was held by a captain general or supreme general (*főgenerális*) who had authority over the whole army and was usually appointed at the beginning of each campaign. There was a general of the Székely, with authority over the soldiers mobilised by the Székely seats of South-Eastern Transylvania. The commander of Oradea fortress was also general of the troops from the western counties, a region also known as *Partium*. Each of these high-ranking officers had a second in command who took their place in case they died on the battlefield or otherwise incapacitated. The supreme general was replaced by the general of the Transylvanian counties who was also chief lieutenant (*főispán*) of Alba County, while the Székely general was replaced by the captain general of Odorhei Seat.[126] These were all temporary military offices, given to prominent

---

126 Apor of Altorja, *Metamorphosis*, p.85.

members of the nobility or the Székely elite at the beginning of each major campaign.

Many permanent office holders in the administrative framework of Transylvania had military duties. In the seventeenth century, most counties had two chief-lieutenants (*főispán*), except for those situated on the western borderland that had only one. One of them remained behind to deal with administrative matters while the other was usually at court or commanding the banner of the county in the army. The Székely seats were also led by two officials, a captain general (*főkapitány*), who commanded the contingents from that administrative unit, and a chief-justice (*főkirálybíró*) with legal and administrative responsibilities. A Székely captain general had many subordinate officers like the vice-captain, lieutenants, standard bearers et cetera.[127]

Some of the most important permanent military offices were held by the commanders of the court guard. Each branch of the court army, cavalry and infantry, had captains, vice-captains and other subordinated officers who held these positions in times of war and peace. In a similar situation were the captains of border fortifications. They were members of the nobility, rewarded with a generous income and invested with a significant military, political and judicial authority in the territories placed under their control. The lower officer ranks included captains of cavalry banners or infantry companies with 100 or less soldiers under their authority. They were followed by a vice-captain or a lieutenant (*hadnagy*) who took command of the banner or company in the absence of the captain. Smaller units of up to 10 soldiers (sometimes even less) were commanded by corporals (*tizedes, decuriones*).

---

127 Apor of Altorja, *Metamorphosis*, pp.85–87.

3

Fortifications, Artillery and Garrisons

The siege was a defining component of seventeenth century warfare. The development of artillery and the art of building fortifications were some of the most dynamic fields of Early Modern warfare. Military architects, engineers, gunsmiths and artillerists became respected war professions, prized by all European monarchs. Governments invested large amounts of resources in building complex defensive systems leading thus the way for the rise of the nation states.[1]

The Ottoman-Habsburg theatre of war in Central Europe was also dominated by siege warfare during the Early Modern period. The frontier between the two was a vast swath of land stretching from the Adriatic Sea to the Carpathian Mountains. Bastioned fortresses, built especially by Italian architects and engineers, but also smaller earth and timber fortifications, called *palanka*, defended the frontier on both sides. The Habsburgs, and to a certain extent the Ottomans, relied on a vast network of fortresses to keep control over the disputed territories in the borderlands.[2]

Following a similar pattern, but obviously on a different scale, the Transylvanian Principality built and consolidated a strong defensive system consisting of older medieval fortifications, modern bastioned fortresses and fortified towns.[3] It was estimated that during the reign of Gabriel Bethlen (1613–1629) the cost of maintaining the defensive system, including the

---

1 Christopher Duffy, *Siege Warfare: The Fortress in the Early Modern World 1494–1660* (London: Routledge & Kegan Paul, 1979), pp.247–249; Jeremy Black, *European Warfare 1494–1660* (London: Routledge, 2002), pp.85–86; Christer Jörgensen, Michael F. Pavkovic, Rob S. Rice, Frederick C. Schneid, Christopher L. Scott, *Fighting Techniques of the Early Modern World. AD 1500 ~ AD 1763: Equipment, Combat Skills, and Tactics* (New York: Thomas Dunne Books, St. Martin's Press, 2005), pp.170–209.

2 Géza Pálffy, 'The Origins and Development of the Border Defence System against the Ottoman Empire in Hungary (Up to the Early Eighteenth Century)', Géza Dávid, Pál Fodor (eds.), *Ottomans, Hungarians and Habsburgs in Central Europe: The Military Confines in the Era of Ottoman Conquest* (Leiden: Brill, 2000), pp.3–71; Duffy, *Siege Warfare*, pp.199–204.

3 Klára Kovács, 'Fortresses-Building in 16th Century Transylvania. The Recruitment of Labour Force', *Transylvanian Review*, Vol. XXI, Supplement No. 2 (2012), pp.163–181; Florin Nicolae Ardelean, 'Political Boundaries and Territorial Identity in Early Modern Central Europe:

wages of permanent garrisons, reached the amount of 150,000 florins per year in addition to the 300,000–400,000 spent when the Transylvanian army was on campaign.[4]

Transylvanian fortifications can be divided in two major groups, based on their geographical position. First, the hinterland fortifications were situated within the confines of the old voivodeship, inside a perimeter marked by the Carpathian Mountain range. The second group, arguably the most important, consisted of the western borderland fortresses, situated in the eastern parts of the Hungarian Kingdom which acknowledged the authority of the Transylvanian prince. During the first half of the seventeenth century, Gabriel Bethlen and George Rákóczi I managed to expand their control over seven more counties in Upper Hungary: Szabolcs, Szatmár, Ugocsa, Bereg, Zemplén, Borsod and Abaúj.

At the height of his power Prince Gabriel Bethlen had stationed a significant number of soldiers in his fortification.[5]

Transylvanian Garrisons in 1626 (1,600 cavalry and 2,050 infantry)

Fortress	Cavalry	Infantry	Total number of soldiers
Alba Iulia	300	300	600
Vințul de Jos	50	50	100
Deva	50	100	150
Făgăraș	100	100	200
Bran	200	300	500
Chinari (Várhegy)	200	300	500
Prejmer	200	300	500
Ciuc	200	300	500
Odorhei	50	50	100
Iernut	50	50	100
Gherla	50	50	100
Chioar	50	50	100
Mănăștur	30	30	60
Șimleu	50	50	100
Tășnad	20	20	40

    The Western Frontier of Transylvania during the Sixteenth Century', *Territorial Identity and Development*, 6/1 (2021), pp.21–38.
4   Harai, *Gabriel Bethlen*, p.202.
5   Szilády, Szilágyi (eds.), *Török-Magyarkori*, p.479.

With a few exceptions, the above-mentioned fortresses were situated in the hinterland of the principality. This is a rough estimation of the defending forces, one which probably included soldiers from the court guard (especially in the case of Alba Iulia) in addition to the members of resident garrisons.

The following table shows some of the fortifications from the western borderlands, including Oradea fortress, the centrepiece of this defensive system.[6]

The Garrison of Oradea fortress and other fortifications on the western frontier of Transylvania in 1626

Fortress	Cavalry	Infantry	Total number of soldiers
Oradea	500	500	1,000
Ineu	300	400	700
Șiria	200	200	400
Gyula	1,000	1,000	2,000
Szarvas	300	300	600
Nádudvar	200	200	400
Debrecen	200	200	400
Kálló	200	200	400
Ecsed	200	300	500
Satu Mare	200	300	500
Mukachevo	100	100	200

The source is not completely accurate as it includes the fortress of Gyula, which was under Ottoman occupation at the time. However, the high number of soldiers correctly indicates the fact that this region was one of the most militarised in the whole principality. The high proportion of cavalry troops (3,700 cavalry and 3,400 infantry) emphasises the importance of cavalry warfare in these parts of Europe and the importance of irregular combat in a fluid and volatile frontier area.

---

6   Szilády, Szilágyi (eds.), *Török-Magyarkori*, p.475.

Plate A. Cavalryman from the guard of the Prince and a sub-captain of the court infantry (first half of the seventeenth century)
See Colour Plate Commentaries for further information.
(Illustration by Catalin Draghici © Helion & Company 2024)

Plate B. Mounted nobleman from the county banners (middle of the seventeenth century)
See Colour Plate Commentaries for further information.
(Illustration by Catalin Draghici © Helion & Company 2024)

Plate C. Székely foot soldier (first half of the seventeenth century)
See Colour Plate Commentaries for further information.
(Illustration by Catalin Draghici © Helion & Company 2024)

Plate D. A Wallachian *seimen* in the service of Prince Michael Apafi (1661–1690)
See Colour Plate Commentaries for further information.
(Illustration by Catalin Draghici © Helion & Company 2024)

Plate E. Young Transylvanian nobleman from the court guard (middle of the seventeenth century)
See Colour Plate Commentaries for further information.
(Illustration by Catalin Draghici © Helion & Company 2024)

Plate F. A Green Rifleman (middle of the seventeenth century)
See Colour Plate Commentaries for further information.
(Illustration by Catalin Draghici © Helion & Company 2024)

Plate G. A 'carbine cavalryman' from the guard of Prince Michael Apafi I (1661–1690)
See Colour Plate Commentaries for further information.
(Illustration by Catalin Draghici © Helion & Company 2024)

Plate H. German Mercenary in the Army of Transylvania (first half of the seventeenth century)
See Colour Plate Commentaries for further information.
(Illustration by Catalin Draghici © Helion & Company 2024)

The Western Frontier of Transylvania in the Seventeenth Century

Caransebeş and Lugoj

The Banat of Caransebeş and Lugoj was situated on the southernmost stretch of the western Transylvanian frontier, bordering the Ottoman province (*villayet*) of Timişoara. This region was entrusted to a high official, the *ban*, who exercised political, administrative, judicial and military authority in the name of the Transylvanian prince. This was an area of intense military activity during the seventeenth century although Transylvania remained a loyal vassal of the Ottoman Empire. It is a clear indication of the fact that irregular warfare in the borderlands was not entirely restricted by official relations between states. Many patents of nobility were issued during this period for the inhabitants of the Banat and many coats-of-arms were illustrated with a 'decapitated Turk'.[7]

Caransebeş and Lugoj were two important fortified urban settlements. Given the general insecurity of the border area most of the nobility had residences inside one of these well defended towns. The defensive enceintes had been built in previous centuries and modernised in the seventeenth century. Lugoj benefited from extensive works of consolidation during the reign of Gabriel Bethlen (1613–1629). In 1624, the Diet voted a tax of one florin for each *porta* for the constructions that were taking place in Lugoj. All had to pay this tax with the exception of Bihor County, who contributed to the construction of Oradea fortress.[8] A significantly larger contribution, of 10 florins for each *porta*, was established in 1627. However, the money was divided between the needs of Lugoj fortress and the construction of a house in Istanbul for Transylvanian envoys.[9]

George Rákózi I (1631–1648) continued to strengthen the fortifications of the two towns by gathering taxes and by bringing serfs from the neighbouring counties to fulfil their work obligations. A tax of one florin for every single *porta* was established in 1632 for the construction work taking place at Lugoj and Ineu, paid by the counties but also by the Saxons and Székely.[10] A few years later, in 1637, the serfs of Hunedoara County were sent to work on the fortifications of Caransebeş.[11] In 1650 the two fortifications from the Banat were supplied by 26 settlements situated in their vicinity but the income from these was insufficient.[12] Further taxes and work contributions from

---

7   Adrian Magina, 'Înnobilările din Lugoj în secolul al XVII-lea', Ligia Boldea, Rudolf Gräf (eds.), *Vocaţia istoriei: Studii în memoria profesorului Nicolae Bocşan* (Cluj-Napoca: Mega, 2017), pp.81–90.
8   MCRT, vol. VIII, p.233.
9   MCRT, vol. VIII, p.368.
10 MCRT, vol. IX, p.281.
11 MCRT, vol. IX, p.597.
12 MCRT, vol. XI, pp.105–112.

the hinterland were necessary to sustain the defensive line along the western borderland.

The whole region was occupied by the Ottomans in 1658, in the early phase of the punitive expedition directed against the rebel Prince George Rákózi II. When he was confirmed in his position by the sultan, Prince Ákos Barcsay agreed to surrender the two fortified towns with their surrounding districts. The Turks placed garrisons of 1,000 men in each town and took over the existing arsenals and supplies.[13] A significant wave of refugees, commoners and nobles alike, migrated to neighbouring Transylvanian counties.[14]

Ineu

The most significant achievement of Transylvania in the Long Turkish War (1591–1606) was the re-conquest of Lipova and Ineu, on the southern sector of the western frontier. At the end of the war, the Ottomans immediately requested the return of the two fortifications. When Gabriel Bethlen was elected and confirmed Prince of Transylvania in 1613, he promised the sultan he would settle the matter of the two disputed strongholds. The defenders of Lipova refused to surrender to the Ottomans and thus Bethlen was forced to besiege his own fortress. The garrison was counting on Habsburg help, but they only received vague promises from Vienna. After a 12-day siege, the rebels surrendered, and Gabriel Bethlen was able to fulfil half of his promise.[15]

Considering the great internal turmoil caused by the surrender of Lipova, Bethlen decided to keep the fortress of Ineu and managed to convince the Ottoman envoys that this was only a temporary delay. In the following decades, Ineu remained within the boundaries of the Transylvanian Principality. By the end of the sixteenth century, it was already a modern fortification with two lines of defence (an inner citadel and an outer wall) strengthened with bastions. Although the surrounding region was often devastated by Ottoman raids, the fortress itself was well supplied with weapons and provisions.[16] Additional works to consolidate the defences were commissioned under Captain Gabriel Haller after 1645. The captain of

Fortress of Ineu (Borosjenő) 1658, in Galeazzo Gualdo Priorato, Historia di Leopoldo Cesare..., (digitisation of University and State Library of Saxony-Anhalt in Halle (Saale)

---

13 Cristina Feneșan-Bulgaru, 'Problema instaurării dominației otomane asupra Banatului Lugojului și Caransebeșului', *Banatica*, IV (1977), pp.223–238.
14 Magina, Livia, 'Cross-Border Mobility: War Refugees in Early Modern Transylvania', Florin Nicolae Ardelean et al. (eds.), *From Medieval Frontiers to Early Modern Borders in Central and South-East Europe* (Berlin: Peter Lang, 2022), pp.95–114.
15 Costin Feneșan, *Doi cronicari ardeleni din secolul al XVII-lea* (Timișoara: Editura de Vest, 2001), p.49; Kraus, Cronica Transilvaniei, p.40.
16 Adrian Magina, 'Conscripția și inventarul bunurilor cetății Ineu în anul 1605', *Banatica* 21 (2011), pp.90–104.

FORTIFICATIONS, ARTILLERY AND GARRISONS

Ineu commanded a large garrison supplemented by a significant cavalry detachment provided by the nobility of Zarand County. Each noble family from the area had to send a certain number of armed horsemen, depending on the size of their estates. In 1653 the rate of conscription was established at one horseman for every 20 *portae*.[17]

In 1658 the Ottomans besieged and conquered the fortress of Ineu. The garrison of only 350 men surrendered after four days and thus the Ottomans reclaimed by force, the fortification they had lost more than half a century ago (1595).[18]

Oradea

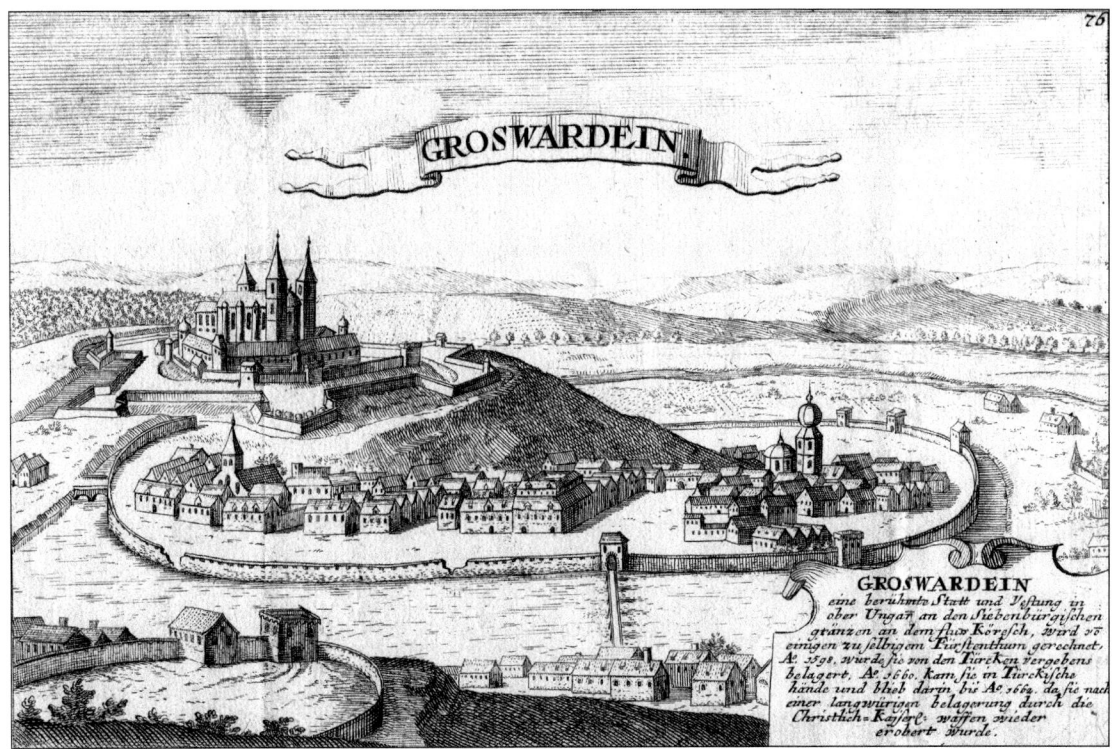

Oradea in the seventeenth century 1 (Țării Crișurilor Museum, Oradea, Romania)

Situated on the Criș (Körös) River, the fortress of Oradea was rightfully considered the 'gateway of Transylvania'. The construction of the bastioned enceinte began in 1568 under John Sigismund Szapolyai and continued for many decades until 1627 when the last bastion was erected. The height of the walls ranged between seven and 11 metres (23–36ft), built with various materials like stone, brick, earth and wood.[19] Throughout his reign Gabriel

---

17 Constituțiile Aprobate, pp.161–162.
18 Eugen Glück, 'Contribuții cu privire la istoricul cetății de la Ineu', *Ziridava*, XIII (1981), pp.131–147.
19 Klára Kovács, Cetatea din Gherla. Răspândirea fortificației în sistem bastionar italian în Transilvania (Cluj-Napoca: Phd. Thesis, Babeș-Bolyai University, 2009), pp.138–147.

Bethlen made constant efforts to complete the construction of this important fortification. In 1614, Captain Francis Rhédey was instructed to use one-quarter of the incomes from Bihor, Crasna and Middle Szolnok Counties for the fortress of Oradea. An Italian architect, Giacomo Resti da Verna, arrived in the winter of 1618 to supervise the construction site. Maintenance and consolidation work was performed regularly. The defensive ditch was deepened, and the counterscarp was reinforced at its base with a stone and brick wall during the Rákózi princes.[20]

Given its strategic importance, Oradea was well supplied with artillery. An inventory drafted in 1632 shows a large variety of cannons and smaller artillery pieces.[21]

Artillery of Oradea Fortress 1632 (bastions and gate tower)

The New (Bethlen) Bastion	The 'King's Son' Bastion	The Red Bastion	The Golden Bastion	The 'Csonka' Bastion	The Gate Tower
One cannon bearing the coat of arms of Bebek family from Szádvár (Upper Hungary), seven pounds[22]	One siege cannon in the casemate	One cannon named 'Younger Brother', 20 pounds	One Tompér cannon, 16 pounds	One falcon of Emperor Maximilian, four pounds	One falconette, four pounds
One cannon from the Margrave of Jägendorf, 10 pounds	Two 'Herczegh' cannon, 10 pounds	Two siege cannon with chains, 20 pounds	One Falconette named 'Younger Brother', three pounds	Two 'Herczegh' cannon, 10 pounds	One rotating falconette, One pound
One Buquoy[23] cannon, 10 pounds	One falcon of Emperor Maximilian, seven pounds	One cannon named 'Older Brother', 35 pounds	Two Falcons named 'Poor Prince', five pounds	One old 'Rudolphus' falconette, three pounds	One cannon of Stephen Báthory, 30 pounds
One cannon fabricated in Košice (Kassa), 28 pounds	One falcon, five pounds	One cannon named 'Stag', 40 pounds	Two falcons named 'Prince', five pounds	One cannon of Stephen Báthory, 28 pounds	One ribauldequin (organ gun) with nine barrels

---

20 Kovács, *Cetatea din Gherla*, pp.161–164.
21 Paul Gyulai, 'Inventarul cetății Oradea la 1632', *Acta Musei Napocensis*, X (1973), pp.665–673; Margit Nagy, *Várak, kastélyok, udvarházak, ahogy a régiek látták: XVII–XVIII. századi erdélyi összeírások és leltárak* (București: Kriterion, 1973), pp.70–73.
22 In sevententh century Transylvania, the 'Cluj pound' = 0.3895 kg was most common, and was slighlty less heavier than a modern English pound = 0.453 kg.
23 Charles Bonaventure de Bucquoy.

FORTIFICATIONS, ARTILLERY AND GARRISONS

One Tompér cannon, 16 pounds	One small falconette called 'Stag', three pounds	One falcon of Emperor Maximilian, seven pounds	One cannon bearing the coat of arms of Bebek family form Szádvár (Upper Hungary), 10 pounds	One falcon of Emperor Rudolph, seven pounds	One ribauldequin (organ gun) with eight barrels
One 'Charming Prince' cannon, 10 pounds	One small Falconette, Two pounds	One Tompér cannon, 14 pounds	One cannon of Stephen Báthory named 'Tenor', 28 pounds	One canon named 'Kurta', 50 pounds	
Four Buquoy cannons, 40 pounds	One cannon of Stephen Báthory, 28 pounds	One Buquoy cannon, 30 pounds		One cannon named 'Dragon', 30 pounds	
Three 'Poor Prince' cannons, 10 pounds	One ruined cannon, 30 pounds	One siege cannon with chains, seven pounds		One siege cannon with chains, 22 pounds	
One 'Little Hawk' cannon of Michael the Brave, five pounds	One ruined cannon from Košice (Kassa), 18 pounds	Two small falconets (tarack), two pounds		One falconette named 'Younger Brother', three pounds	
One 'Big Hawk' cannon of János Hommonay, 20 pounds	Two mortar cannons, 20 pounds	One unidentified cannon		One falcon named 'Poor Prince', five pounds	
One 'Herczegh' cannon, 10 pounds					
Three unidentified cannons					
One cannon fabricated in Košice (Kassa), 20 pounds					
One falconette (*tarack*), Two pounds					
Total: 21 artillery pieces	**Total**: 12 artillery pieces	**Total**: 12 artillery pieces	**Total**: Eight artillery pieces	**Total**: 11 artillery pieces	**Total**: Five artillery pieces

A total number of 69 artillery pieces were distributed among the bastions and the gate tower. Those who drafted the inventory used the term cannon (*ágyú*) for pieces above 10 pounds and up to 50 pounds, but there are a few exceptions of smaller pieces placed in this category as well. Two mortars (*mozsár*) of 20 pounds each can also be included in this group, which adds up to a total of 49 pieces of heavy artillery. Smaller pieces (20 in total), which can be included in the light artillery category, ranged between one and seven pounds. In the document they are referred to as falcons (*falkoni*) (4-, 5-, and 7-pounders) and falconets (*tarack*) (1-pounders up to 4-pounders). Two Ribauldequins (organ guns), with eight and nine barrels respectively were placed in the gate tower.

The document provides other interesting details like the individual names of cannons, accompanied at times by the name of the first owner or the place of fabrication. Some of the cannon were several decades old, cast during the second half of the sixteenth century, like those bearing the names of Habsburg Emperors, Maximilian II (1564–1576), Rudolph II (1576–1612) and Transylvanian rulers like Stephen Báthory (1571–1586) and Michael the Brave (1600–1601). A sizeable number of cannons bear the name of the Habsburg general Charles Bonaventure de Buquoy and were captured by Prince Gabriel Bethlen during the siege of Nové Zámky, in 1621.

Gunpowder, saltpetre, hand firearms (muskets and harquebuses) and other military equipment was deposited in a few storehouses situated inside and outside the fortified enceinte.

FORTIFICATIONS, ARTILLERY AND GARRISONS

Storehouses of Oradea Fortress in 1632

Lower storehouse	Upper storehouse	Gunpowder storehouses
963 – 40-pound shots	306 muskets	537 *mázsa*[24] and 15 pounds of gunpowder deposited in two storehouses
1,116 – 3-pound shots	100 muskets given to the German infantry	343 *mázsa* and 13 pounds of gunpowder deposited in two towers
1,302 – 30-pound shots	174 harquebuses	
26 – 25-pound shots	150 lances	
91 – 22-pound shots	146 breastplates	
346 – 20-pound shots	32 soldiers' helmets (*sisak*)	
299 – 14-pound shots	19 German helmets	
1,400 – 5-,6- and 7-pound falcon shots	11 round shields	
1,360 – 4-pound falcon shots	28 flags captured last year (1631)	
4,656 – 2- and 3-pound falconette shots	10 flags from the time of the late prince (Gabriel Bethlen)	
12 new ropes (66 pounds)		
14 old ropes (56 pounds)		
23 very old, damaged ropes (59 pounds)		
Six very old, damaged ropes		
Two cannon wheels with ropes		
One set of Dutch cannon wheels		
Six old pieces of pewter		
80 pounds of saltpetre		

An impressive number of artillery shot (14,859) was deposited in the two main storehouses, together with various weapons and military equipment. More than 500 firearms were available inside the fortress, including both muskets but also older harquebuses. The total quantity of gunpowder recorded is very large, over 48 tonnes. This source clearly indicates that Oradea, the most important fortification of the Transylvanian Principality, had enough military supplies to withstand prolonged sieges.

---

24   1 *mázsa* = 100 *font* (pounds) = 38.95 kg.

It was estimated that 5,000 soldiers were necessary for an efficient defence of such a fortress.²⁵ In reality, such a large number of defenders were never gathered inside the walls of Oradea. During the siege of 1598 Oradea was defended by 2,000 soldiers, both locals and Habsburg mercenaries. In 1660, when the fortress was conquered by the Ottomans after 46 days of siege, the defenders counted only 300 professional soldiers aided by townsmen who had sought refuge inside the fortress.²⁶

Săcuieni

Further north, the defensive system of Transylvania relied on another bastioned fortification at Săcuieni (Székelyhíd). The construction of the modern fortress began under David Zólyomi, a rich and powerful nobleman, who owned the estate until 1634 when he was put on trial for treason and all his proprieties were confiscated. The construction continued under Prince George Rákózi I who understood the strategic importance of a stronghold situated in the marshy area of the Eriu (Ér) River. The fortress had four bastions built upon a foundation enforced with pillars of hard maple. The base of the bastions and curtain walls was made of stone, while the sections above water level were built in brick. After Oradea was conquered by the Ottomans in 1660, Săcuieni remained the most important Transylvanian fortification in Bihor County. Nevertheless, during the troubled years of the Ottoman punitive expeditions in Transylvania (1658–1661) Săcuieni opened its gates to a Habsburg garrison.²⁷

A few years later, in 1664, the garrison rebelled against the Habsburgs and pledged its loyalty to the Prince of Transylvania, Michael Apafi I. This unexpected achievement proved to be a double-edged sword. On one hand Transylvania regained an important stronghold on its western frontier which was seriously weakened after the fall of Oradea. However, Săcuieni had become a source of discord in Ottoman-Habsburg relations and the maintenance of the fortress, and maintaining its garrison was a heavy financial burden for Transylvania. Although the captain of Săcuieni was entitled to gather taxes from several urban and rural settlements in the area, including the large town of Debrecen, he faced numerous difficulties because in the borderlands, the authority of the Transylvanian ruler was often challenged by its powerful neighbours. Both the Ottomans and the Habsburgs demanded taxes form those living on the Transylvanian frontier, thus contributing to the weakening of the authority of the prince. In the course of 1664, from April to December, Captain Martin Boldvai could hardly gather 6,900 florins, which were barely enough for paying the monthly wages of the 150 German mercenaries. As the tensions were rising, Apafi and his councillors wanted to secretly surrender the fortress to the Habsburgs but the war between the two empires ended

---

25 Kovács, *Cetatea din Gherla*, p.139.
26 Ardelean, *Organizarea militară*, pp.171–172.
27 Liviu Borcea, 'Contribuții la istoria cetății Săcuieni (comitatul Bihor) în secolele XV-XVII', *Anuarul Institutului de Istorie și Arheologie din Cluj-Napoca*, 26 (1983–1984), pp.319-332.

before this plan could be set in motion. One of the provisions of the Vasár peace treaty (10 August 1664) demanded the demolition of Săcuieni fortress. The work began without delay and was finished in February 1665.[28]

Huszt

The fortress of Huszt (today Хуст in Ukraine) was built on a high ridge overlooking the Tisa River in Maramureș County. It was a modern fortification, with Italian style bastions, which was controlled at various points in time by both the Habsburgs and the Transylvanians.[29] When Gabriel Bethlen was elected prince in 1613, Huszt was in the hands of the Habsburgs, but the new ruler of Transylvania managed to retake this important borderland stronghold through diplomatic means. According to the treaty of Trnava (Nagyszombat) in 1615, signed by Matthias of Habsburg and Gabriel Bethlen, the fortresses of Huszt and Chioar were returned to the Principality of Transylvania. On 11 July 1615, the officials appointed by Bethlen reached the fortress of Hustz and the garrison, composed mostly of local soldiers, swore an oath of allegiance to their new ruler and his representative, the captain.[30]

Soon after this event, the Prince and Diet agreed to organise ample repair work and consolidation at Huszt and other fortifications around the country. The nobility had to send six serfs and one cart pulled by four oxen, for every 10 *portae* (fiscal units), which were expected to work for three whole weeks at the designated fortress.[31] A small garrison resided inside the fortress at all times. According to documents issued in the second half of the seventeenth century the size of the permanent garrison was made up of 69–70 soldiers, mostly locals but also some German mercenaries.[32] In the winter of 1685–1686, the Habsburg commander Federico Veterani entered Maramureș County, leading five regiments (one infantry, four cavalry). This was done with the approval of Transylvanian authorities which were already negotiating a pact with Viennese envoys. In this context, the fortress of Huszt passed once again, but this time for good, under the authority of the Habsburgs.[33]

The Expansion of the Western Frontier in Upper Hungary

The first campaign (1619–1621) of Gabriel Bethlen against the Habsburgs in the Thirty Years' War was concluded with the Peace Treaty of Mikulov

---

28 Ágnes Szalai, 'Aceasta fiind cetate de graniță în locul Oradiei...' Rolul guvernământului princiar în cadrul tratativelor referitoare la cetatea de graniță Săcueni', Teréz Oborni (ed.), *"Oradea cum e ocrotită": Lupte pentru Oradea în epoca modernă timpurie. Studii despre istoria Țării Bihorului* 7 (Oradea: Fundația Culturală Varadinum, 2020), pp.151–184.
29 Alajos Deschmann, 'Huszt vára – a máramarosi sóbányák őre', *Műemlékvédelem*, 35/ 1-4 (1991), pp.156–164.
30 MCRT, vol. VII, pp.274–277.
31 MCRT, vol. VII, pp.274–277.
32 SJAN CJ, Colecția socoteli princiare, 46 Evidențe nominale de efective militare, f.19, 230.
33 Bethlen, *Descrierea*, pp.185–186.

(Nikolsburg), in late December 1621. According to this treaty, Bethlen was granted possession of seven counties in Upper Hungary (Szabolcs, Szatmár, Ugocsa, Bereg, Zemplén, Borsod and Abaúj). This territorial gain was consolidated through the peace treaties with the Habsburgs signed at Vienna (1624) and Bratislava (1626). When Prince Bethlen died in 1629, the seven counties were returned to the Habsburgs. George Rákózi I followed in the footsteps of his predecessor and joined the Protestant faction in the Thirty Years' War. After an inconclusive campaigning 1644–1645, he signed a new treaty with the Habsburgs at Linz (December 1645) and regained the seven Hungarian counties until his death in 1648. There was a special provision regarding the counties of Szabolcs and Szatmár which were inherited by his successor, George Rákóczi II and remained within the boundaries of the Transylvanian Principality until 1659.

Fortress of Satu Mare (Szatmár) second half of the seventeenth century, in Galeazzo Gualdo Priorato, Historia di Leopoldo Cesare..., (digitisation of University and State Library of Saxony-Anhalt in Halle (Saale))

The region represented by the seven eastern Hungarian counties had several major fortresses and fortified towns, which had been built to oppose further Ottoman expansion. Among them was Satu Mare (Szatmár), an important modern fortification with five bastions, built between 1565 and 1573. The Habsburgs and the Transylvanians fought for the possession of this fortress and the surrounding region during the second half of the sixteenth century, but it was the Habsburg Kings of Hungary who held authority over the fortress for most of the time. Completely surrounded by the waters of the Someș (Szamos) River, Satu Mare had an especially important strategic position and was supplied by a vast network of rural and urban settlements.[34] While Satu Mare was in the hands of the Transylvanian princes its role as a border fortress was diminished and consequently its estate was reduced. According to a conscription document drafted in 1630 only 751 serf families lived in the settlements surrounding this fortification.[35]

Košice was the most important fortified city in the newly acquired territories of Gabriel Bethlen. Under the Habsburgs, the city was the leading military and financial centre in Upper Hungary as headquarter of the captain general and of the Szepes chamber. The Transylvanian prince counted on the financial help of the chamber and on the weapons provided by the arsenal of the city.[36] Košice was defended by a medieval stone wall with 23 towers

---

34 Adalbert Burai, 'Despre cetatea de tip italian din Satu Mare', *Studii și Comunicări. Satu Mare* I (1969), pp.143–160.
35 MNL OL, Urbaria et Conscriptiones, E 156 – a. - Fasc. 047. - No. 005, f.1–9.
36 Klára Papp, 'Várad, Debrecen és Kassa szerepe Bethlen Gábor fejedelemsége idején', Veronka Dáné et al. (eds.), Bethlen Erdélye, Erdély Bethlene: Bethlen Gábor trónra lépésének 400.

maintained and defended by the local craftsmen guilds. In the second half of the sixteenth and throughout the seventeenth century a second wall, provided with modern Italian type bastions, was constructed.[37] In the Early Modern age, Košice was the most important centre of weapon production in the region. Several inventories drafted during this period indicate significant amounts of weapons and war materials stored inside the city. For example, in 1647, while the city was under the authority of the Transylvanian prince, the arsenal of the city held: 147 double harquebuses (*Doppelhaken*), 57 muskets, 41 cannons and nine and a half tonnes of gunpowder.[38]

The territorial gains in Upper Hungary of Gabriel Bethlen and George Rákóczi I represented the most important political achievement of Transylvania, rightfully marking the 'golden age' of the principality. It was a prosperous region, which greatly increased the revenues of the prince and helped transform Transylvania into a regional military power.

The Reorganisation of the Western Frontier After the Fall of Oradea (1660)

The main western defensive line of Transylvania collapsed during the Ottoman campaigns against the rebel Prince George Rákóczi II (1658–1660). Caransebeș and Lugoj were surrendered to the Ottomans in 1658, Ineu was conquered during the same year and Oradea was taken after a 46-day siege in 1660. Five years later, in 1665, the fortress of Săcuieni was demolished as a consequence of Habsburg-Ottoman negotiations. In this unfavourable context, Prince Michael Apafi I and his councillors organised a second line of defence along the Carpathian Mountain range. The main fortifications of this new western defensive system were Deva (Déva), Cluj (Kolozsvár), Bologa (Sebesvár), Șimleu Silvaniei (Szilágysomlyó) and Chioar (Kővár).

Deva

Built on top of a high hill overlooking the Mureș valley, Deva was an older medieval fortress modernised in the sixteenth and seventeenth centuries. One of the most important improvements was made under Prince Gabriel Bethlen, who ordered the construction of a semi-circular bastion in 1623–1624.[39]

The size and organisation of the defending garrison is revealed by a document from 17 January 1684. Returning from the siege of Vienna (1683), Prince Michael Apafi spent some time in Deva where he inspected the garrison and received an oath of fealty from the soldiers. The garrison was composed of 156 infantry, divided in two distinct groups, namely those who

---

évfordulóján rendezett konferencia tanulmányai : 24–25 október 2013, Kolozsvár (Cluj-Napoca: Societatea Muzeului Ardelean, 2014), pp.537–548.

37 János Krcho, 'Standing watch in Kassa' City Walls and Watchtowers and their Phases of Construction', *Periodica Polytechnica Ser. Architecture*, 36/1–4 (1992), pp.189–213.

38 György Domokos, 'A kassai királyi hadszertár fegyverzete és felszerelése a XVI-XVII. században az inventáriumok tükrében', *Hadtörténelmi Közlemények*,110/4 (1997), pp.667–749.

39 Gheorghe Anghel, *Cetăți medievale din Transilvania* (București: Editura Meridiane, 1972), p.96.

resided inside the fortress (63 soldiers) and those who lived in the 'new town' at the foot of the hill (93 soldiers). The first group was organised in six units of nine to 11 men each. Five of them included local soldiers, Hungarians and Romanians, while the sixth unit was composed of German mercenaries. Three of the soldiers were designated as artillerists. The second group was significantly larger and was organised in 10 units, ranging between seven and 11 soldiers each. Their names indicated that most of them were local soldiers, Hungarians and Romanians. Some are called Váradi (meaning from Oradea), Lugasi (from Lugoj) or Karansebesi (from Caransebeș) indicating that they were probably migrants from the regions that had been lost to the Ottomans in previous decades.[40]

Cluj

One of the most prosperous urban settlements of Transylvania, Cluj was transformed into a borderland fortification after the fall of Oradea. The change of status and the proximity of hostile Ottoman garrisons had a significant impact on the social and economic life of the urban community.

Cluj was defended by a stone wall enforced with 18 towers, of which three were gate towers. In the beginning of the seventeenth century, Cluj did not have a specific military role, being situated at a safe distance from all borders of the country. Nevertheless, a small permanent garrison of 22 men defended the gates and towers of the city in 1614. When the army of the principality was mobilised for campaigns, Transylvanian towns were also each expected to send their detachments, newly recruited for the occasion. In 1618, Cluj sent a group of 80 guardsmen in the main army, while in 1634 the size of their detachment was reduced to 40 soldiers.[41] Although their numbers were rather limited, the monthly wages of garrison were a significant financial burden, representing between 15–20 percent of the yearly expenses of the town.[42]

In the second half of the seventeenth century, the garrison of Cluj was increased to a few hundred mercenary soldiers, both cavalry and infantry.[43] The expanded garrison was no longer sustained exclusively by the local community. A general tax was levied throughout the entire country to cover the expenses of borderland garrisons, including the main military force stationed in Cluj.[44]

During this period, the captain of Cluj became the most important permanent office in the military hierarchy of the country, leading not only the garrison of Cluj but also the soldiers stationed in other fortifications such as Șimleu Silvaniei, Cehu Silvaniei, Bologa and Gherla. One of the most notable personalities to hold this position was Dénes Bánffy who in addition

---

40   MCRT, vol. XVIII, pp.186–190.
41   Izsán, 'Between Soldier and Guard', pp.195–202.
42   Csaba Izsán, 'A zsoldos darabontok számadásai és a város védműveinek javítási költségei Kolozsvár 17. századi számadáskönyveiben', Áron Tőtős et al. (eds.) *Ezerarcú Erdély. Politika, társadalom, kultúra* (Kolozsvár: Erdélyi Múzeum-Egyesület, 2019), pp.341–343.
43   MCRT, vol. XIV, pp.123–124.
44   MCRT, vol. XVII, p.255.

to the above-mentioned military offices was also lord-lieutenant (*ispán*) of Cluj and Dăbâca counties and member of the princely council. Transylvania was on the brink of a civil war when a noble faction led by Michael Teleki accused Bánffy of treason. In 1674, the captain of Cluj mobilised his troops, including 400 German mercenaries who served in his border fortifications, and a significant amount of artillery. His adversaries relied mostly on Székely and noble levies and were at a clear disadvantage. However, Teleki was able to avoid a direct confrontation and convinced his rival to submit to a trial. After prolonged debates, the judges sentenced Bánffy to death, on account of secret negotiations with the Habsburgs. The sentence was carried out with haste before a letter of pardon signed by Prince Apafi could reach in the hands of the judges.[45]

Bologa

A stone fortress on the main road connecting Oradea to inner Transylvania, Bologa served as an outpost for Cluj. After 1660, this old fortification was improved with two semi-circular artillery towers, 11 metres tall (about 36 feet) and three metres thick (almost 10 feet).[46] Sustaining a defensive system in the second half of the seventeenth century was a heavy financial burden for the country and the revenues generated by the estates of border fortifications were no longer sufficient. During the meetings of the Diet, Dénes Bánffy and Michael Teleki, the two most influential councillors of the prince, often argued regarding this topic. Bánffy insistently requested more money for the frontier area while Teleki argued that these expenses would bring ruin to the whole country.[47] Until 1674 Bánffy had the upper hand and even modest fortifications like Bologa were maintained in good condition and defended by large garrisons. Although it was one of the smallest fortresses on the western border, Bologa was defended by 100 soldiers, namely 60 cavalry and 40 infantry.[48] After the execution of Dénes Bánffy, Bologa lost its role as a frontier outpost and its defences were neglected.[49]

Șimleu Silvaniei

Șimleu Silvaniei was the main residence of the Báthory family, who ruled Transylvania at the end of the sixteenth century. The construction of the fortification began in the first decades of the sixteenth century, when the Báthory's of Somlyó were already established as members of the high nobility in the Kingdom of Hungary. The inner citadel had a rectangular footprint with four large round towers. In the seventeenth century, one of the towers served as storage place for gunpowder and ammunition. Work on a second

---

45 Bethlen, *Descrierea*, pp.134–148.
46 Anghel, *Cetăți medievale*, p.97.
47 MCRT, vol. XIV, p.131.
48 MCRT, vol. XIV, p.155.
49 Nagy, *Várak, kastélyok*, pp.177–178.

enceinte, with modern angular bastions, began in the last decades of the sixteenth century.

Șimleu was owned by various members of the Báthory family until 1594 when it was included in the royal estate by Prince Sigismund Báthory. In 1660, various sections of the fortification were set on fire by Turkish and Tatar raiders, but in the following years Șimleu was repaired and became part of the new fortified border of the principality. Dénes Bánffy bought the fortress and its estate in 1670 and built an additional palisade which served as a third line of defence. After the death of its owner in 1674, Șimleu was once again integrated into the royal estate of the country and the garrison was placed under a captain designated by the prince and his councillors. This important military office was held for many years by Francisc Bialis, an Italian from Genoa, who served in the Transylvanian army until the Habsburg conquest. He died a few years later in 1693.[50]

The fortress needed regular maintenance work which was secured through the obligations of Transylvanian serfs to perform a certain number of days of 'free labour' (*gratuitus labour*) not only for their landlords but also for the country where required. For example, in 1679 the serfs from Crasna and Middle Szolnok counties performed their 'free labour' obligation at Șimleu fortress.[51] The garrison of the fortress consisted of both local soldiers and German mercenaries who received regular wages. They were strong enough to defend the fortress and organised occasional raids across the border into Habsburg controlled territories.[52]

Chioar

The fortress of Chioar was built during the second half of the thirteenth century, in the aftermath of the Mongol invasion of 1241. In the following centuries, the fortress and its estate were owned by various noble families. When Transylvania was separated from the rest of the Hungarian kingdom in the second half of the sixteenth century, Chioar became a border fortification, often besieged and occupied by Habsburg troops. At the beginning of the seventeenth century, it was controlled by a Habsburg garrison, until 1615 when it was given back to Transylvania after the peace treaty of Trnava (Nagyszombat), signed by Matthias of Habsburg and Gabriel Bethlen. Throughout the following decades, the fortress remained under the authority of Transylvanian princes who appointed captains from among their most trusted councillors. The captaincy of Chioar was considered an important office in the military hierarchy of the principality, remunerated with an annual salary of 1,000 florins and other material benefits.[53]

---

50 Kovács, *Cetatea din Gherla*, pp.171–179.
51 MCRT, vol. XIV, p.663.
52 MCRT, vol. XV, p.303.
53 David Prodan, *Iobăgia în secolul al XVII-lea*, vol. II (București: Editura Științifică și Enciclopedică, 1987), p.59.

FORTIFICATIONS, ARTILLERY AND GARRISONS

The defence of Chioar was entrusted to a mercenary garrison and a considerable number of semi-privileged soldiers, known as 'riflemen', who resided in the villages of the local district. The numbers of these men increased significantly towards the middle of the seventeenth century, during the reigns of the two Rákóczi Princes, and they were often also mobilised for foreign campaigns.[54] The soldiers of the permanent garrison (*praesidium*) resided inside the fortification and received regular wages. A regulation issued in 1665, under the captaincy of Michael Teleki, indicates that the defenders of the fortress were both local soldiers and German mercenaries. The two groups were often at odds and many disputes had to be settled through resorting to harsh punishments for the offenders.[55]

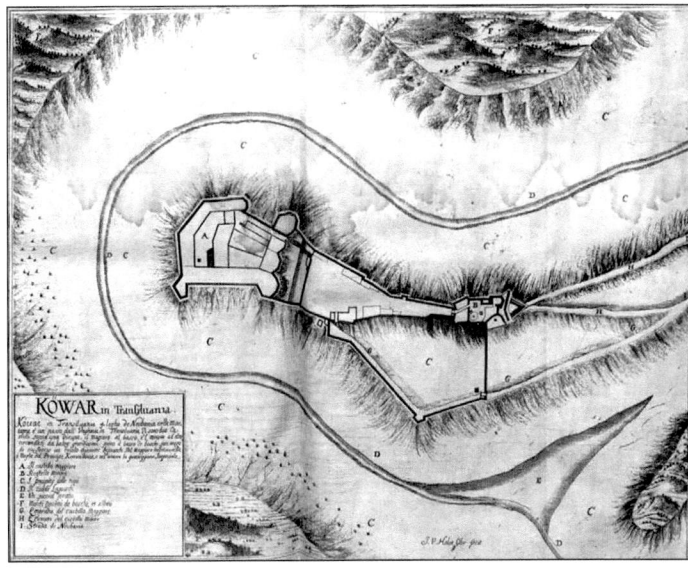

Plan of the fortress of Chioar (Kővár) second half of the seventeenth century, in Galeazzo Gualdo Priorato, Historia di Leopoldo Cesare, (digitisation of University and State Library of Saxony-Anhalt in Halle (Saale))

Hinterland Fortifications

The northern, eastern and southern borders of Transylvania were set along the Carpathians. These high mountains provided a natural obstacle, although not an insurmountable one. There was no need to build a chain of fortifications along this border but, nevertheless, Transylvanian princes held some important strongholds in these areas. In addition, the Saxons had built defensive walls around their most important settlements, which were improved and still functional during the seventeenth century.

Alba Iulia

The walls of Alba Iulia defended the main residence and court of the Prince of Transylvania. In the seventeenth century the estate of Alba Iulia included 22 settlements which provided for the needs of the princely court, with its administrative and military apparatus.[56] Soon after he was elected Prince of Transylvania, Gabriel Bethlen took initiatives to improve the defences of his main residence. The work progressed slowly in the beginning, mostly because

---

54   Valer Hossu, *Nobilimea Chioarului* (Baia Mare: Biblioteca Județeană „Petre Dulfu", 2003), pp.102–116.
55   Jozef Koncz, 'Magyar hadi szabályzatok gyüjteménye. Hadi edictum Kővár vára részére 1665-ből', *Hadtörténelmi Közlemények*, IV (1891), pp.429–434.
56   Emőke Gálfi, 'A gyulafehérvári udvarbírák és területi hatáskörük Bethlen Gábor uralkodásának első szakaszában', Veronka Dáné et al. (eds.), *Bethlen Erdélye, Erdély Bethlene: Bethlen Gábor trónra lépésének 400. évfordulóján rendezett konferencia tanulmányai: 24–25 október 2013, Kolozsvár* (Cluj-Napoca: Societatea Muzeului Ardelean, 2014), pp.319–327.

the Transylvanian Estates failed to provide all the necessary resources, money contributions and labourers. Nevertheless, in 1619 when Bethlen was preparing for his first campaign against the Habsburgs in the Thirty Years' War, the new walls and bastions of Alba Iulia were already taking shape. The plan was to build four bastions, one by the prince himself (with resources from the treasury) and the other three by the Transylvanian Estates (Nobility, Saxons and Székely). By the end of Bethlen's reign only two bastions were built, the one built from the princely treasury and the one constructed by the Saxons. The nobles and the Székely were unable to fulfil their initial promise, but Bethlen's successors made no attempts to continue the project.[57] The vulnerability of Alba Iulia was shown during the Ottoman campaign of 1658 when the town was left defenceless and most buildings inside the enceinte were burnt to the ground.

Alba Iulia also hosted the most important arsenal and gun foundry in Transylvania, founded in the second half of the sixteenth century. Weapon production continued into the seventeenth century. George Rákóczi I was particularly focused on improving his artillery and the capacity of his arsenals. It is estimated that during his time the foundries of Sárospatak (in Upper Hungary) and Alba Iulia produced about 300 cannons, especially light and medium pieces.[58]

Făgăraș

Făgăraș was the strongest fortification on the southern border of Transylvania, the favourite residence of the princesses and a secure place to safely keep the princely treasury. The building of the bastioned enceinte began in the last decades of the sixteenth century and continued under the rule of Gabriel Bethlen (1613–1629) and George Rákóczi I (1630–1648). The four bastions and the curtain walls were nine to 10 metres high and 1.20–1.80 metres thick. The façade was enforced with brick layers while the inside of the walls was filled with earth. The whole fortress was surrounded by a deep ditch, 40–75 metres wide.[59] The construction was mostly done with local resources provided by the vast estate of Făgăraș which included 52 settlements, inhabited by 3,087 serf families.

Throughout the seventeenth century, the fortress was provided with a sizeable number of cannon and substantial amounts of shot and gunpowder. An inventory drafted in 1632 mentions 26 pieces of heavy artillery, mortars, bombards, falcons and 125 harquebuses. A few years later, in 1637, 30 cannons of diverse sizes were accounted for, together with a large variety of hand weapons, such as muskets, Polish rifles, Janissary rifles, carbines, Teschen rifles, spears, and shields.[60]

57　András Kovács, 'Gábor Bethlen and the Construction of the New Seat of the Transylvanian Princedom', *Hungarian Historical Review*, 2, no.4 (2013), pp.880–888.
58　Szabó, 'The Army of the Principality', p.54.
59　Anghel, *Cetăți medievale*, pp.122–124.
60　Prodan, *Iobăgia XVII*, vol. II, pp.433–437; Claudia Sima, 'Arsenalul militar al cetății Făgăraș din secolul al XVII-lea', *Acta Terrae Fogarasiensis*, VIII (2019), pp.73–81.

FORTIFICATIONS, ARTILLERY AND GARRISONS

The resident garrison was composed of a mixture of local soldiers and foreign mercenaries, mostly Germans. In 1684 Făgăraș was defended by 91 soldiers of whom 38 were Hungarian infantry, 41 were German infantry and 10 were artillerists.[61] The surrounding district was inhabited by a semi-privileged group with military obligations, the boyars of Făgăraș. They were similar to nobility in terms of privileges and obligations with one major difference; their status was recognised only within the territorial limits of their district. They were unable to acquire proprieties beyond the boundaries of Făgăraș unless they were promoted to ranks of the 'true nobility' (*una eademque nobilitas*). According to a regulation issued in the second half of the seventeenth century, the boyars performed military service as cavalry, equipped with chainmail and armed with a lance and a gunpowder weapon.[62] In a conscription document drafted in 1632 a total number of 158 boyars (heads of families) were registered together with 98 nobles, freemen and guardsmen. They all had an obligation to perform military service at the fortress of Făgăraș and join the army of the prince when summoned.[63] In 1683, when Michale Apafi prepared his troops for the siege of Vienna, 70 boyars from Făgăraș were mustered.[64]

Gherla

The fortress was built in the middle of the sixteenth century, in the shape of an irregular quadrilateral with four bastions and one semi-bastion. During the Long Turkish War (1591–1606) Gherla suffered considerable damage and was in dire need of repairs. Gabriel Bethlen made constant efforts to consolidate this important stronghold and to renovate the princely residence inside its walls. Local resources but also craftsmen and labourers from the neighbouring counties and districts were brought to Gherla to work under the supervision of an Italian architect, Giovanni Landi. Work was temporarily suspended when Bethlen died in 1629 and resumed a few years later, after George Rákóczi I secured his position as ruler of Transylvania. The expansion and consolidation of the ditch was one of the costliest endeavours in this period. The most important contribution of George Rákóczi II was the construction of

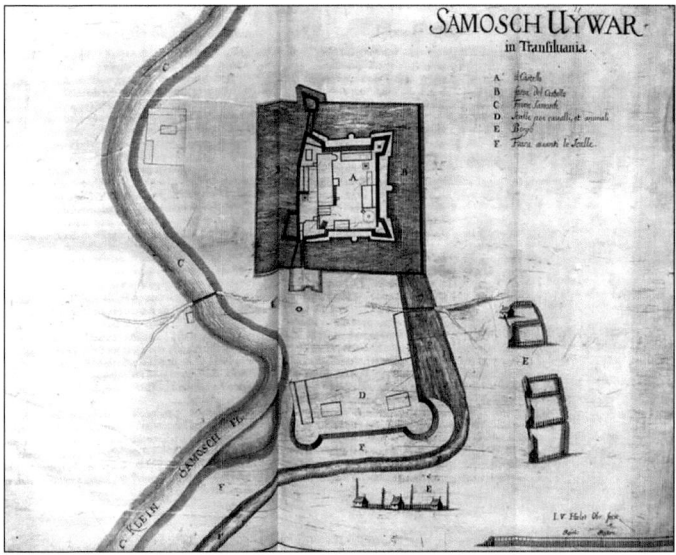

Plan of the fortress of Gherla (Szamosújvár) second half of the seventeenth century, in Galeazzo Gualdo Priorato, *Historia di Leopoldo Cesare*, (digitisation of University and State Library of Saxony-Anhalt in Halle (Saale)

---

61 SJAN CJ, Colecția socoteli princiare, 46 Evidențe nominale de efective militare, f.201.
62 Costea, *Solam virtutem*, p.78.
63 David Prodan, 'Boieri și vecini în Țara Făgărașului în sec. XVI-XVII', *Din istoria Transilvaniei. Studii și evocări* (București: Editura Enciclopedică, 1991), p.43.
64 Veress, *Documente*, vol. XI, 1886, pp.196–197.

a new palace inside the fortification. There is no evidence of significant changes or constructions during the second half of the seventeenth century.[65]

Although Gherla served mostly as a residence for the princely family, it had a strong garrison and a good supply of artillery and gunpowder. An inventory drafted in 1654 mentions a permanent guard of 99 infantry soldiers, divided into nine units (*tized*). Several light artillery pieces were placed in the bastions together with large numbers of smaller gunpowder weapons indicating that in case of necessity the number of defenders could be increased to several hundred men.[66] Another inventory from 1675 presents a comparable situation regarding the artillery, with a total number of 36 cannon recorded. The vast majority were light pieces, with shot weighing between one and 10 pounds, and there was only one heavy cannon with shot weighing 25 pounds. In addition, the inventory mentions 110 lances, 116 harquebuses and a wide variety of siege tools.[67]

Gurghiu

Positioned on the eastern border of the Principality of Transylvania, Gurghiu was an older medieval fortress strengthened with four modern bastions throughout the second half of the sixteenth and first half of the seventeenth century. The construction of the fourth and last bastion began in 1640. The walls of the fortress were six metres high (almost 20 feet). Inside the fortification there were 28 rooms, some used as living quarters and others for storage.[68] The royal fortification was provided with a modest estate consisting of two market towns and 16 villages in 1652. This estate gradually diminished and in 1672, during the reign of Michael Apafi I, only nine villages were left to supply the fortification and its garrison.[69]

According to an inventory drafted in 1651 Gurghiu was rather well supplied with gunpowder weapons, there being six cannons (35-pdrs, 12-pdrs and 8-pdrs), nine mortars, two bombards, 125 harquebuses and 64 muskets. The garrison consisted of 64 free men who lived in the villages of the estate. They worked the land and tended to their households like the other peasants, but they also performed guard service in the fortress, once every three weeks. When the fortress was threatened, they were all mobilised.[70] The fortress provided shelter for the local community but occasionally it was also a place of refuge for the prince. In 1660, for example, Ákos Barcsay retreated to Gurghiu with a guard of 106 soldiers while his reign was threatened by John Kemény. The fortress provided only temporary shelter because Prince

---

65 Kovács, *Cetatea din Gherla*, pp.49–64.
66 MNL OL, Gyulafehérvári Káptalan Levéltára, Lymbus, XXVII/1.
67 Gabriel-Virgil Rusu, 'O mărturie documentară despre Cetatea Gherla la 1675', *Studia Universitatis Babes-Bolyai – Historia*, 1–2 (2003), pp.65–94.
68 Liviu Ursuțiu, Domeniul Gurghiu (1652–1706): Urbarii, inventare și socoteli economice (Cluj-Napoca: Argonaut, 2006), pp.5–6.
69 Béla Szádeczky, *I Apafi Mihály fejedelem udvartartása. Bornemisza Anna gazdasági naplói*, (Budapest: Magyar Tudományos Akadémia könyvkiadóhivatala, 1911), pp.276–277.
70 Ursuțiu, *Domeniul Gurghiu*, pp.6–7.

Barcsay was eventually captured and killed by his rival.[71] After the Habsburgs strengthened their position in Transylvania, they decided to destroy the fortress of Gurghiu in 1708.[72]

Fortified Saxon Towns

Some of the most important urban centres of Transylvania were situated in the seats and districts of the Saxons. These prosperous communities received royal privileges to defend their settlements with stone walls during the fourteenth and fifteenth century and continued to improve their defences in the following years.[73] By the seventeenth century, the most important towns of the Saxons like Sibiu, Brașov, Sighișoara, Mediaș, Bistrița and Sebeș were well defended by stone walls, towers and, in some cases, modern bastions.

The most important town of the Transylvanian Saxons, Sibiu was also one of the strongest fortifications in the southern part of the country. Three modern bastions were already added to the medieval enceinte during the second half of the sixteenth century, while the fourth and fifth bastions were built in the first decades of the seventeenth century.[74] Like all other major urban settlements in Transylvania, Sibiu employed a small group of town guards (*trabanten*) who were usually tasked with the defence of the town gates. In the sixteenth century their number was usually between 16 and 18 men but was increased later to 20 to 22 men. Account registers testify to the fact that these *trabanten* received regular wages at the same level as soldiers from the field army.[75] The other Saxon towns had similar permanent garrisons (20 to 30 town guards)[76] which were supplemented in case of necessity by hiring additional mercenaries or by obtaining troops from the army of the prince.

In an age when territorial boundaries were vague and fluid, fortifications played a crucial role in securing political and practical control over the land. The distinct types of fortifications in Transylvania were essential in ensuring the survival of the principality as an autonomous state for one and a half centuries. The new principles of military architecture had reached Transylvania without any delay and by the end of the sixteenth century several fortifications were built according to modern principals, and older, medieval fortresses were re-enforced with bastions and other innovative elements of defence. The modernisation of the defensive systems continued in the seventeenth century, especially under Gabriel Bethlen (1613–1629) and George Rákózi I (1631–1648). Construction and maintenance were ensured through the use of local resources. Food provisions were essential

---

71   Kraus, Cronica Transilvaniei, p.385.
72   Ursuțiu, *Domeniul Gurghiu*, p.6.
73   Radu Lupescu, 'The medieval fortifications of Sibiu', Olaf Wagener (ed.), „*vmbringt mit starcken turnen, murn*". Ortsbefestigungen im Mittelalter (Frankfurt am Main: Peter Lang, 2010), pp.351–362.
74   Kovács, *Cetatea din Gherla*, pp.99–106.
75   Julia Derzsi, *Delict și pedeapsă: Justiție penală în orașele săsești din Transilvania în secolul al XVI-lea* (Cluj-Napoca: Egyetemi Műhely, 2022), pp.195–201.
76   Izsán, 'Between Soldier and Guard', pp.194–197.

for the welfare and efficiency of fortresses. As mentioned previously each major fortification was surrounded by an estate, consisting of rural and urban settlements, which provided financial revenue and food supplies for the military and administrative personnel of the fortress, who were usually entitled to regular food rations (*praebenda*). The most common provisions found in fortress inventories were cereals (grain, oats, and millet), bacon, lard, cheese, wine, vinegar and occasionally smaller quantities of vegetables and dried fruits.[77] At the same time, major fortifications with an important strategic position benefited from resources gathered from the whole country in the form of special taxes or the mobilisation of the workforce from neighbouring counties.

In the sixteenth century, the defence of fortifications was entrusted to small permanent garrisons and larger groups of semi-privileged soldiers who lived in nearby villages and towns. In the following century, the size of permanent garrisons was increased, reaching up to 100 soldiers or even more, while the semi-privileged soldiers such as guardsmen and 'riflemen' were maintained mostly on estates from the hinterland and were considered to be members of the princely banner.

Another interesting development is the significant increase of firepower, especially in the first half of the seventeenth century, provided by various arsenals and substantial amounts of gunpowder. Cannons were produced in local foundries in Transylvania and Upper Hungary and were mostly small and medium pieces. Heavy cannon were captured during the Thirty Years' War and brought to Transylvania by the armies of Gabriel Bethlen, as can be seen by the mention of six Buquoy cannons in the inventory of Oradea fortress drafted in 1632.

---

77 Livia Magina, 'Rezerve de alimente în cetățile Principatului Transilvaniei', Zeno Karl Pinter, Anca Nițoi, Claudia Urduzia (eds.), *Relații interetnice în Transilvania: Militaria Medievalia în Europa Centrală și de Sud-Vest* (Sibiu: Astra Museum, 2018), pp.179–186.

4

Military Campaigns, Battles and Sieges

The First Campaign of Gabriel Bethlen in the Thirty Years' War, September 1619–December 1621

The expedition began on the first day of September 1619 when the Transylvanian army of about 18,000 soldiers set out from its main camp situated in the vicinity of Cluj.[1] Before attacking the Habsburgs in Hungary, Bethlen made sure that most of the nobility and the local population were on his side and saw him as a liberator.

The *hajdú* were eager to fight against the Habsburgs and captured several fortifications even before the Transylvanian army crossed the border. George Rákóczi, a leading figure among the Protestant Hungarian nobles, also joined the Transylvanian faction and besieged the fortified city of Košice, residence of the captain general in Upper Hungary. The inhabitants, mostly Protestants, rebelled against the Habsburg garrison, seized the artillery and opened the gates during the second day of the siege. Thus, in just a few days, Bethlen and his partisans held control over a significant part of Eastern Hungary. Over the next month Bethlen divided his troops into two armies and marched towards Bratislava (Pozsony) without encountering major opposition. The main army, under his personal command, advanced on a northern route, from Košice to Trnava. The second army was entrusted to Francis Rhédey and followed a southern road along the Ottoman frontier, capturing some of the most important fortifications on its way, such as Fiľakovo (Fülek) and Nové Zámky.[2]

---

1 *Chronicon Fuchsio-Lupino-Oltardinum sive annales Hungarici et Transsilvanici*, vol. I, (ed.) Josephus Trausch, (Coronae: Impressum per Johanne Gött, 1847), p.294.
2 János B. Szabó, 'Bethlen Gábor, az újjászervező. A kora újkori hadügyi fejlődés Kelet-Közép-Európában: az Erdélyi Fejedelemség példája a XVII. század első felében (2.rész)', *Hadtörténelmi Közlemények*, 127/1 (2014), pp.54–55; János B. Szabó, 'Gábor Bethlen's Armies in the Thirty

THE ARMY OF TRANSYLVANIA 1613-1690

Gabriel Bethlen in front of Bratislava, 1619, by Matthäus Merian and Aegidius Sadeler II. (Public domain)

After the Ottoman conquest of Buda in 1541, Bratislava became the centre of political authority in Habsburg Hungary. The palatine (the most important office given to Hungarian nobles under Habsburg rule) resided in this city and the Diet gathered there most of the times. In 1619 the position of palatine was held by Sigismund Forgách, who refused to admit the troops of general Tieffenbach (12,000 men and three canons) inside the city. The army of Bethlen defeated the Habsburgs outside the walls of the city and the Transylvanian prince entered triumphantly on 14 October.[3]

In the following weeks Bethlen joined forces with the Bohemian rebels and threatened the seat of the Habsburgs, Vienna. Some of his troops, under the command of Francis Rhédey, joined the Bohemian army of Matthias von Thurn and approached Vienna from the north. Meanwhile the soldiers of Henri Duval Dampierre and Charles Bonaventure de Longueval, Count of Bucquoy, prepared to face the attackers. The Habsburg army, estimated at about 20,000 men, engaged the Bohemian-Transylvanian vanguard at Ulrichskirchen from 24–26 October.[4] Bethlen himself arrived with reinforcements during the third day of battle but the Habsburg commanders decided to retreat closer to Vienna. With the arrival of the Transylvanian reinforcements the anti-Habsburg coalition now held numerical superiority with about 32,000 soldiers but were unable to deal a decisive blow. Many Hungarian nobles refused to fight beyond the borders of the kingdom and the arrival of a cold winter would have made a siege exceedingly difficult.

Meanwhile, back in Eastern Hungary, George Drugeth of Hommona, Bethlen's old rival, arrived with an army of 7,000–8,000 Cossacks and Polish soldiers. Having superior numbers, he was able to defeat George Rákóczi and threatened to attack Transylvania. Without the promised financial support from the Habsburgs, the army of Drugeth scattered and returned home, but by the time things had settled in the east the opportunity to mount an attack on Vienna had passed.[5]

Negotiations for an armistice with the Habsburgs began on 16 January 1620 and Bethlen was recognised as ruler (prince) of Hungary. In the meantime, he decided to renew his alliance with Frederic V of Bohemia and prepared to continue the war in spring. The prince spent the winter in Košice and some of his troops were quartered in the surrounding area. In

---

Years' War', Gábor Kármán (ed.), *The Princes of Transylvania in the Thirty Years' War* (Paderborn: Brill Schöningh, 2022), pp.59–61.

3 Peter, 'The Golden Age of the Principality, pp.70–71
4 Ödön Olchváry, 'Bethlen Gábor első támadása II. Ferdinánd', *Hadtörténelmi Közlemények*, III (1890), pp.347–348.
5 Ștefania Gáll Mihăilescu (ed.), *Memorialul lui Nagy Szabó Ferencz din Târgu Mureș (1580–1658)* (București: Kriterion, 1993), pp.169–170.

March he sent a group of delegates to the Ottoman sultan to report on the situation in Hungary, including the state of his army at the time. The troops in camp at that moment were 8,000 cavalry, mostly lancers (*kopjásunk*) and 6,000 infantry. All had their wages paid for the following month. The county banners had spent winter at home but were ready to join the rest of the army. The Transylvanian army was only partially mobilised. Among them were 3,000 *hajdú* from the western borderlands and 600 Székely cavalry.

The conscription rate was established at one horseman and five infantry for every six *porta* (fiscal unit), but unfortunately the prince gives no estimation of the total size of these conscripted detachments. The Saxons sent 500 infantry and a considerable financial contribution of 12,000 florins. The lesser nobility was not expected to take part in the campaign but instead had to pay a redemption tax, which was used for the wages of mercenary units. The free cities also paid a special war tax, and the resulting money was enough to pay the wages of 500 infantry. The banners of the Transylvanian counties were estimated at 1,700 cavalry and 1,500 infantry. The Hungarian counties were expected to bring larger contingents of 9,700 cavalry and 7,700 infantry. In addition, some of the largest landowners in Hungary were expected to come with their own retinues of 500 soldiers each (200 cavalry and 300 infantry), including Széchy, Szaniszló Thurzó, Imre Thurzó and George Rákóczy. Other high-ranking nobles were expected to bring their own retinues and thus Gabriel Bethlen counted on an army of 41,000 soldiers even without fully mobilising his Transylvanian troops.[6]

The Army of Gabriel Bethlen in March 1620 (23,600 cavalry and 17,400 infantry)

Cavalry	Provider	Infantry	Provider
8,000	Mercenary (mixed origins)	6,000	Mercenary (mixed origins)
3,000	*Hajdú* (Transylvania)	500	Saxons (Transylvania)
600	Székely (Transylvania)	500	Free cities (Hungary)
1,700	Counties (Transylvania)	1,500	Counties (Transylvania)
9,700	Counties (Hungary)	7,700	Counties (Hungary)
200	Széchy (Hungary)	300	Széchy (Hungary)
200	Szaniszló Thurzó (Hungary)	300	Szaniszló Thurzó (Hungary)
200	Imre Thurzó (Hungary)	300	Imre Thurzó (Hungary)
200	George Rákóczy	300	George Rákóczy

Of course, we must keep in mind that this was a rough estimation and Bethlen had all the reasons to boast about his military strength to the Ottomans. The total number of soldiers is extremely high and reflects the military potential of the territories that were under Bethlen's rule at the time rather than the actual size of his active forces. Some interesting

---

6 Szilády, Szilágyi (eds.), *Török-Magyarkori*, vol. III, p.218.

conclusions can be drawn from this document. First of all, we can observe that the proportion of cavalry was higher than that of infantry (57.6 percent compared to 42.4 percent). Bethlen relied on a high number of mercenaries who received regular wages and were kept in quarters close to the war zone (14,000 soldiers). The number of troops from Transylvania was rather limited (4,300 soldiers without counting the borderland *hajdú*), indicating that the prince still had to rely on the Diet to mobilise certain elements of the army.

Hostilities resumed at the end of April and Stanislaw Thurzó, captain general of the Hungarian army, was sent to reinforce the Bohemian rebels with 3,000 soldiers. A plea for military support was also sent to Sultan Osman II but he was not ready to begin another war with the Habsburgs at the time. On 27 June the Hungarian Diet gathered in Banská Bystrica and reaffirmed their support for the Transylvanian prince and his fight against the Catholic Habsburgs. Just before the end of the meeting, on 25 August, the representatives of the Hungarian estates elected Gabriel Bethlen as King of Hungary. It was a great achievement for a Transylvanian prince but not without precedent as Stephen Bocskai had also managed to hold both titles, Prince of Transylvania and King of Hungary, in 1604–1606.[7]

With an army of 11,000 soldiers Bethlen launched a renewed offensive against the remaining Habsburg garrisons in Hungary. Throughout September 1620 his troops conquered several important fortifications, further consolidating his authority in the region. However, the arrival of General Dampierre halted the advance of the Transylvanian-Hungarian army at the beginning of October. The Habsburgs made a bold move against the most important city in the area, Bratislava, which was defended by one of the most loyal supporters of the Transylvanian prince, George Rákóczi, with an army of 6,000 *hajdú* and 1,000 guardsmen (infantry). Shortly after the siege began, Dampierre lost his life on the battlefield and, soon after, his army retreated without achieving its goal.[8]

The Protestant faction suffered a significant blow on 8 November 1620 when the Bohemians lost the battle of White Mountain. A detachment of Transylvanian and Hungarian cavalry, estimated at about 1,500–2,000 men, was present on the battlefield but they were unable to change the outcome of the confrontation. According to some sources, Bethlen's cavalry did not perform well and fled the battlefield. Initially the number of Transylvanian troops was much higher, about 5,000–6,000 soldiers, but many of them had already left the camp of Matthias von Thurn because of unpaid wages and lack of provisions. The night before the battle, the Transylvanian camp was attacked by a detachment of Habsburg cavalry and suffered 200 casualties. In addition, the reinforcements commanded by the Transylvanian chancellor, Simon Péchy (3,000 cavalry), were unable to reach the battlefield in time.[9]

---

7 Harai, *Gabriel Bethlen*, pp.109–114.
8 Kraus, Cronica Transilvaniei, pp.48–50.
9 Szabó, 'Bethlen Gábor (2)', pp.57–59; Szabó, 'Gábor Bethlen's Armies', pp.65–68; Lajos Kropf, 'Bethlen Gábor lovassága a fehérhegyi csatában,1620', *Hadtörténelmi Közlemények*, XI (1910), pp.460–461.

MILITARY CAMPAIGNS, BATTLES AND SIEGES

In the south, Ottoman border troops conquered the fortress of Vác in November 1620. Prince Bethlen and Ottoman officials had discussed the matter of this fortress in previous months, but they were unable to reach an understanding.[10] This incident was a clear indication that the Ottomans were not willing to start another war with the Habsburgs and would rather expand their control along the frontier with Hungary. This incident had a significant impact on the relation between Bethlen and the Hungarian estates, with the former losing faith in the ability of the Transylvanian prince to defend their lands from Turkish aggression.[11]

During the winter of 1620–1621 Bethlen concentrated on negotiating a favourable peace treaty with the Habsburgs while strengthening the border fortifications. Most troops were kept in service and were billeted in various locations around Bratislava (Pozsony) and Nitra (Nyitra) counties. A register compiled at the order of the prince contains information about 12,610 soldiers (10,210 cavalry, 1,700 infantry, and 700 soldiers from the court guard of the prince) and their winter quarters, in 105 different settlements. Most of these soldiers were *hajdú* recruited in the counties of Bihor and Szabolcs.[12]

As hostilities resumed in the spring of 1621 many nobles, especially in the western parts of the kingdom, were reconsidering their political options and pledged allegiance to Ferdinand II. Officers and common soldiers mutinied against their former employer and joined the ranks of the Habsburg army. Francis Rhédey, the most experienced Transylvanian commander, was captured by enemy troops and died soon after. The Habsburg offensive began successfully with the capture of Bratislava and Nitra. In June 1621, they reached the fortified town of Nové Zámky defended by a garrison of 3,500 infantry and 200 cavalry, commanded by Stanislaw Thurzó. Bethlen, who had taken residence in Košice, sent 4,000–6,000 Transylvanian troops under the command of John Bornemisza to help his loyal Hungarian subjects.

The Habsburg army consisted of about 10,000 infantry, 4,000 cavalry, four heavy siege cannon and seven smaller artillery pieces. There were not enough troops for a complete blockade of the town and not enough artillery to breach the defensive walls. Thurzó was able to bring in new supplies even after the siege began and kept constant contact with the commanders of the relief force. The battle lasted several days and began with an unexpected attack performed by the Transylvanian cavalry. Bornemisza approached the Habsburg camp during the night and ordered the assault just before dawn when the enemies would least expect it. The arrival of a relief force and their constant harassment had a strong demoralising effect on the besiegers. On 10 July, General Bucquoy was killed in a skirmish and thus ended the siege of Nové Zámky. Without their leader and decimated by plague and famine, the remaining Habsburg troops retreated towards Bratislava.[13]

---

10 Gábor Kármán (ed.), *The Correspondance of the Beylerbeys of Buda 1617-1630* (Budapest-Szeged: Research Centre for the Humanities, Institute of History, 2022), pp.146–148.
11 Balázs Sudár, 'Ottoman Auxiliary Troops in Gábor Bethlen's Armies 1619–1626', Gábor Kármán (ed.), *The Princes of Transylvania in the Thirty Years' War* (Paderborn: Brill Schöningh, 2022), pp.138–140.
12 Seres, 'Bethlen Gábor hadainak', pp.1,050–1,066.
13 Kraus, *Cronica Transilvaniei*, pp.51–52; Szabó, 'Bethlen Gábor (2)', pp.60–61.

For the rest of the year Bethlen was on the offensive. Several smaller fortifications were captured but the new Habsburg garrison of Bratislava resisted the repeated assaults of the Transylvanian army. A long siege was extremely hard to maintain due to the lack of provisions and gunpowder, so Bethlen had to give up on retaking this major strategic point on the Danube. Nevertheless, when winter arrived, most of Hungary was once again in the hands of the Transylvanian prince. It was time, once again, for peace negotiations but this time Bethlen was in a much better position to make demands.[14]

After three long years of intermittent fighting Gabriel Bethlen and Ferdinand II of Habsburg signed a peace treaty at Mikulov (Nikolsburg) on the last day of December 1621. The conditions of the agreement were very favourable to Transylvania, but the prince had to give up his claim to the Hungarian throne. In exchange he was granted possession over seven counties in Eastern Hungary (Szabolcs, Szatmár, Ugocsa, Bereg, Zemplén, Borsod and Abaúj) with five important fortresses and towns (Košice, Mukacevo, Tokaj, Tarcal and Ecsed). The Habsburgs also promised an annual sum of 50,000 florins for maintaining the fortifications in the seven Hungarian counties. Bethlen became a prince of the Holly Roman Empire as owner of the Duchy of Oppeln and Ratibor.[15]

This military campaign had a particularly important political outcome but lacked any large-scale direct confrontations. The army of Bethlen included troops from Transylvania but also a considerable number of soldiers from Royal Hungary (*hajdú* from the western borderland but also Protestant nobles from Hungary and their retinues). Sieges were usually of short duration and most fortifications surrendered after a few days under artillery fire. Military success was achieved through wise logistic decisions rather than prowess on the battlefield. The presence of the Transylvanian army on the eastern flank of the Habsburgs was important from a strategic point of view as it prevented the concentration of troops against the other members of the Protestant faction.

The Second Campaign of Gabriel Bethlen in the Thirty Years' War, August 1623–May 1624

As the war between the Catholics and Protestants continued in Europe, Gabriel Bethlen was looking for a new opportunity to reclaim the crown of Hungary. He renewed his alliances with the members of the Protestant faction and convinced the Ottomans to send military aid against the Habsburgs.

The march of the Transylvanian army, 10,000 men strong, began on 15 August from a camp situated in the vicinity of Cluj. They travelled first to Oradea on the western frontier and then to Košice, where they arrived almost one month later on 13 September. In the meantime, Ottoman troops

---

14   Harai, *Gabriel Bethlen*, pp.109–136.
15   Volkmer, *Siebenbürgen*, pp.344–346; Harai, *Gabriel Bethlen*, pp.137–139.

MILITARY CAMPAIGNS, BATTLES AND SIEGES

advanced towards the same destination, commanded by the Pasha of Bosnia. Another important objective for Bethlen was to join his Protestant allies, Ernst von Mansfeld and the Margrave of Jägendorf.

Although the support of the Hungarian estates was limited, Bethlen advanced easily towards the western parts of the kingdom of Hungary. Smaller fortresses were occupied without major losses and many local garrisons decided to pledge their loyalty to the conqueror. When they reached the walls of the city of Trnava, an army of about 10,000 Ottoman soldiers joined their ranks.[16] It is estimated that by the end of October, Bethlen had a large but heterogeneous army of about 30,000 soldiers including Transylvanians, Ottomans, Germans, Hungarians, Wallachians and Moldavians. The Habsburgs, on the other hand, had a much smaller force, of about 10,000 soldiers, under the command of General Hyeronimus Carafa de Monte-Negro. Albrecht von Wallenstein, who later became one of the most famous general in the Thirty Years' War, was an infantry captain in his army. With smaller numbers but superior firepower, Monte-Negro built a fortified camp in the vicinity at Hodonín. Bethlen realised that a general assault would have been very costly and decided to encircle the enemy and starve them out. He relied on his light cavalry to disrupt any attempts of the enemy to find provisions outside their camp.[17]

A thorough description of the military operations at Hodonín is provided by John Kemény, future Prince of Transylvania, in his memoires. At the time Kemény was a young page (16 years old) in the entourage of Prince Bethlen. This was his first experience of war, and the young nobleman was not lacking in courage. From the beginning of the campaign, he joined a group of Serbian, Croat and Polish mercenaries who were in the service of the Transylvanian prince and followed them on plundering forays and skirmishes with the enemy troops as they were approaching the river Morava. By the time the Transylvanian army arrived, General Monte-Negro had built a well-fortified camp, outside the walls of Hodonín. On the exposed side of the camp, his soldiers dug a deep ditch and built a tall wood and earth rampart. The Habsburg soldiers were mostly on foot. They had four times more infantry than the Transylvanians, but almost no cavalry.

During the first phase of the siege Bethlen was content to keep the enemy under heavy artillery fire and used his light cavalry to capture or kill any enemy who dared venture outside the fortified camp. One day, while the prince was inspecting the enemy fortification his horse was killed by artillery shot. Unscathed by the unfortunate event, Bethlen continued his inspection showing courage and determination in front of his own officers. During the first weeks of the siege, the Habsburgs assaulted the besiegers during the night several times. However, these skirmishes were of little consequence because they had only a few detachments of heavy cavalry (cuirassiers) and were unable to break the blockade. On the other hand, Bethlen had an extremely tough time convincing his officers to organise an assault against the well-defended rampart. The deep ditch was a serious obstacle and the

---

16 Sudár, 'Ottoman Auxiliary Troops', pp.146–147.
17 Szabó, 'Bethlen Gábor (2)', pp.63–65; Szabó, 'Gábor Bethlen's Armies', pp.72–76.

besiegers tried to cross it with improvised wooden bridges but suffered heavy casualties as they were very exposed to enemy fire.[18]

The siege lasted only a few weeks, until the Hungarian Palatine Stanislaw Thurzó, former ally and captain general of Gabriel Bethlen, convinced the Transylvanians to conclude a temporary ceasefire and thus saved the imperial army from starvation. Bethlen had his own reasons for choosing diplomacy over war. The weather was very cold and life in camp was miserable for both besieged and besiegers. The Ottomans were not accustomed to winter campaigns and wanted to return home with the considerable plunder they had been able to gather so far. Under these circumstances the Transylvanian prince agreed to a 10-month armistice. A new peace treaty was signed on 8 May 1624 in Vienna before the armistice expired. The agreement was similar with the one established at Mikulov two years before. This time Bethlen gave up his control of the Duchy of Opplen and Ratibor, which generated revenues of 300,000 florins per year, in exchange for more territories in Hungary.[19]

The Third Campaign of Gabriel Bethlen in the Thirty Years' War, 1626

Transylvanian diplomats contacted Dutch, English, French and Venetian ambassadors in Istanbul to prepare a new offensive against the Habsburgs. Bethlen was acknowledged as the most important member of the Protestant faction on the eastern flank of the Catholic League and his military intervention was considered vital for a successful outcome for the campaign.

This time Bethlen was able to muster a force of 20,000 men, most of them *hajdú* from the borderlands of Transylvania and Hungary. Their march followed the same route as in 1623 but the local population was no longer enthusiastic about the defender of the Protestant faith and his army. The Count (*ispán*) of Trencsén and Liptó, Gaspar Illésházy, was the only notable supporter of Bethlen in Hungary during this campaign and he was entrusted with the recruitment of local mercenaries (400 infantry and 200 cavalry) for the Transylvanian army. Illésházy helped the Protestant army of Mansfeld and John-Ernest of Saxe-Weimar once they crossed the border into Hungary at the beginning of September. Their troops made incursions into the lands of towns and nobles who were loyal to Ferdinand II but avoided any major confrontations. Wallenstein himself crossed the border into Hungary and attacked the Ottoman army that was besieging the fortress of Nógrád. Bethlen wanted to join forces with Mansfeld and Saxe-Weimar, but the two generals decided to retreat towards the Bohemian border because they did not want to risk an encounter with Wallenstein. On 30 September, the Transylvanians arrived at Dregélypalánk where they met their Ottoman allies, the troops of the newly appointed Beylerbey of Buda, Mürteza Pasha.[20]

---

18   Ioan Kemény, *Memorii (1607–1662)*, (Cluj-Napoca: Casa Cărții de Știință, 2002), pp.55–59.
19   Harai, *Gabriel Bethlen*, pp.148–154.
20   Kármán (ed.), *The Correspondance*, pp.314–317.

This time the Ottoman aid was substantial (17,000–20,000 men) as the sultan gave the order for all the soldiers from the Hungarian borders to join his Transylvanian vassal.[21] Both factions wanted to avoid a direct confrontation and Bethlen continued his march towards Széchény where he finally reached Mansfeld and his troops. They continued to advance towards Bars while the Transylvanian cavalry harassed Wallenstein's army which was also marching in the same direction.[22]

Once again, a detailed description of the campaign was made by John Kemény in his memoires. He was 19 years old and served as standard bearer of the Transylvanian prince. Due to the scarcity of provisions the Transylvanian army marched divided, and many captains plundered the countryside without the consent of the prince. Their abusive behaviour damaged the reputation on Bethlen in Hungary and greatly diminished his chances of reclaiming the crown. Wallenstein was a redoubtable enemy, and Bethlen did not want to face him before joining forces with his allies.

Although the two armies were close and smaller skirmishes were unavoidable, a decisive confrontation was postponed. Eventually the Transylvanian army and the 8,000 soldiers of Mansfeld and Saxa-Weimar met at Széchény. The newly arrived troops were well armed and disciplined but they were tired from the long march and had been obliged to leave their artillery behind. After a few days of rest, the Protestants moved towards the Habsburg army which was prepared for battle. This time it was Wallenstein who refused to engage the enemy and retreated westwards. He decided to occupy an easily defendable position in the vicinity of Hlohovec and divided his troops into three different camps. As soon as they arrived, the Transylvanians organised smaller detachments of cavalry (several hundred each) and began harassing the enemy camps. Kemény himself joined such a detachment and attacked a village where several Habsburg officers had taken up quarters. Most of the common soldiers were killed while the officers were taken prisoner. Among them was Heinrich von Schlick, artillery general and commander of the imperial lifeguard. Kemény recognised him as a high-ranking official and insisted that he should be spared and ransomed. He was eventually released and continued his successful career in the Habsburg army reaching the position of Field Marshal and President of the War Council (*Hofkriegsrat*).[23]

Over the following weeks the two armies maintained their positions and engaged in small skirmishes. The Habsburg army suffered an outbreak of plague and by the beginning of November Wallenstein had lost more soldiers to the disease than fighting with the enemy. Hunger and cold weather made life miserable for both factions and the prospect of negotiations was becoming increasingly appealing. At a certain point, the Ottomans were ready to depart for their winter quarters, but Bethlen ordered his Transylvanian soldiers to surround their camp and threatened to kill all who would dare leave the battlefield. In the end the Turkish commander decided to remain and ordered

---

21 Sudár, 'Ottoman Auxiliary Troops', pp.149–150.
22 Szabó, 'Bethlen Gábor (2)', pp.65–67.
23 Kemény, *Memorii*, pp.80–85.

Gerard Mercator's map of Transylvania, from the edition published in 1641 (National Library, Warsaw)

the execution of some of the officers who instigated the rebellion.[24]

On 12 November Wallenstein and Bethlen signed a ceasefire as both armies were exhausted from their long marches and the lack of provisions. In the meantime, Transylvanian diplomats were sent to various European courts and ensured the inclusion of Gabriel Bethlen in the Treaty of the Hague. On 20 December 1626, a new peace treaty was signed between the Transylvanians and the Habsburgs at Bratislava confirming the provisions of the previous agreements signed at Mikulov (1623) and Vienna (1624).[25]

The political and military achievements of Gabriel Bethlen in his conflict with the Habsburgs are remarkable considering the significant difference in size and resources between the two states. At the time of this confrontation, Ferdinand II relied on an annual income of about four to five million Rhenish florins while the Prince of Transylvania had only a little over one million Rhenish florins per annum. In addition, the Habsburgs were able to gather considerable sums of money through credit and subsidies from their allies in the Holy Roman Empire and Spain.[26]

Bethlen was able to mobilise an army of 10,000–30,000 men in Transylvania, without counting the troops sent by the Ottomans, Wallachia, Moldavia or the soldiers recruited in Hungary. The costs of maintaining this army were extremely high, reaching 300,000–400,000 florins per year, during the campaigns against the Habsburgs.[27] He avoided decisive battles, and his military actions were meant to support his diplomatic endeavours. He was an adept of guerrilla warfare focused on securing logistical advantages over his enemy in order to gain the upper hand in negotiations.

The success of the prince was partially determined by his ability to gain the support of the Hungarian estates and the local population, especially the Protestants. However, this support was quite strong during the first campaign but then gradually declined or turned to outright hostility.[28] Bethlen used his army as an efficient political instrument and the aim of his war was to obtain a favourable peace, which he did quite successfully.

24　Kemény, *Memorii*, pp.86–87.
25　Harai, *Gabriel Bethlen*, pp.167–171.
26　István Kenyeres, 'The Fiscal Capacity and War Expenses of Transylvania and the Habsburg Monarchy during the Rules of Gábor Bethlen and Ferdinand II: A Comparison', Gábor Kármán (ed.), *The Princes of Transylvania in the Thirty Years' War* (Paderborn: Brill Schöningh, 2022), p.129.
27　Harai, *Gabriel Bethlen*, pp.201–202.
28　Pálffy, 'The Kingdom of Hungary' pp.16–19.

The Campaign of Prince George Rákóczi I in the Thirty Years' War, 1644–1645

Following in the footsteps of his predecessor, George Rákóczi I declared war on the Habsburgs because he wanted to defend the Protestants of Hungary and the privileges of the Hungarian estates. Of course, his reasons were much more complex and, like Bethlen before him, he wanted to expand his control over territories in Eastern Hungary and to consolidate his diplomatic relations with other European states.

The war plans of Rákóczi depended greatly on an alliance with France and especially one with Sweden, the most important enemies of the Habsburgs in this phase of the Thirty Years' War. In 1642 Lennart Torstensson led a successful campaign in Moravia and occupied the town of Olomouc, a particularly important strategic point situated in the vicinity of the Hungarian border. Thus, Transylvania's most important ally was in a favourable position to provide aid and to coordinate their military actions against the Habsburgs. After long negotiations, a treaty between France, Sweden and Transylvania was signed on 16 November 1643 and one of the provisions referred to an exchange of troops between the allied armies whereby 3,000 Swedish infantry were supposed to serve in the Transylvanian army while Rákóczi promised to send 3,000 cavalry to join the army of Torstensson.[29]

Preparations for war were intensified in Transylvania and especially within the personal domains of George Rákóczi in Hungary. Even before his election as prince, Rákóczi was one of the wealthiest and most influential nobles from the eastern parts of the Hungarian kingdom. He had strong garrisons in the fortresses of Mukacevo, Ónod, Sárospatak and Szerencs, and the support of other Protestant nobles from the area who were able to muster up to 2,000 men. Given the various resources available it can be estimated that his army was about 15,000 men strong. Two-thirds were light cavalry while the rest of the army consisted of light infantry troops recruited among the Székely seats and the *hajdú* communities of the borderlands. His best infantry detachments were the 'blue guardsmen' from the court army and the 1,000 German musketeers which were settled in Transylvania by his predecessor, Gabriel Bethlen.[30] In addition, Rákóczi received 6,000 soldiers from his ally in Wallachia and about 1,000 Moldavian horsemen.[31] The Ottoman sultan had also given his consent for this campaign, but his effective support was limited to 1,000–1,500 soldiers.[32] While his army matched the standards of the age in terms of size, Rákóczi faced great difficulties in providing wages and provisions for his troops, hence the reason why he always demanded financial support from his allies.

---

29 Czigány, 'The 1644–1645 Campaign', pp.90–91.
30 Czigány, 'The 1644–1645 Campaign', p.94.
31 Constantin Rezachevici, 'Efectivele oştilor din Ţara Românească şi Moldova în veacul al XVII-lea' *Studii şi Materiale de Muzeografie şi Istorie Militară*, nr. 6, (1973), p.104.
32 Mahmut Halef Cervioğlu, 'Ottoman Foreign Policy during the Thirty Years' War', *Turcica*, 49 (2018), pp.220–221.

The campaign began in February 1644. Rákóczi divided his army and attacked the enemy from three directions. He led the largest contingent through the county of Bihor on a southern route. A second army was entrusted to his son, Sigismund, who was ordered to cross the frontier of Transylvania into Hungary from the northwest. John Kemény commanded the third army which was tasked with subduing the towns and counties beyond the northern sector of the border.

The troops entrusted to Kemény were mobilised from the Transylvanian hinterland and included the Székely detachments of Ciuc and Odorhei, together with the banners of three counties, namely Dăbâca, Turda and Inner Solnoc. Their total number was estimated at 8,000 men. Initially these troops were gathered in a camp, close to the town of Dej, and marched northwards as soon as all the soldiers were gathered together. After they crossed the border into Satu Mare county, controlled by the Habsburgs at the time, they occupied some minor fortifications and the important mining town of Baia Mare, without encountering significant opposition. The situation changed drastically when they reached the fortress of Satu Mare.

Satu Mare was an Italian style of fortification on the lower course of the Someș River, built during the second half of the sixteenth century. It was the most important stronghold of the Habsburgs situated beyond the Tisa River and was defended by a sizeable garrison and well supplied with munitions and artillery. The townsmen of Mintiu welcomed the Transylvanian troops and provided them with provisions and helped establish the best locations for setting up artillery platforms. A few days after the siege began, Kemény's soldiers crossed the frozen waters of the river and occupied the other settlement (Satu Mare) thus surrounding the fortress. Nevertheless, the defenders were determined to resist despite the fact that they were significantly outnumbered.

The garrison was composed of two distinct groups, that is, German mercenaries and local Hungarians. The number of German mercenaries was estimated at about 400 men while the number of local troops remains unknown, but their numbers were probably the same or slightly higher. Throughout the siege they organised several sorties, but they suffered significant loses. On the other side of the walls, Kemény did not want to risk a direct assault although numbers were in his favour, and his artillery was insufficient to create a breach in the thick wall of the fortifications. His only option was a long blockade, but he was running out of time. After three weeks of siege the food stocks of the defenders dwindled, and dissention began to break out between the German and Hungarian soldiers of the garrison. The Transylvanians became aware of this internal conflict after capturing a messenger who was tasked with bringing urgent help from neighbouring Habsburg garrisons. Kemény was ready to exploit this internal conflict by sending propaganda messages into the fortress, but he received urgent orders from the prince who needed him and his troops in Košice. Thus, the siege was lifted after almost one month and a small garrison of less than 1,000 men had been able to resist an army at least eight times larger.[33]

The other Transylvanian commanders were more successful, and the main contingent was able to subdue the fortress of Kálló, which surrendered without resistance. On 12 March, the Transylvanian army conquered Košice, the most important military and financial centre in Upper Hungary. The Ottomans had given their consent for this campaign and approved only the conquest of the seven counties from Eastern Hungary, which had belonged to Transylvania in the time of Gabriel Bethlen. However, Rákóczi ordered his troops to advance beyond the limits set by the sultan and occupied fortifications in other neighbouring Hungarian counties.[34]

Although the Swedish army of Torstensson of about 15,000 men was diverted from Moravia for an offensive in Denmark,[35] Rákóczi decided to continue his campaign in Hungary. The Aulic War Council in Vienna had taken some preventive measures, such as sending additional troops, mustering the loyal nobility and paying the outstanding wages of the garrisons, but this was not enough the stop the advance of the Transylvanian army.

Rákóczi maintained his initial approach and kept his troops divided into three columns, for strategic and especially logistic reasons. It was much easier to gather provisions for smaller armies and his main objective at this point was to gain control over as many fortifications as possible. The largest detachment of about 6,000 men, commanded by György Kapronczay, advanced westwards along the valley of the Váh river. A second, smaller group, of 2,000 soldiers under Pál Bornemisza targeted the urban settlements situated in the mining area of the Hron valley, while the third Transylvanian army was entrusted to Rákóczi's son, Sigismund, and was ordered to besiege the fortress of Fiľakovo.[36]

Transylvanian envoys in Istanbul made constant efforts to convince the sultan and other Ottoman dignitaries to approve of the further expansion of Rákóczi's rule in Hungary and to provide military support against the Habsburgs. While military assistance was not officially denied, the Ottoman help was not significant either and consisted of less than 3,000 soldiers from the borders. On the other hand, Habsburg diplomats tried to convince the Ottomans to withdraw their support for the Transylvanians for the sake of maintaining the peace between the two empires.[37]

In the meantime, the Habsburgs decided to take a more decisive approach to the Transylvanian threat and sent an army of 4,849 cavalry, 330 dragoons and 4,713 infantry under the command of Johann Götz, to confront the enemy troops that were advancing along the Váh river. The Transylvanians were attacked at Hlohovec by imperial cavalry and lost 300 soldiers, including their commander, Kapronczay. The remaining troops

---

33   Kemény, *Memorii*, pp.196–200.
34   Czigány, 'The 1644–1645 Campaign', pp.96–97.
35   Paul Douglas Lockhart, *Denmark, 1513–1660: the rise and decline of a Renaissance monarchy* (Oxford: Oxford University Press, 2007), pp.205–206.
36   Czigány, 'The 1644–1645 Campaign', pp.97–98.
37   Czigány, 'The 1644–1645 Campaign', pp.98–99.

retreated towards Fiľakovo where they joined the detachment commanded by Sigismund Rákóczi. Pál Bornemisza made a similar move and thus the Transylvanian army in Hungary was reunited but unable to face the superior enemy. Rákóczi's men had been on campaign for more than two months and suffered many casualties, mostly due to famine and sickness.

The local population was quite hostile to the Transylvanian army and finding provisions became extremely hard. Under these circumstances, the prince decided on a retreat to Upper Hungary where he enjoyed the support of the nobility and of the Protestant population. Here he strengthened the garrisons of the most important fortifications (Prešov: 500 soldiers, Košice: 2,000 soldiers, Sárospatak: 1,100 men and Tokaj: 700 men) and moved the rest of his army closer to Transylvania. The Habsburg army, commanded by Johann Götz and Miklós Esterházy, advanced without encountering serious opposition until they reached the town of Košice in early June. In the meantime, the size of the defending garrison was increased to 3,000, without including the detachments of light cavalry camped outside the walls and ready to harass the besieging army. The Habsburg army lacked heavy artillery and storming the walls of Košice was likely to be a very risky and costly endeavour. Pressured by the constant harassment of the locals who organised themselves in small armed bands, the Habsburgs were having a very hard time gathering the necessary provisions. Once again, the offensive was abandoned due to logistical failings and the Habsburg army retreated towards Western Hungary.[38]

Peace negotiations had already begun in May although the two armies continued to fight. The Habsburgs needed to move soldiers to other fronts while Rákóczi was having trouble paying the wages of his soldiers. On top of that, the main camp of the Transylvanian army was devastated by an outbreak of plague. Both factions dispatched smaller detachments and engaged in raids and skirmishes until August, when Johann Götz was able to muster soldiers and resources for another major offensive. The Habsburg army followed the same route and recaptured some fortifications which had previously surrendered to the Transylvanians. Previously Rákóczi had moved his main army east of the Tisza River, closer to the Transylvanian border. When a *hajdú* vanguard of 2,000–3,000 men crossed the river, they were attacked by a strong detachment of German infantry and Hungarian cavalry. Rákóczi's men were taken by surprise and lost the battle. The Habsburgs took a few hundred prisoners, 2,000 horses, 1,500 cattle and 200 wagons. In spite of this early success and although he must have been aware of his enemy's weakness, Götz retreated once again without dealing a decisive blow. The rest of the year continued without significant changes and while the Prince of Transylvania was satisfied with having secured control over the seven counties in Upper Hungary the Habsburgs were also content to maintain their rule over the central and western parts of the Hungarian Kingdom.[39]

The year 1645 began well for the Protestant cause. After a successful campaign against Denmark, the Swedish army was finally able to move

---

38 Czigány, 'The 1644–1645 Campaign', pp.99–103.
39 Czigány, 'The 1644–1645 Campaign', pp.103–106.

MILITARY CAMPAIGNS, BATTLES AND SIEGES

towards Vienna. On 6 March they won a decisive battle against a Bavarian and Habsburg army at Jankov (Jankau). Johann Götz, commander of the imperial army, was amongst the casualties. Torstensson continued his successful offensive and conquered a significant part of Lower Austria, threatening the imperial capital Vienna.[40]

Swedish and Transylvanian armies during the unsuccessful siege of Brno (Brünn), May-August 1645. Painting by Hieronymus Benno Bayer and Hans Jörg Zeiser (Muzeum města Brna – Špilberk)

George Rákóczi was eager to resume hostilities because the situation was much more favourable for him this time. He mustered 6,000 cavalry and 1,200 infantry which were sent as a vanguard to join the Swedish army. They first contacted the troops commanded by General Robert Douglas under the walls of Trnava. The Transylvanian vanguard did not significantly alter the balance of war as most of the soldiers were reluctant to fight beyond the borders of Hungary. When Prince Rákóczi approached Moravia with another 12,000 troops he received clear orders from the Grand Vizier which prohibited him from continuing the war against the Habsburgs.[41] In spite of this serious threat, Rákóczi decided to hold his positions in Hungary and sent most of his troops to help the Swedish army that was besieging Brno. Although Torstensson made two attempts to storm the walls of the town,

---

40 Geoffrey Parker, *The Thirty Years' War* (London: Routledge, 2006), p.153.
41 Cervioğlu, 'Ottoman Foreign Policy', p.224.

THE ARMY OF TRANSYLVANIA 1613-1690

the Habsburg garrison resisted them both successfully. On 15 August, the Transylvanian army retreated because of the sultan's order and because they had reached a favourable agreement with the Habsburgs. The peace treaty was finally signed at Linz on 16 December 1645 and its provisions were very similar to the previous treaties between Bethlen and the Habsburgs. Rákóczi still ruled over the seven counties in Eastern Hungary and received some fortresses and estates as personal property from Ferdinand III. Later, when the Peace Treaty of Westphalia was concluded, the contribution to the war by Transylvania was acknowledged by all the signatories of the treaty.[42]

Transylvanian officers in 1645. From the painting of siege of Brünn (Brno), by Hieronymus Benno Bayer and Hans Jörg Zeiser (Muzeum města Brna – Špilberk)

Compared to Bethlen's campaigns against the Habsburgs, Rákóczi's expedition was less impressive in terms of achievements, but he faced far less favourable conditions. First and foremost, he had almost no support from the Hungarian estates beyond the seven eastern counties. His troops travelled through hostile territory and faced serious logistical problems. As a consequence, he also had problems in raising the money to finance the war. From a strategic point of view Rákóczi was even more cautious than his predecessor and avoided almost all major hostilities with the enemy. The focus of the campaign was to assume control over as much territory as possible by conquering smaller fortifications and their zones of influence over the countryside.

The Battle of Șoplea, 26 June 1655

The princes of the Rákóczi family had established close ties with the rulers of Wallachia and Moldavia, because they needed trustworthy allies in order to pursue their ambitious external policy. At times, the fulfilment of this political project required military interventions across the Carpathians. In 1655 the alliance between Transylvania and Wallachia was endangered by a massive uprising in the army of Constantin Șerban, who had proven to be a faithful ally of the Transylvanian prince.

---

42   Czigány, 'The 1644–1645 Campaign', pp.107–111.

MILITARY CAMPAIGNS, BATTLES AND SIEGES

The rebellion began on 27 February 1655 when soldiers serving at the court in București, Serbian mercenaries (*seimeni*) and guardsmen (*dorobanți*), attacked Constantin Șerban and his entourage as they were returning home after the Sunday Mass. Many boyars and their families were brutally slaughtered on the spot, but the voivode managed to escape. He had lost control over some of the most important elements in his army, the military servants (*slujitori*) and the *seimeni*, which were at the time the most important group of foreign mercenaries in Wallachia.[43] Although he could not rule and was essentially kept hostage by his own soldiers, Constantin Șerban was able to communicate in secret with his allies from Transylvania and Moldavia. His repeated pleas for help were received with great concern in Transylvania, where George Rákóczi II managed to convince the Diet and the Princely Council to organise a military campaign in Wallachia. The Ottomans were also in favour of this intervention because they were eager to restore stability in the territories of their northern vassals and had resorted to such tactics on several previous occasions.

The ruler of Moldavia, Gheroghe Ștefan, and Ottoman troops from the Danubian borderland (Silistra) were expected to support the Transylvanian army in its attempt to quell the rebellion in Wallachia. When news of an imminent attack from Transylvania reached București on 23 May, the rebels moved towards the northern border and reinforced the defences of Târgoviște. As the Transylvanian army was marching across the Carpathians, Constantin Șerban found refuge at Silistra where he decided to wait until things had settled down. The various groups of military servants (*slujitori*) who had joined the rebellion decided to elect a new ruler, Hrizea din Bogdănei, a boyar who had held important offices at court in previous years but had lost his position because of Constantin Șerban.[44]

On 22 June, George Rákóczi II crossed the border into Wallachia and marched southwards until 26 June when he reached the village of Șoplea, on the Teleajen River. Gheorghe Ștefan of Moldavia also crossed the border after 2,000 Tatars had reached his camp and was heading in the same direction with the intention of joining the Transylvanian army, but he did not arrive in time to take part in the battle.

Information regarding the size of the armies involved in this conflict varies from one narrative source to another. One of the most accurate and balanced perspective seems to be provided by Moldavian chronicler Miron Costin who claims that Rákóczi had about 12,000 soldiers.[45] The size of the rebel army was estimated at about 12,000–16,000 men with a sizeable number of cannons (30–33 pieces), much more than the 12 field guns brought by the Transylvanian army.[46]

---

43 Nicolae Stoicescu, *Curteni și slujitori: Contribuții la istoria armatei române* (București: Editura Militară, 1968), pp.60–176; pp.195–201.
44 Lidia Demény, Lajos Demény, Nicolae Stoicescu, *Răscoala seimenilor sau răscoală populară?* (București: Editura Științifică, 1968), pp.130–133.
45 Miron Costin, *Opere*, p.172.
46 Demény, Demény, Stoicescu, *Răscoala seimenilor*, p.138; Neagoe, Peligrad, 'Lupta de la Șoplea', p.6.

The Transylvanians were the first to arrive on the battlefield, early in the morning of 26 June, and set their camp close to the riverbank. Around noon the first detachments of Wallachian guardsmen *(dorobanți)* arrived with some of the artillery, which they positioned on a high hill overlooking the river. The battle began with their artillery salvos which were not aimed accurately and, according to a contemporary observer, 'most cannonballs flew over the Transylvanian camp'. Hrizea divided his army in three main groups (battalions). The largest part of the army remained in camp while the vanguard had already occupied a high hill overlooking the Transylvanian camp as mentioned before. The third battalion, with a substantial number of cannon pulled by oxen, planned to approach the Transylvanian camp from the riverside. It was a torrid summer afternoon and when the Wallachian rebels approached the Teleajen River they were unable to stop the oxen from diving into the cool waters dragging with them their carriages, cannons and gunpowder supplies.

With an important part of their artillery sunk in the river, the *seimeni* were now vulnerable to a Transylvanian cavalry charge. Taking advantage of the lack of coordination in the army of Hrizea, Rákóczi ordered a swift assault directed mostly against the Wallachian vanguard, which included the largest number of cannons and held the high ground. The attack was performed by a mixed detachment of cavalry and infantry. The Transylvanian captain general, John Kemény, personally led the cavalry charge. The infantry consisted mostly of German mercenaries armed with muskets, commanded by Andrew Gaudy (Gawdy), an officer of Scottish origin in Transylvanian service. The Transylvanian infantry was supported by a detachment of dragoons, commanded by Captain Mansfeld. Some cavalry banners were directed against the second enemy formation which was struggling to reclaim their sunken cannons, while most of the mounted troops performed a flanking manoeuvre around the hill occupied by the Wallachian vanguard. Rákóczi's German mercenaries approached the hill head-on and used their superior firepower to scatter the enemy troops who were defending the artillery.[47]

According to Miron Costin, once the Germans reached a favourable position 'they all shot at the same time', which is one of the few indications of the use of volley fire tactics in the Transylvanian army. The captured cannons were redirected against Hrizea's main camp where panic had already started to set in. Many captains and boyars surrendered; some joined the Transylvanians while others ran away with the intention of reaching Constantin Șerban. The battle began around noon and lasted until sundown, but the outcome was decided in the first few hours. For the longest part of the day, Transylvanian cavalry chased the fleeing rebels and looted their camp.[48]

Although the two armies were similar in size (about 12,000 men each), the Transylvanians had a clear advantage in terms of leadership and cohesion.

---

47 Kraus, *Cronica Transilvaniei*, p.181; Demény, Demény, Stoicescu, *Răscoala seimenilor*, pp.143–145.
48 Miron Costin, *Opere*, p.172; Neagoe, Peligrad, 'Lupta de la Șoplea', pp.7–8; Ardelean, *Organizarea militară*, pp.354–356.

The rebels had more field guns than their adversaries, but due in part to the misfortune with the thirst-crazed oxen they were unable to use those that remained to them efficiently. Rákóczi had brought a respectable number of mounted troops, which were highly effective against the light infantry which formed the bulk of Hrizea's army.[49] Thus, the Transylvanian prince was able to achieve a decisive victory in Wallachia and Constantin Șerban resumed his reign with a great debt of gratitude towards Rákóczi. Two years later, when the prince departed for his ill-fated campaign in Poland, the ruler of Wallachia functioned as a loyal ally, providing military and diplomatic support.

The Polish Campaign of George Rákóczi II, 1657

The greatest ambition of George Rákóczi II was to win the Crown of Poland. Knowing the tragic outcome of this endeavour, many historians have concluded that it was a foolish ambition, one doomed to failure from the beginning. However, a careful analysis of contemporary sources and the general political and military context would indicate that George Rákóczi II had a decent plan and a strong enough army to achieve his goal. First of all, the campaign was well prepared for from a diplomatic point of view. In previous years Rákóczi had built up an extensive network of allies, which included Sweden, the Cossacks, Moldavia, Wallachia and a group of Polish nobles who backed his claim for the crown. Constant diplomatic efforts were also made at the Habsburg court and with the Ottomans in trying to appease their anger, but they were unsuccessful.[50]

Prince George Rákóczi II did not take the decision to embark on this campaign on his own. Many Transylvanian nobles were in favour of an alliance with Sweden and a military intervention in Poland. There were of course some, like Francis Rhédei, the lord-lieutenant of Maramureș, who advised against this military action. His main argument was that the Cossacks were untrustworthy allies.[51]

After he concluded an alliance with Sweden at Iernut (Rádnot) on 6 December 1656, the prince sent out orders to mobilise his troops. The various components of the Transylvanian army were expected to muster, with haste, in various locations across the country, including Cluj, Oradea, and Debrecen. The *hajdú* from the western borderland gathered in Nánás, a small market town in Szabolcs county, on 11 December 1656, where they awaited further orders from their General, Gábor Bakos.[52] Some preparations

---

49 Demény, Demény, Stoicescu, *Răscoala seimenilor*, p.140.
50 Gábor Kármán, 'II. Rákóczi György 1657. évi lengyelországi hadjáratának diplomáciai háttere', *Századok*, Vol. 146 (2012) pp.1049–1084; Eugène Pavelesco, *Georges II Rákoczy prince de Transylvanie (1648–1660). Essai sur sa politique extériure* (Iași: «Versuri și Proză», 1924), pp.71–73.
51 Sándor Gebei, 'II. Rákóczi György lengyelországi hadjárata, 1657', *Hadtörténelmi Közlemények* 105/2 (1992), pp.31–32.
52 Gebei, 'II. Rákóczi György', p.32.

had been made well in advance. The gunsmiths had been busy casting new cannons, the Saxon towns were ordered to prepare an unprecedented number of horses and carts for the baggage train, while the smiths of Aiud made 4,000 lances decorated with gold for the army. There was a certain sense of fervour and enthusiasm behind the preparations for this campaign. The prince showed no restraint in the display of wealth and power as was befitting for somebody with royal ambitions. His close entourage was mounted on 120 Turkish horses adorned with expensive harnesses. A witness to these lavish preparations, the Saxon chronicler Georg Kraus, commented that the prince and his soldiers looked like they were preparing for a wedding instead of going to war.[53]

Transylvanian and Swedish soldiers during the campaign in Poland 1657. Etching based on the drawings by Erik Dahlbergh from Samuel Pufendorf's De rebus a Carolo Gustavo Sveciae rege Gestis Commentatorium Libri septem, 1696 (National Library, Warsaw)

An estimation of the size of Rákóczi's army at the beginning of the campaign is rather difficult to arrive at because contemporary sources do not differentiate between combatants and camp followers. In this particular context the presence of allied troops (Wallachians, Moldavians, Cossacks and Swedish) further adds to the confusion. One of the most generous estimations was made by Georg Kraus who claimed that the prince was leading an army of 60,000 men supported by 80 cannons.[54] A more accurate account is provided by the commander of the Swedish troops, Heinrich Coelestin von Sternbach, written in February 1657. Although the army of Rákóczi had been on the march for almost two months at the time and might have suffered the usual loses one would expect due to attrition, they still had 18,000 cavalry and 5,000 infantry.[55] The allied troops from Moldavia and Wallachia numbered 6,000 men, a total more or less confirmed by other

---

53 Kraus, *Cronica Transilvaniei*, pp.185–194.
54 Kraus, *Cronica Transilvaniei*, p.185.
55 Alexander Szilágyi, *Transsylvania et Bellum Boreo-Orientale: Acta et Documenta*, vol. II (Budapest: Magyar Tudományos Akadémia, 1891), pp.273.

sources (4,000–5,000 soldiers).⁵⁶ Regardless of the variations in absolute numbers, all sources indicate that Rákóczi was at the head of an impressive military force, a composite 'coalition army'. A noteworthy detail is the high percentage of cavalry, which ensured a high degree of mobility to an army adapted for the strategic and logistical realities of East-Central Europe.

Transylvanian soldiers during the campaign in Poland 1657. Etching based on the drawings by Erik Dahlbergh from Samuel Pufendorf's De rebus a Carolo Gustavo Sveciae rege Gestis Commentatorium Libri septem…, 1696 (National Library, Warsaw)

In the cold winter days of December 1656, banners and companies of soldiers from all over the country began marching towards the county of Maramureş, in the northern part of Transylvania on the border with Poland. The meeting point was established at Visk (today Vîşkovo, in Ukraine), a small market town on the banks of the Tisza River, close to the Carpathian Mountains. On the last day of December, the Transylvanian prince and his councillors drafted a manifest addressed to 'the people of Poland', claiming that their intervention was for the sake of restoring peace, all freedoms and privileges would be respected and last but not least, that Rákóczi had been invited to take the throne in the past and decided to act on the basis of that invitation.

As more and more troops continued to gather, the prince organised a short Diet, which concluded on 17 January 1657. It was a brief meeting meant to establish some last details regarding the campaign and the gathering of a new tax for the war effort.⁵⁷ Soon after the order to march was given and the Transylvanians, together with their Moldavian and Wallachian allies, started a perilous journey through the snow-covered mountain passes into the lands of the Polish-Lithuanian Commonwealth. On 2 February they had

---

56   Grigore G. Tocilescu, Alexandru I. Odobescu (eds.), *Documente privitoare la Istoria Românilor* (colecţia Hurmuzaki), vol. I/Supplement I (Bucureşti: Ministerul Cultelor şi Instrucţiunii Publice şi Academia Română, 1886), p.243; Costin, *Opere*, p.176.
57   MCRT, vol. XI, pp.245–248.

already reached Sînovîdne and were expecting to meet with their Cossack allies in a few days at the settlement of Stryi. The Transylvanians arrived first and waited in vain for the Cossacks who had begun their march later than expected, under the command of Hetman Anton Jdanovics. The two armies met only later, on 17 February in the Sambor-Przemyśl region. After the merger, the coalition army reached an impressive size of 50,000 men.[58]

Transylvanian and Cossacks soldiers crossing Vistula River at Zakroczym in March 1657, during the campaign in Poland. Transylvanian cavalry appears to be unarmoured, but many soldiers are armed with lances. Etching based on the drawings by Erik Dahlbergh from Samuel Pufendorf's De rebus a Carolo Gustavo Sveciae rege Gestis Commentatorium Libri septem…, 1696 (National Library, Warsaw)

In the meantime, Crown Marshal Jerzy Lubomirski and his troops were besieging Krakow, controlled at the time by Sweden. When news of the arrival of the Transylvanian army reached his camp, he decided to abandon the siege and retreated on his estate of Lancut, near Przemyśl.[59] The prince tried to convince him of his good intentions and win his support but in vain. It was now obvious that Rákóczi was not welcomed in Poland and that his claim to the throne was far from being unanimously accepted. Instead of retreating back to Transylvania he decided to continue his pursuit for the Polish throne and ordered his captain general, John Kemény, to attack the estates of Lubomirski. The Transylvanians met little resistance because the Crown Marshal had already left the area. Rákóczi's soldiers showed no restraint and savagely pillaged the countryside. They acted in a similar way as they advanced towards Krakow, while the animosity of the local population grew. Bands of armed peasants and also smaller detachments of the regular army constantly harassed the Transylvanians who were now facing great difficulties in finding sufficient food supplies.[60]

Diplomatic efforts were not abandoned although the military campaign had already begun. While Rákóczi was marching his troops across the

---

58 Gebei, 'II. Rákóczi György', pp.34–36.
59 Robert I. Frost, *The Northern Wars: War, State and Society in Northern Europe 1558-1721* (Harlow: Pearson Education, 2000), p.178.
60 Gebei, 'II. Rákóczi György', pp.37–39.

MILITARY CAMPAIGNS, BATTLES AND SIEGES

Polish border, the Ottomans sent their first envoys to Transylvania with a clear message, ordering the prince to stop all hostile actions in Poland and return home.[61] Rákóczi decided to neglect these threats hoping that after he had secured his claim the crown, the anger of the Ottomans would be easily appeased with generous gifts and promises of obedience.

Meeting between Prince George Rákóczi II and Charles X Gustav, King of Sweden, at Ćmielów on 12 April 1657, during the campaign in Poland. Etching based on the drawings by Erik Dahlbergh from Samuel Pufendorf's De rebus a Carolo Gustavo Sveciae rege Gestis Commentatorium Libri septem…, 1696 (National Library, Warsaw)

As per their agreement, the Swedish troops handed over Krakow to the Transylvanians. Rákóczi spent only two days in the city and left János Bethlen with 2,000 soldiers to guard this important strategic point. A handful of Swedish soldiers remained behind to provide assistance to their Transylvanian allies while the prince resumed his march northwards with the intention of joining King Charles X Gustav. The two monarchs met on 13 April, at Ćmielów, and both of them were disappointed with what they found. Apparently, the King of Sweden questioned the quality of the Transylvanian-Cossack host while Rákóczi was unsatisfied with the small size of the Swedish army (10,000–12,000 soldiers). Charles Gustav was intent on confronting the army of John Casimir in a decisive battle and the Transylvanians agreed to this plan. However, the Polish commanders had no intention of risking a direct confrontation at that time. On 30 April, the army of the Swedish-Transylvanian-Cossack coalition crossed the Vistula at Zawichost and tried to encircle the enemy in the Zamość-Lublin-Brest area, but the highly mobile Polish troops were able to avoid the trap.[62]

---

61 Eudoxiu de Hurmuzaki, *Documente privitoare la Istoria Românilor*, vol. IX/ Part 1 (București: Ministerul Cultelor și Instrucțiunii Publice și Academia Română, 1897), pp.82–83.
62 Gebei, 'II. Rákóczi György', pp.45–46.

THE ARMY OF TRANSYLVANIA 1613-1690

Transylvanian and Cossack armies crossing the Vistula River during the campaign in Poland 1657. Etching based on the drawings by Erik Dahlbergh from Samuel Pufendorf's De rebus a Carolo Gustavo Sveciae rege Gestis Commentatorium Libri septem…, 1696 (National Library, Warsaw)

Unable to deal a decisive blow against their enemy, Charles Gustav and Rákóczi had to settle with the conquest of Brest in Lithuania. The town surrendered on 17 May after a short siege. One of the reasons for the brevity of the siege might have been their small supply of gunpowder and lack of heavy artillery. According to a brief inventory completed after the capture of the city, the arsenal of Brest included seven tonnes of gunpowder, 3,000 musket shot, 200 iron shot for cannons and culverins, 34 iron and bronze culverins, one damaged cannon, five damaged culverins, 31 large muskets and four bombards.[63]

Two or three days after the capitulation of Brest, Charles Gustav and most of his troops retreated westward. News of the planed Danish attack on Sweden had already reached him although he did not disclose his true intentions to the Transylvanians. A small force, commanded by Marshal Sternbach was left with Rákóczi. The Swedish commander began to take Cossacks, as well as Moldavians and Wallachians into his service, weakening thus the position of Rákóczi within the coalition.[64] Nevertheless, he remained the leader of this composite army and he also decided to turn westwards in the hopes of reuniting with the rest of the Swedish army. On 12 June they were camped below the walls of Warsaw, where town authorities decided to surrender almost without opposition.[65] Although he had taken some of the most important urban centres in the Polish-Lithuanian Commonwealth (Krakow, Brest, Warsaw) the Prince of Transylvania was far from being in control. His army was suffering from a severe lack of supplies and internal dissent had reached a critical point. On top of that Charles Gustav ordered

---

63 Szilágyi, *Transsylvania et Bellum Boreo-Orientale*, pp.293–294.
64 Szilágyi, *Transsylvania et Bellum Boreo-Orientale*, p.293.
65 Szilágyi, *Transsylvania et Bellum Boreo-Orientale*, pp.308–312.

MILITARY CAMPAIGNS, BATTLES AND SIEGES

the retreat of the remaining Swedish troops in Rákóczi's army while an unknown epidemic began to spread in Warsaw. At the same time (June 1657) the first Habsburg soldiers arrived at Częstochowa and John Casimir could now count on the help of a powerful ally.[66]

Meeting between Prince George Rákóczi II and Charles X Gustav, King of Sweden, at Modliborzyce on 11 April 1657, during the campaign in Poland. Prince (marked with letter B) is bowing to King, and on his right (marked with letter C) is John Kemény. Etching based on the drawings by Erik Dahlbergh from Samuel Pufendorf's De rebus a Carolo Gustavo Sveciae rege Gestis Commentatorium Libri septem…, 1696 (National Library, Warsaw)

From mid June until the beginning of July, Marshal Jerzy Sebastian Lubomirski and his troops ravaged the northern parts of Transylvania. Many villages and estates from the counties of Bereg, Ugocsa and Satu Mare were ruthlessly pillaged in response to the destruction by Rákóczi's soldiers of the personal estates of the Crown Marshal at the beginning of the campaign. Personal revenge was probably not the only reason behind this attack as Lubomirski was hoping to pressure the Transylvanian army into retreating back home.[67] According to the Moldavian chronicler Miron Costin, the Polish magnate was leading a small army of only 4,000 soldiers.[68] Both local and central authorities responded quickly to the Polish threat. The counties which were directly affected by the incursion mobilised the local banners, but their numbers were significantly reduced because many nobles were with the prince in Poland. The deputy of the prince, Ákos Barcsay, ordered a general levy and was able to gather 1,200 infantry and 4,000 cavalry. It was enough to face the Polish raiders but by the time they reached the northern parts of the principality, Lubomirski was already gone.[69]

---

66   Gebei, 'II. Rákóczi György', pp.48–51.
67   János B. Szabó, '„Sors bona nihil aliud" Az 1657. évi erdélyi ‚Blitzkrieg' kudarca Lengyelországban', Ildikó Horn et al (eds.), *Művészet és mesterség: tisztelgő kötet R. Várkonyi Ágnes emlékére* (Budapest: L'Harmattan, 2016), pp.231–250.
68   Costin, *Opere*, p.177.
69   Enyedi, 'II Rákóczi György', pp.230–234.

THE ARMY OF TRANSYLVANIA 1613-1690

Transylvanian soldiers in the Swedish camp at Modliborzyce, 11 April 1657, during the campaign in Poland. Etching based on the drawings by Erik Dahlbergh from Samuel Pufendorf's De rebus a Carolo Gustavo Sveciae rege Gestis Commentatorium Libri septem…, 1696 (National Library, Warsaw)

By the end of June 1657, the balance of war in the Polish-Lithuanian Commonwealth had changed drastically. King John Casimir was now in a much better position with both the Habsburgs and the Ottomans sustaining his cause. George Rákóczi II was abandoned by his main ally, Charles Gustav X of Sweden, who had to return home to deal with a Danish attack. In this unfavourable context the Transylvanians decided to return to Krakow and join with the garrison they had left there a few months ago. However, the Habsburg army of Hatzfeld was very close to Krakow and heading in that direction, and posed the risk of a direct confrontation, which at this point would have been very disadvantageous for the Transylvanian army. As Rákóczi and his war council were debating their next move, the Polish nobles who had followed him so far abandoned him and left the camp, while the Cossacks were preparing to cross the Vistula River at Zawichost. The prince shelved his plan of reaching Krakow and decided to follow the Cossacks. This proved to be a particularly unsuccessful move. The crossing of the river was done with some haste, and this resulted in many losses, and supply wagons and cannons had to be left behind or intentionally sunk in the river. Rákóczi was trying to return home but he could not take the shortest and most obvious route through the Carpathian Mountain passes because he feared an encounter with Lubomirski. He therefore decided to make a long detour through the territories of his supposed allies, the Cossacks and Moldavia.[70]

As the campaign approached its tragic end, the Transylvanian army was gradually wasting away. The prince left troops in several major towns and fortifications along the way, such as Pinczów, Brest, Waldeck and Krakow, where the Transylvanian garrison was estimated at 2,000–3,100 men. On 19 July 1657, a sizeable number of Rákóczi's soldiers, about 3,000–4,000 Székely, county troops, Moldavians and Wallachians had left the main army and were already heading for the Transylvanian border.[71] In the unfavourable

---

70 Gebei, 'II. Rákóczi György', pp.53–57.
71 Szabó, 'Sors bona', p.235; Gebei, 'II. Rákóczi György', p.58.

MILITARY CAMPAIGNS, BATTLES AND SIEGES

conditions generated by such a hasty retreat, Rákóczi's composite army was significantly affected by internal conflict and dissent. The Cossacks realised that their alliance with the Transylvanian prince no longer had purpose and were the first to retreat, across the Bug River. It still remains unclear if their retreat began before or after Rákóczi sent his envoys to the Polish camp.[72] Sensing the weakness of their enemy, Polish commanders intensified their attacks against the Transylvanians. Among them, the most determined was Stefan Czarniecki. With his 10,000 soldiers he attacked the rearguard of the Transylvanian army at Magierów on 11 July and captured a considerable number of wagons loaded with loot and supplies. However, with the exception of Magierów, the other skirmishes were rather inconclusive, with both armies sharing similar rates of success and failure. After the middle of July, the strength of the Polish-Lithuanian army grew with the arrival of Lubomirski, Sapieha and Potocki, but their troops also suffered from attrition.[73] No faction was at a clear advantage and the Polish commanders, with the exception of Czarniecki, were considering halting the pursuit after the Transylvanians crossed into Cossack territory. However, at this point Rákóczi decided it was time to begin peace negotiations.[74]

Mounted musicians accompanying Prince George Rákóczi II, campaign in Poland in 1657. Etching based on the drawings by Erik Dahlbergh from Samuel Pufendorf's *De rebus a Carolo Gustavo Sveciae rege Gestis Commentatorium Libri septem...*, 1696 (National Library, Warsaw)

On 20 July 1657 at Czarny Ostrów, the Transylvanian army suffered another large-scale attack and had to abandon most of their supply wagons and spoils of war. A few days later, on 22–23 July the prince met with Polish commanders at Czarny Ostrów and agreed to all their peace conditions, including the payment of reparations for the war of 1,200,000 gold coins. On 24 July, the prince wrote a letter to János Bethlen, commander of the Transylvanian garrison in Krakow, informing him of the treaty that had been recently signed with the Polish hetmans and ordered him to return home as soon as a good opportunity arose.[75] Soon after, with a small entourage of about 300 guards, the prince headed home for Transylvania while the main army was entrusted to the captain general, John Kemény.

Rákóczi travelled with great haste and on 26 July he finally reached Câmpulung, in Moldavia, near the Transylvanian border.[76] The remaining Transylvanian army of about 4,000–5,000 soldiers advanced slowly along the same route and on 27 July they made camp near Trembowla (Terebovila in Ukraine). The Tatars had been ordered by the Ottoman sultan to attack the enemies of the Polish-Lithuanian Commonwealth and for several weeks

---

72 Szabó, 'Sors bona', pp.249–250.
73 Szilágyi, Transsylvania et Bellum Boreo-Orientale, pp.316–318.
74 Szabó, 'Sors bona', pp.241–242.
75 Szilágyi, Transsylvania et Bellum Boreo-Orientale, pp.313–314.
76 Gebei, 'II. Rákóczi György', pp.58–59.

they pillaged the territories of the Cossacks and pursued the remnants of the Transylvanian army. They finally caught up with them at Trembowla where Kemény had established a fortified camp. The weakened Transylvanian army resisted for three days and were determined to hold out much longer knowing the fate that awaited them if captured by the Tatars. On the fourth day Kemény was convinced to leave his camp under the pretext of conducting negotiations. In his absence the Tatars mounted a large-scale assault and with the help of some treacherous Wallachian *seimeni*, they were able to breach the defences and swarmed into the Transylvanian camp, overrunning it.

Later, the captain general himself wrote a short account of the tragic events that led to the defeat and capture of the Transylvanian army by the Tatars, entitled 'The ruin of the Transylvanian army' (*Ruina exercitus Transylvaniae*). Kemény begins by describing the deplorable state of his remaining troops, exhausted after long marches and constant skirmishes with the enemy. Fear of Tatar captivity was already affecting the morale of the soldiers who were forced to place their trust, and their lives, in the hands of some untrustworthy Polish scouts. The war council understood the dire situation and agreed (or even suggested) that Prince Rákóczi should leave with a small escort to avoid the risk of being captured. The captain general and other leading nobles including Francis Kornis, Pál Béldi, Péter Huszár and Tamás Damokos remained behind to maintain the morale and cohesion of the army.

Tatars and also groups from the Polish-Lithuanian army continued to attack the Transylvanian rearguard despite the treaty signed not long before. As more Tatars stalked his army Kemény decided to set up camp and placed the few remaining light cannons (eight pieces) in firing positions. There were only a few detachments of Székely infantry remaining, but most mounted troops were also equipped with gunpowder weapons, so they had enough firepower to keep the Tatars at bay. Small detachments of light cavalry performed occasional sorties and pursued the fleeing Tatars without straying too far away from the camp. By the end of the first day the Transylvanians had suffered significant losses, including two leading officers, Miklós Jármi, captain in the field army and Captain Mansfeld of the German dragoons. The fighting continued for two more days and nights.

On the morning of the fourth day (31 July), Kemény left the camp to negotiate an armistice and secure a peaceful retreat but as he was exchanging courtesies with the Tatar leaders, he heard a great commotion in their camp. The entire horde rushed towards the Transylvanian camp which from the distance appeared to be darkened by a black cloud of arrows. The Tatars were able to breach the defences of the camp with help of a group of Wallachian *seimeni* who turned against their former allies. In a few hours, the remnants of the once proud army of the Transylvanian principality were captured and enslaved by the Tatars.[77] Some nobles were ransomed by their families and were able to return home after a few years. The fate of many others, whether nobles or commoners, remains unknown but can be guessed at.

---

77 János Kemény, 'Ruina exercitus Transylvaniae', in Éva V. Windisch (ed.), *Kemény János és Bethlen Miklós művei* – Magyar Remekírók (Budapest: Szépirodalmi Könyvkiadó, 1980), pp.314–321.

The news of the Tatar victory was received with great joy at the Sublime Porte and the Transylvanian envoys were imprisoned in the Seven Towers.[78] The Grand Vizier had decided to punish harshly the disobedient vassals of the Crescent. In the following years (1658–1661), Ottomans and Tatar armies swept across the territories of Transylvania and thus ended the 'Golden Age' of the principality.

Considering the harsh political consequences suffered by Transylvania, it is tempting to conclude that this campaign was a grave mistake and a complete failure. However, we must consider the complex political context that led to this outcome and influenced the performance of the Transylvanian army. They travelled about 1,700–1,800km, mostly in hostile territory, facing serious obstacles in sourcing supplies and provisions. The campaign began in winter and continued during a rainy spring, through woodland and over marshy terrain. In spite of these difficult conditions the highly mobile troops of the Transylvanian prince managed to advance with surprising speed. From 23 June, when they left Warsaw and until they reached Czarny Ostrów on 20 July 1657, they advanced almost 600km in less than a month, although they did have to leave behind some of their infantry and baggage train. Mounted troops represented a high proportion (about 78 percent) in the Transylvanian army. The prince himself mentions that he was able to organise fast-moving vanguards, which included a respectable number of dragoons, to reach and hold important objectives on their route.[79] Rákóczi and his allies managed to occupy the most important towns and fortifications along the way but, contrary to expectation, this did not ensure effective control over the land. Their garrisons remained more or less isolated and faced great difficulties in obtaining provisions.

When he set out on this campaign Rákóczi relied on the good faith of his allies and on the benevolence, or at least neutrality, of his two great neighbours, the Habsburgs and the Ottomans. He could not have foreseen that in 1657 the political interests of the two empires would converge, and both would offer direct or indirect support to King John Casimir of Poland. Charles Gustav X and Bohdan Khmelnytsky followed their own agenda in the Polish-Lithuanian Commonwealth and regarded Transylvania as means to an end. In consequence there was little cohesion in the army of the Swedish-Transylvanian-Cossack coalition. Rákóczi often blamed the Cossacks for their brutality in pillaging the countryside but his own troops were equally responsible for much destruction. Internal disputes, especially between Transylvanians and Cossacks, were common and had a negative effect on the overall morale of the army.

This was a campaign without major battles, with the exception of the last stand against the Tatars near Trembowla. Ambushes, skirmishes and raids in search of plunder were the most common form of military action. The constant attacks by the Polish-Lithuanian troops, directed mostly against the rearguard and the baggage train had a devastating effect in the long

---

78 Eudoxiu de Hurmuzaki, *Documente privitoare la Istoria Românilor*, Vol. V/ Part 2, (București: Ministerul Cultelor și Instrucțiunii Publice și Academia Română, 1886), pp.34–35.
79 Szabó, 'Sors bona', pp.236–237.

term. Attrition affected Rákóczi's forces (Transylvanians, Wallachians and Moldavians) and they were significantly reduced in numbers by this stage in the campaign. The 29,000 soldiers under arms as recorded in January 1657 had reduced alarmingly to roughly 4,000 men at the end of July, and most of these were captured by the Tatars in the battle that concluded this unfortunate campaign.

The Battle of Florești (Szászfenes), 22 May 1660

In the spring of 1660, Seidi Ahmet, Pasha of Buda, marched his troops across the border of Transylvania with the purpose of defeating and capturing the rebel prince, George Rákóczi II, who had disobeyed the orders of his liège lord, Sultan Mehmet IV. The Turkish army faced little resistance as they marched through the western borderlands of the principality because Rákóczi had moved most of his troops inland and was besieging the Saxon town of Sibiu. As he was advancing through the territories of Bihor, Middle Szolnok and Crasna counties, Seidi Ahmet forced the local nobility to swear fealty and take up arms against any of their fellow countrymen who still recognised the authority of the rebel prince.[80]

Prince Rákóczi had no intention of avoiding a direct confrontation, so he took most of his loyal troops and marched towards Cluj, in the centre of Transylvania. While some of his soldiers were left behind to maintain a blockade around Sibiu, where his rival Barcsay had taken refuge, Rákóczi managed to gather about 8,000 men. Seidi Ahmed had a larger army of about 10,000 men, including 6,000 of his own troops, a few thousand soldiers from Moldavia and Wallachia (1,000–3,000 men) and an unknown number of Transylvanians from the counties of Bihor, Crasna and Middle Szlonok.[81]

The army of George Rákóczi II took up position in a field on the left banks of the Someș River, facing the west end of Florești (Szászfenes) village, in the vicinity of Cluj. On his left flank, Rákóczi placed 10 banners of cavalry from the field army (about 1,000 men), commanded by Gergely Kovács and the Székely banners of Ciuc and Gheorgheni. The Prince himself led the central detachment, consisting of 500 mounted *hajdú* from Ónod, the German infantry of Andrew Gaudy and a group of recently conscripted peasants (600 Romanians) led by an Orthodox priest from the village of Ciurila. A few field guns, eight in number, were placed on a small hill in front of the central body. The right flank was secured by the Székely banners of Odorhei, Trei Scaune and Mureș. The court cavalry, county nobility and other mounted troops from Oradea were placed in a second line of battle. Rákóczi wanted to give the impression that he had a large force under his command, so he ordered his camp followers, servants and wagon drivers to set up a third battle line.

The Ottomans and their allies had travelled peacefully beneath the walls of Cluj and established a camp along the road which connected Florești to

---

80 Kraus, *Cronica Transilvaniei*, pp.337–338.
81 Costin, *Opere*, pp.198–199.

MILITARY CAMPAIGNS, BATTLES AND SIEGES

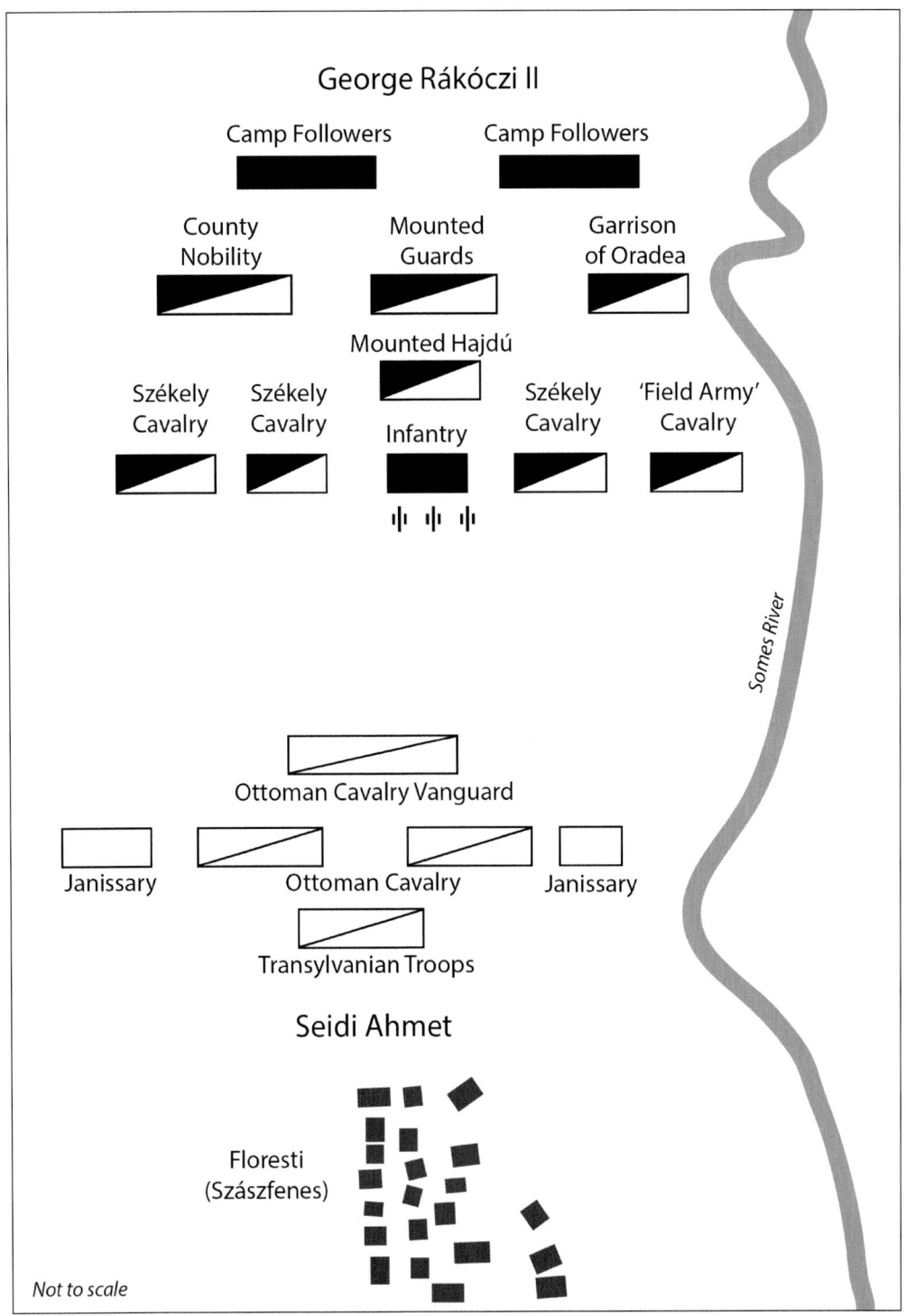

Map 2 The Battle of Florești (Szászfenes) 22 May 1660

Gilău. As soon as Rákóczi's troops were in sight, Seidi Ahmet ordered his men to take up their battle positions. Hussein Pasha was placed in the vanguard with 20 banners of cavalry (roughly 2,000 men). The Pasha of Buda took command of the main cavalry detachment situated in the centre, while the Transylvanians were positioned in the rearguard. Both flanks of the Ottoman army were secured by infantry detachments, who tried to take advantage of the higher ground.[82]

The battle began around eight o'clock in the morning with an assault by the cavalry of Hussein Pasha. Rákóczi ordered Gergely Kovács and his cavalry from the left flank to mount a counterattack. The Ottomans had lost some of their momentum because they had to cross over marshy terrain and were scattered by the Transylvanian cavalry. Soon after, the Ottoman left flank (cavalry and infantry) attacked the central Transylvanian detachment where the conscripted infantry occupied the first line. Forced into close combat with a superior enemy, the conscripted peasants were scattered and many of them died on the battlefield. In the meantime, the right flank of the Transylvanian army (Székely and Court cavalry) had also engaged in combat and was beginning to lose cohesion under the relentless attack of the Ottomans. Rákóczi himself rushed in their direction hoping to increase their morale and rally the wavering troops but was caught up in a skirmish with several Turkish and Wallachian soldiers who were eager to claim the head of the rebel prince. Outnumbered by his enemies, Rákóczi was forced to retreat and seek safety in a ditch and lost his helmet in the process. He would have perished on the spot if not for his personal guard who caught up in time to retrieve his severely wounded body from the clutches of the enemy. Unable to continue the battle, Rákóczi was placed in a carriage and taken to Oradea.[83]

Without their leader, the Transylvanian army began to dissolve and scatter. Running away was the best option for those who had formed the second battle line, mostly cavalry, because their horses were rested and therefore, they had a better chance of escaping their pursuers. Without the support of mounted troops, the infantry was attacked from three sides and pushed towards the Someș River. Only a few soldiers escaped by swimming across the river, while the vast majority were cut down on the battlefield.[84]

In this battle, the Ottomans had some obvious advantages that led to their victory. Primarily the Pasha of Buda commanded a larger army and had a better position on the battlefield, occupying the higher ground on his left flank. However, the outcome of the battle was decided by the mistake of the Transylvanian prince who recklessly engaged in a skirmish and received several mortal wounds. His guard carried him to Oradea alive, but he was tormented by a high fever caused by his infected wounds. After several days of agony he died, on 7 June 1660, leaving behind a country ravaged by war

---

82　Kraus, *Cronica Transilvaniei*, pp.342–344.
83　Ioan Lupaş, *Documente istorice transilvane, 1599–1699* (Cluj, Cartea Românească, 1940), pp.298–299.
84　József Jármy, 'II. Rákóczy György szász-fenesi csatája, megsebesülésének és halálának körülményei. (Második és befejező közlemény.)', *Erdélyi Múzeum* 19/4 (1902), pp.223–225.

MILITARY CAMPAIGNS, BATTLES AND SIEGES

and with an insecure future. His body was transported to Ecsed and then to Sárospatak, the most important estate of the Rákóczi family, where he was laid to rest on 4 April 1661.

The Siege of Oradea, 1660

On 15 April 1660, a large Ottoman force commanded by Köse Ali began its march towards the Hungarian border. Its purpose and destination were not noticeably obvious in the beginning. Although the Pasha of Buda was already in Transylvania and had obtained a decisive victory against the rebel Transylvanian prince, the sultan was not yet satisfied with the punishment inflicted upon his disloyal vassals. Prince Barcsay and the supreme captain of Oradea, Gabriel Haller, were already 'guests' in the army of Seidi Ahmed who received orders to join the army of Köse Ali and obey his orders. The Ottoman troops combined forces in the vicinity of Arad and continued their march along the Western Transylvanian frontier. It soon became clear that their real objective was Oradea, the 'gateway' of Transylvania. Gabriel Haller refused to use his influence and authority to convince the garrison to surrender. At the same time, Barcsay sent letters of encouragement to the officers in Oradea, asking them to defend the fortress at all costs and to

Oradea in the seventeenth century 2 (Țării Crișurilor Museum, Oradea, Romania)

ignore any further letters or messages sent in his name, which might try to persuade them to do otherwise.[85]

As soon as they received the letters of warning from the hostage prince, the garrison began preparations for the siege. All kinds of supplies were taken inside the fortified perimeter and some of the townsmen and their families decided to join the garrison. Many soldiers from the regular garrison of Oradea had left the fortress to accompany the body of George Rákóczi II to Ecsed. There were only 300 professional soldiers inside the fortress at the time, most of them German, Cossack and Wallachian (seimeni) mercenaries, who had been sent by Barcsay a few weeks before the siege. A considerable number of townsmen who had taken refuge inside the fortress took up arms, raising the total number of defenders to 850.[86] Máté Balogh assumed command of the garrison and sent pleas for help in Transylvania and in Hungary. The principality was already ravaged by almost three consecutive years of war and there were no more troops to send to Oradea at such a short notice. The Habsburgs considered the option of helping the defenders of the fortress but in the end, they decided to keep their peace with the Ottomans.[87]

The vanguard of Ottoman army reached Oradea on 11 July. By that time, the defenders had retreated inside the fortress and burnt all buildings outside the walls. On 14 July Oradea was completely surrounded by enemy troops. Evliya Çelebi, the renowned Turkish traveller and writer, accompanied the army of Köse Ali in this campaign and left a detailed first-hand account of the siege. According to his narrative, as soon as they arrived, the Ottomans dug trenches and erected ramparts, preparing thus for a prolonged siege. Four artillery platforms, mounting a total of 29 siege guns, were set up around the fortress. The largest battery, consisting of 10 cannon was positioned on a high hill situated in the vicinity of the fortifications. The fortress was kept under daily artillery fire while Ottoman sappers were digging zigzag approach trenches and underground galleries.[88] Oradea was well supplied with cannons and gunpowder but there were no trained artillerists inside the fortress when the siege began. Nevertheless, the defenders made effective use of their cannon, and kept the Ottomans at bay during the first weeks and destroyed eight of their artillery pieces.[89]

The ditch of the fortress proved to be a serious obstacle for the besieging army and prevented them from mounting a general assault in the first days of the siege. Eventually, with the help of a local woman who wanted to free her son from captivity, the Turks found the location of a sluice and managed to drain most of the water from the ditch. In the meantime, a Tatar army camped close to Oradea and new troops from Anatolia joined the besieging army.[90] All these events had a major negative effect on the morale of the defenders. If that were not enough, on 14 August their main gunpowder storehouse

---

85 Szabó, 'Asedierea cetății Oradea', pp.138–140.
86 Kraus, Cronica Transilvaniei, p.350.
87 Szabó, 'Asedierea cetății Oradea', pp.141–145.
88 *Călători străini*, vol. VI, pp.519–522.
89 Szabó, 'Asedierea cetății Oradea', p.148.
90 *Călători străini*, vol. VI, pp.519–522.

MILITARY CAMPAIGNS, BATTLES AND SIEGES

exploded. It was most likely an accident caused by a careless guard, but it had terrible consequences for the garrison. They lost a significant quantity of gunpowder and a sizeable number of men.

One of the favourite siege techniques of the Ottomans was digging mining galleries, a technique which was applied with great success at Oradea in 1660. Although artillery fire had produced considerable damage to the bastions and curtain walls of the fortress, the defenders were able to block the collapsed sections of the wall with debris. After many days of hard labour, a mining gallery reached one of the five bastions of Oradea (the Red Bastion). Ottoman sappers loaded the tunnel with a large amount of gunpowder while the army prepared for a general assault. A massive explosion, which collapsed a large section of the wall and severely damaged the bastion, was the signal for the assault. Against all expectations the defenders managed to repel the Ottomans. They concentrated a sizeable number of soldiers behind the breach, met the enemy with salvos of musketry and then engaged in a bloody melee. By the end of the day the Ottomans retreated after having suffered a considerable number of casualties.[91]

The Transylvanians had also suffered many casualties and lost all hope of help from the outside. On the following day, Ottoman sentinels observed several white flags raised along the walls of the fortress. Soon after, a group of officers from the garrison was dispatched to the Ottoman camp to negotiate a peaceful surrender. On 27 August, the two factions reached an agreement, and the remaining defenders of Oradea were allowed to leave the fortress with their families and personal belongings. Only 300 men were still alive at the end of the siege.[92]

Oradea was taken after 46 days of intensive siege. In spite of the significant difference in numbers (50,000 Ottomans against 850 Transylvanians) the

The Fortress of Oradea today (Țării Crișurilor Museum, Oradea, Romania)

---

91   Kraus, *Cronica Transilvaniei*, pp.372–373; *Călători străini*, vol. VI, pp.523–524.
92   Kraus, *Cronica Transilvaniei*, pp.374–375.

defenders were able to repel all attempts by the enemy to take the fortress by force. The modern defences of Oradea as well as the determination of its garrison, consisting of both volunteers and professional soldiers, were enough to balance the odds. The Transylvanians decided to surrender, after losing almost 65 percent of the garrison, because there was no hope of help from the outside. When Oradea was taken by the Ottomans, Transylvania lost a particularly important border fortification but also its status as regional power.

The Campaigns of Prince Michael Apafi I Against the Habsburgs, (1681–1683)

In 1664, when the peace treaty of Vasvár was signed, the Habsburg-Ottoman rivalry in Europe had reached a new milestone. Although the two empires had ceased open conflict there was no peace in Central and Eastern Europe. In the following years, the Ottomans focused their military strength on other fronts, in Crete and against the Polish-Lithuanian Commonwealth, while the Habsburgs had to deal with a protracted rebellion in Hungary. In 1681, Imre Thököly, leader of the Hungarian rebels, requested Ottoman assistance against the Habsburgs and promised to become a loyal vassal of the sultan. Thus, the conflict between the two great empires was reignited.[93]

The principality of Transylvania had no way of avoiding the war that was threatening to engulf the borderlands between the two empires. Ever since the early phase of the Hungarian uprising, the so called '*Wesselényi Conspiracy*' (1664–1671), Prince Michael Apafi I together with a significant part of the Transylvanian political elite declared their support for the rebels. This political option was approved by the Ottomans who were preparing to deliver a decisive blow against Vienna and the sultan was counting on his northern vassals (Transylvania, Wallachia, Moldavia and the Crimean Tatars) to provide military and logistical support.

In the summer of 1681, the Ottomans decided to offer military assistance to the Hungarian rebels. Troops from the borders aided by contingents provided by the vassal states were considered sufficient for the task. The pasha of Oradea gathered about 9,000 soldiers from the frontier garrisons while Moldavia provided 3,000 men and Wallachia 4,000. Prince Apafi mustered a small army of 8,000 men in a camp situated near the fortress of Gherla.[94] The Transylvanians began their march on 21 August and headed for the county of Bihor. Their advance was slow, a little over 200km in 15 days, and on 5 September they reached the fortress of Pocsaj. Here they waited several days for their other allies to gather and then turned northwards. They advanced with caution and captured some smaller Habsburg fortifications on their way.

The small garrison of Böszörmény (Hajdúböszörményi, Hungary) surrendered without firing a single shot on 12 September. Six days later,

---

93   Pálffy, *Hungary between Two Empires*, pp.161–162.
94   Szilágyi, 'Az erdély 1681-ik', pp.415–420.

on 18 September, they reached the larger fortification of Kálló (Nagykálló, Hungary), which was defended by a combined garrison, with a separate Hungarian and Italian commanders. The garrison resisted for seven days before opening their gates to the besieging army. From this point, Michael Teleki (captain general of the Transylvanian army) turned his troops eastward, towards the Transylvanian frontier. On their way they besieged two other major Habsburg fortifications at Ecsed (Nagyecsed, Hungary) and Satu Mare, but they retreated after a few days, in each case without capturing either place. The rearguard of the Transylvanian army was attacked by the garrison of Satu Mare soon after they lifted the siege. It was a swift skirmish with 70 casualties inflicted on the Székely banners of Transylvania. On 21 October Apafi's troops were back in Transylvania, at Gherla where the campaign had begun.[95]

An interesting account of this expedition is provided by Miklós Bethlen, a high-ranking Transylvanian noble who was entrusted with the command of the camp watch and with keeping the muster records. Bethlen went to war well prepared, with a retinue of 40 servants, some of them armed according to the traditional custom of the noble insurrection. For the transportation of supplies he prepared five wagons driven by eight oxen each, two carriages driven by eight horses each, a coach with six horses and two more pack horses. Food provisions included a variety of livestock, such as sheep, cattle, hens, one pig, plus fodder for the animals, and various quantities of victuals, vegetables, fresh and dried fruits, wheat flour, biscuit, green peas, lentils, smoked meat, cheese, butter and honey. He also brought copious quantities of wine, for himself and his retinue, but also for sale in the camp market. A small chest of pharmaceuticals ended Bethlen's list of war supplies. According to his account desertion was a big issue in the Transylvanian army. Many soldiers even paid their own captains to be allowed to return home before the end of the campaign. At the same time, individuals and smaller groups of Hungarians joined the Transylvanians as volunteers. The marching speed of the army was rather slow, although the army only had a few pieces of artillery, in the shape of five cannon and two mortars. Not all Transylvanians had been as well prepared as Bethlen and resorted to plundering the countryside in order to gather provisions. There were also internal conflicts between the mercenaries of the field army and the Székely banners who refused to engage the enemy before the former did.[96]

This campaign lacked any spectacular confrontations, and it was simply a diversion meant to reduce the pressure of the Habsburg army on the Hungarian rebels. The Transylvanians were not very motivated to risk their lives for the Hungarian uprising, especially as the relationship between Prince Apafi and Imre Thököly was starting to deteriorate.

A new Ottoman offensive was launched in 1682. Prince Apafi mustered his troops in the same location as in the previous year, near the fortress of Gherla, and set off for Upper Hungary at the beginning of August. Their destination was the fortress of Fiľakovo (Fülek), where a large force of 30,000

---

95   MCRT, vol. XVIII, p.338.
96   Bethlen, *Descrierea*, pp.170–172.

men was gathering, composed of Ottomans from the province of Buda and Hungarian rebels. Apafi, with his small army of 8,000 men, reached the walls of Fiľakovo on 2 September. By that time, the fortress had already been subdued and the Transylvanians were given the task of demolishing the walls.[97] Miklós Bethlen was once again among the Transylvanian nobles who joined the army of the prince. On this occasion he was entrusted with the command of the county banners which formed a small detachment of 700–800 men, both cavalry and infantry.[98] This campaign represented the high point of Thököly's rebellion in Hungary. Before joining the Ottomans under the walls of Fiľakovo he had taken control over the important military and financial centre at Košice. By the end of the year, he was in control of Upper Hungary and the Ottomans recognised him as legitimate ruler of these lands.[99] Michael Apafi was not happy with the ascension of his new neighbour whom he regarded as a rival rather than an ally. On 15 October, the prince and his army returned home.[100]

In 1683, Grand Vizier Kara Mustafa embarked on a massive campaign with the objective of capturing Vienna. Such an endeavour required an unprecedented mobilisation of resources even for the Ottoman Empire. An army of epic proportions (120,000–140,000 men) consisting not only of Ottoman soldiers but also contingents provided by the sultan's vassals marched towards the Habsburg.

In February, a letter from the sultan arrived at the court of the Transylvanian prince, ordering him to prepare for the upcoming expedition. It is estimated that Moldavia, Wallachia and Transylvania contributed with a total number of 13,000 men.[101] Apafi mustered a small army of 6,000, which included various detachments such as Székely banners, boyars from Făgăraș district, musketeers from Chioar district and the banners and companies of the court army.[102] By the year of the siege of Vienna the guard of Prince Apafi had reached the unprecedented size of 1,170 soldiers, organised into 13 cavalry banners (lancers, dragoons and mounted carabineers) and seven infantry companies.[103]

Prince Apafi ordered the mobilisation of troops to a camp at Apahida, near the town of Cluj, on the first day of July. The prince himself arrived a day after and issued a very elaborate series of orders and regulations, consisting of 40 separate articles meant to enforce discipline within the army. A few more days were spent in camp waiting for the rest of the troops to gather. On 8 July the army began its march towards Vienna. They were not very motivated to

---

97 MCRT, vol. XVII, p.339; Szabó, János B., 'Splendid Isolation? The Military Cooperation of the Principality of Transylvania with the Ottoman Empire (1571–1688) in the Mirror of the Hungarian Historiography's Dilemmas', in Gábor Kármán, Lovro Kunčević, (ed.), *The European Tributary States of the Ottoman Empire in the Sixteenth and Seventeenth Centuries* (Leiden and Boston: Brill, 2013), p.328.
98 Bethlen, *Descrierea*, p.174.
99 Pálffy, *Hungary between Two Empires*, p.162.
100 MCRT, vol. XVII, p.339.
101 Nicolae Iorga, *Acte și fragmente cu privire la istoria românilor adunate din depozitele de manuscrise ale apusului,* vol. I (București: Imprimeria Statului, 1895), p.95.
102 Veress, *Documente*, vol. XI, pp.196–197.
103 Ardelean, *Organizarea militară*, pp.205–211.

MILITARY CAMPAIGNS, BATTLES AND SIEGES

join in the war, so they did not exactly rush to reach the Ottomans. After only two days of travelling, they spent an entire day resting near the village of Creaca (Kariká) situated only 80km away from their starting point. By this time the Grand Vizier was already at Győr urging his allies to hurry as he was approaching his final destination of Vienna.

Apafi continued his march through Hungary, reaching Bakonszeg on 28 July and Visegrád on 3 August. A few days later on 7 August the Transylvanians crossed the Danube on the bridge between Esztergom and Štúrovo (Párkány). On 13 August they reached Győr and on the 18 they crossed the Leitha River. On 22 August Apafi reached the main Ottoman camp and was received by the Grand Vizier himself. During the meeting he was informed that his task was to defend the Danube crossing near the fortress of Győr which was still controlled by a Habsburg garrison. Apafi obeyed the orders and on 2 September returned with his small army to the vicinity of Győr. At this point he was more concerned about negotiating with the Habsburgs rather than fighting against them. News of the crushing Ottoman defeat on the Kahlenberg on 12 September swiftly reached the Transylvanian camp.[104]

As the Ottoman army was slowly retreating towards the Hungarian border Apafi secured their crossing point near Győr and remained in the rearguard. Eventually he also left his camp and reached Buda on 4 October. The scarcity of food provisions was becoming felt badly by the retreating army. Apafi had to wait for 10 days in the vicinity of Buda as the situation in his camp was getting increasingly difficult. One of the key issues was finding sources of clean water, a problem which led to an outbreak of disease of epidemic proportions. Only half of the 6,000 Transylvanians who began this journey returned home. The rest of them succumbed to illness and hunger on the road.[105]

On 13 October the Grand Vizier finally granted Michael Apafi the permission to return home, and on 19 October they crossed the Tisa River at Szolnok and slowly continued their journey eastward. Following a different route, they reached the Ottoman fortress of Lipova on 30 October and crossed the border into Transylvania during the course of the following days. On 4 November the army was camped in the vicinity of Deva fortress.[106]

The campaigns of 1681–1683 are a clear indication of the political crisis that affected Transylvania during the second half of the seventeenth century. Barely able to muster 8,000 men, Prince Apafi acted as an obedient vassal of the sultan because he had no other choice. Transylvanian troops only played a marginal role in this campaign, acting as auxiliaries of the Ottoman army. After the siege of Vienna (1683), the Habsburgs gained the upper hand and gradually expanded their empire to the detriment of the Ottomans. When the Hapsburg expansion reached the borders of Transylvania a few years later, Apafi together with most of the local elite were ready to accept the political change.

---

104 MCRT, XVIII, pp.11–13.
105 Szabó, 'Splendid Isolation', pp.329–330.
106 MCRT, XVIII, pp.14–15.

Conclusion

For almost one and a half centuries (1541–1690), Transylvania was a distinct state on the maps of Early Modern Europe. The history of this small east-central European state was entangled with the Habsburg-Ottoman rivalry that for decades dominated the political situation in these parts of the continent. Over the course of the seventeenth century Transylvania did not just survive in the shadow of its imperial neighbours, it thrived and became a regional power.

Its armies were a constant threat for the Habsburgs during the Thirty Years' War. Gabriel Bethlen and George Rákóczi I led successful campaigns in the west, concluded advantageous peace treaties and expended their dominion over important territories in Eastern Hungary. By the middle of the century the military strength and political prestige of Transylvania was so great that its ruler was considered a suitable candidate for the Polish-Lithuanian throne. With a strong army and a vast diplomatic network, George Rákóczi II tried to take the throne through military strength but without the consent of the Ottomans. Although at the time the odds seemed to be in his favour, he miscalculated the reaction of his liège lord, the Sultan, who organised a massive punitive campaign against his disobedient vassal, and thus ended the 'golden age' of the Principality. The last decades of an autonomous Transylvania coincided roughly with the rule of Prince Michael Apafi I, who managed to restore stability in a country that had lost significant territories in just a few years. With the reduced resources at his disposal Apafi continued to play an important role in the region, as long as the balance of power between the two empires was maintained. When the Habsburgs gained the upper hand after they successfully defended Vienna in 1683, it was just a matter of time before they expanded their dominion over Transylvania.

Throughout the seventeenth century, the army of Transylvania was in an almost constant process of change and adaptation. The social background of those who performed military service was truly diverse. Some medieval military structures such as the noble and Székely levies or the peasant and Saxon militias were maintained but their role was less significant. The proportion of those who received regular or temporary wages was on the rise. *Hajdú* troops from the western borderland, soldiers from the court guard or those enlisted in the field army were paid for longer or shorter periods of time. In addition to local troops, the princes of Transylvania also recruited foreign mercenaries. Germans (infantry and dragoons) are among

CONCLUSION

the most numerous outsiders who joined the armed forces of the principality. They were usually included in the court army or in the permanent garrisons of borderland fortifications. Moldavians and Wallachians were also well represented among the foreigners who served in the Transylvanian army.

The cavalry represented the most important branch in the Transylvanian army. Throughout the seventeenth century, the proportion of mounted troops was extremely high, at between 50–78 percent. Transylvanian cavalry was very versatile and consisted mostly of light and semi-heavy riders. The lance, sabre, and long sword (*hegyestőr* or *pallos*) remained some of the most common offensive weapons, but firearms were also widely used.

The infantry was mostly regarded as an auxiliary element subservient to the mounted arm. Local levies were usually organised as light infantry detachments almost exclusively armed with gunpowder weapons. The recruitment of German infantry was an attempt to adapt to the latest standards of infantry warfare based on the use of heavy muskets and volley fire.

Artillery was deployed during sieges but also in pitched battles. The local foundry of Alba Iulia continued to provide a substantial number of medium and light cannons, but many artillery pieces were acquired abroad, either purchased or captured on campaign.

For defensive purposes, Transylvania relied on a good network of fortifications, most of them modernised according to the latest principles of military architecture. Fortresses were usually well provided with permanent garrisons, often reaching up to several hundred men, artillery arsenals and gunpowder supplies. Their capacity to resist was high, as shown by the example of Oradea fortress which held out for a 46-day siege in 1660 with a ratio of one defender for every 50 attackers. However, without help from the outside and dwindling food supplies, garrisons were eventually faced with the inevitability of not submitting and were forced to surrender.

The performance of the Transylvanian army on the battlefield varied greatly from one situation to another. While the participation of Gabriel Bethlen and George Rákóczi I in the Thirty Years' War is generally acknowledged as a remarkable success, their expeditions were not very spectacular in terms of military achievements. Nevertheless, the peace treaties concluded with the Habsburgs were very advantageous for Transylvania and thus we can conclude that both princes made excellent use of their armed forces by obtaining important political and material advantages with low military loses. Transylvanians, like most of their east-central European neighbours, were very proficient in irregular warfare. The high proportion of lightly armed cavalry favoured skirmishes and ambushes while large-scale pitched battles were usually avoided.

Most Transylvanian rulers from the seventeenth century strived to build up an efficient military system and they succeeded to a certain extent. The principality was able to muster a redoubtable army for such a modestly sized state, an army which had the power to upset or maintain the balance of power in the region. However, when Transylvania became the direct target of its imperial neighbours, its armed forces were simply overwhelmed. Both Ottomans and Habsburgs contributed to the fall of the autonomous principality. First the Ottomans seriously weakened their northern vassal through a devastating campaign meant to punish the rebel prince George Rákóczi II (1658–1660). Ironically, they had only paved the way for their rivals, the Habsburgs, who occupied Transylvania several decades later.

Colour Plate Commentaries

Plate A. Cavalryman from the guard of the Prince and a sub-captain of the court infantry (first half of the seventeenth century)

The court guard, with its cavalry and infantry detachments, constituted a core of professional soldiers in the army of the Principality of Transylvania. The number of soldiers employed in the personal retinue of the Prince increased during the reigns of Gabriel Bethlen (1613–1629) and George Rákóczi I (1630–1648), especially while Transylvania was involved in the Thirty Years' War. Mounted troops were mostly equipped as shock cavalry, with lances, sabres and long swords (*hegyestőr* or *pallos*) attached to the saddle of the horse. In addition, these elite cavalrymen also used firearms (especially pistols) for distance combat. As members of the princely banner they could afford expensive defensive equipment, consisting mostly of steel breastplates and *sisak* (lobster tail/zischägge) helmets. Some sources mention the custom of wearing animal pelts over the armour. In 1640, when the future Prince George Rákóczi II was appointed captain of Oradea, he entered the fortress in the company of 80 members of the court cavalry, among whom 23 were wearing tiger and leopard hides (…*aulicicirciter 80, ex quibus 23 pellibus tygridis et panterae seu leopardi vestiti*).

In 1630, Princess Catherin of Brandenburg, wife of the late Prince Gabriel Bethlen, issued a patent of nobility for Miklós Nagy, sub-captain of the guard infantry (…*certorum militum nostrorum peditum praetorianorum Vice Ductoris*). The coat of arms is considered an accurate representation of such an officer and forms the main source for the illustration. The sub-captain wears yellow riding boots, a red mantle (*mente*) and a blue dolman (*dolmány*), typical for the members of the infantry guard since the reign of Stephen Báthory (1571–1586). This is most probably ceremonial dress and his only weapons are a sabre and a mace. The mace is carried as a symbol of office, and was usually associated with leading positions in the military hierarchy.

Plate B. Mounted nobleman from the county banners (middle of the seventeenth century)

The obligation of the nobility to attend regular musters and participate in military campaigns was maintained throughout the seventeenth century. Following the medieval tradition, the nobility was expected to fight on horseback. Although many of the impoverished lesser nobles couldn't afford a war horse and the necessary equipment, the majority of the Transylvanian nobility was able to procure mounts and the typical weapons of the light cavalry: lance, sabre and long sword (*hegyestőr* or *pallos*). Gunpowder weapons, such as pistols, were also very common in this period. The Ottoman cultural influence can be observed in some of the typical clothes of a Transylvanian noble such as the embroidered dolman, the silk sash and the fur trimmed *mente*. The riding boots were usually brightly coloured in yellow or red (as in this case).

Plate C. Székely foot soldier (first half of the seventeenth century)

Foot soldiers (*pedites pixidari/gyalogpuskás*) were one of the groups within the Székely community who performed military service in exchange for tax exemptions. While nobles and leaders (*primipili/lófők*) formed cavalry units, those who could not afford war horses joined the ranks of the infantry. According to the muster lists issued in 1614, 3,546 men could have served in this capacity in the army of Prince Gabriel Bethlen. Although they were never fully mobilised, their numbers increased in the following decades in the context of the anti-Habsburg campaigns. They were light infantrymen armed with muskets, sabres and a hand axe with a long wooden shaft (*fokos*).

Plate D. A Wallachian *seimen* in the service of Prince Michael Apafi (1661–1690)

Inspired by the Ottoman *seğban* infantry, *seimenii* were initially Balkan mercenaries in the service of Wallachian and Moldavian rulers. In the second half of the seventeenth century some of them were employed in Transylvania. During the long reign of Prince Michael Apafi (1661–1690), a small unit of such mercenaries, between 27 and 79 men, served in the court army. Some contemporary observers compared them to Ottoman janissaries. They wore baggy trousers, long fur hats and were armed with sabres and long Turkish muskets. It is noteworthy that they received the highest monthly wage (5 florins) in the princely guard which at the time also included German, Polish and Hungarian soldiers.

COLOUR PLATE COMMENTARIES

Plate E. Young Transylvanian nobleman from the court guard (middle of the seventeenth century)

The sons of prominent noble families were sent to the court for education and as a sign of loyalty to the ruling prince. In some documents they are presented as a distinct group, the court youth (*udvariifjak*), within the mounted guard of the prince. They served as cavalry and were sometimes accompanied by mounted servants. The Saxon chronicler, Georg Kraus, mentions that these young nobles often indulged in debauchery and were a bad example to the young Prince George Rákóczi II. They wore wolf pelts as a distinctive adornment and were armed with sabres and maces. Towards the second half of the seventeenth century, the mace was perceived as a symbol of social status rather than a sign of military office.

Plate F. A Green Rifleman (middle of the seventeenth century)

The Green Riflemen were initially organised as an elite group of sharpshooters by Prince George Rákóczi I (1630–1648) who had a great passion for hunting. They were considered as part of the court guard but they resided on the various estates of the princely family (Chioar, Iernut, Gilău, Gherla and Alba Iulia). During the reign of the Rákóczi family, their numbers varied between 60 and 300 men. Their distinctive clothing was a green dolman. All of them had good quality weapons, and the rifleman shown in the illustration is armed with an expensive Teschen rifle.

Plate G. A 'carbine cavalryman' from the guard of Prince Michael Apafi I (1661–1690)

Throughout the seventeenth century, most mounted soldiers in the Transylvanian army carried firearms, and pistols were used as secondary weapons, even by lancers and other types of shock cavalry. Carbines (*karabély*) were particularly commonly used in the second half of the seventeenth century and Prince Michael Apafi I organised a distinct unit, armed with such weapons, in his mounted guard. It was a small group of 75 men within a detachment of 588 men, dominated by lancers. However, those who served in the 'carbine cavalry' unit (*karabélyosok*) received the highest wages among the Prince's mounted troops.

Plate H. German Mercenary in the Army of Transylvania (first half of the seventeenth century)

In the seventeenth century, Transylvanian rulers hired a significant number of German mercenaries to compensate for the lack of an efficient local infantry. Gabriel Bethlen was the first to organise a regiment of German infantry during his campaigns against the Habsburgs in the Thirty Years' War. Later, they were settled on an estate of the Prince and continued to serve in the court guard. Armed with heavy muskets and accustomed to 'volley fire' tactics, German mercenaries were very much appreciated within the principality. During the second half of the seventeenth century many soldiers of German origin were employed in the garrison of border fortifications in addition to the locally recruited soldiers.

Bibliography

Archival Sources

Magyar Nemzeti Levéltár Országos Levéltára (MNL OL), F 7 Armales.
Magyar Nemzeti Levéltár Országos Levéltára (MNL OL), Gyulafehérvári Káptalan Levéltára, Lymbus.
Magyar Nemzeti Levéltár Országos Levéltára (MNL OL), Urbaria et Conscriptiones, E 156 – a.
Serviciul Județean al Arhivelor Naționale, Cluj (SJAN CJ), Colecția socoteli princiare, 46 Evidențe nominale de efective militare.

Edited sources

Apor of Altorja, Péter, *Metamorphosis Transylvaniae* (translated by Bernard Adams), (London and New York: Routledge, 2010).
Bethlen, Nicolae, *Descrierea vieții sale de către el însuși* (Cluj-Napoca: Casa Cărții de Știință, 2004).
Călători străini despre Țările Române, vol. V, Maria Holban, Maria Matilda Alexandrescu-Dresca Bulgaru, Paul Cernovodeanu (eds.), (București: Editura Științifică și Enciclopedică, 1973).
Chronicon Fuchsio-Lupino-Oltardinum sive annales Hungarici et Transsilvanici, vol. I, (ed.) Josephus Trausch, (Coronae: Impressum per Johanne Gött, 1847).
Costin, Miron, *Opere*, edited by Petre P. Panaitescu (București: Editura pentru Literatură, 1965).
Dáné, Veronka, (ed.), *Torda vármegye jegyzőkönyvei 1607–1658*, vol. I (Cluj-Napoca: Societatea Muzeului Ardelean, 2009).
Demény, Lajos (ed.), *Székely oklevéltár. Új sorozat 4. Székely népesség-összeírások*, 1575–1627 (Kolozsvár: Az Erdélyi Múzeum-Egyesület Kiadása, 1997).
Demény, Lajos (ed.), *Székely oklevéltár. Új sorozat 5. Székely népesség-összeírások, 1635* (Kolozsvár: Az Erdélyi Múzeum-Egyesület Kiadása, 1997).
Enyedi, István, 'II Rákóczi György veszedelméről 1657–1660', in *Erdély történelmi adatok*, IV (Kolozsvár: nyomatott az ev. ref. főtanoda betüivel, 1862).
Herlea, Alexandru, Marcu, Liviu (eds.), *Constituțiile Aprobate ale Transilvaniei (1653)* (Cluj-Napoca: Editura Dacia, 1997).
de Hurmuzaki Eudoxiu, *Documente privitoare la Istoria Românilor*, Vol. V/ Part 2, (București: Ministerul Cultelor și Instrucțiunii Publice și Academia Română, 1886).
de Hurmuzaki, Eudoxiu, *Documente privitoare la Istoria Românilor*, vol. IX/ Part 1 (București: Ministerul Cultelor și Instrucțiunii Publice și Academia Română, 1897).

Iorga, Nicolae (ed.), *Documente privitoare la Istoria Românilor*, (Hurmuzaki collection) vol. XV/2 (București: Academia Română și Ministerul Cultelor și Instrucțiunii Publice, 1913).

Kármán, Gábor (ed.), *The Correspondance of the Beylerbeys of Buda 1617–1630* (Budapest-Szeged: Research Centre for the Humanities, Institute of History, 2022).

Kemény, Ioan, *Memorii (1607–1662)* (Cluj-Napoca: Casa Cărții de Știință, 2002).

Kemény, János, 'Ruina exercitus Transylvaniae,' in Éva V. Windisch (ed.), *Kemény János és Bethlen Miklós művei – Magyar Remekírók* (Budapest: Szépirodalmi Könyvkiadó, 1980), pp.314–321.

Koncz, Jozef, 'Magyar hadi szabályzatok gyüjteménye. Hadi edictum Kővár vára részére 1665-ből', *Hadtörténelmi Közlemények*, IV (1891), pp.429–434.

Lupaș, Ioan, *Documente istorice transilvane, 1599–1699* (Cluj: Cartea Românească, 1940).

Mihăilescu, Ștefania Gáll (ed.), *Memorialul lui Nagy Szabó Ferencz din Târgu Mureș (1580–1658)* (București: Kriterion, 1993).

Nagy, Margit, *Várak, kastélyok, udvarházak, ahogy a régiek látták: XVII–XVIII. századi erdélyi összeírások és leltárak* (București: Kriterion, 1973).

Szádeczky, Béla, *I Apafi Mihály fejedelem udvartartása. Bornemisza Anna gazdasági naplói*, (Budapest: Magyar Tudományos Akadémia könyvkiadóhivatala, 1911).

Szádeczky, Lajos (ed.), *Székely oklevéltár*, vol. VI (Kolozsvár: Magyar Történelmi Társulat Kolozsvári Bizottsága, 1897).

Szilády Áron, Szilágyi Sándor (eds.), *Török-Magyarkori Állam-Okmánytár I. Török-Magyarkori történelmi emlékek. Okmánytár*, III (Pest: Eggenberger, 1868).

Szilágyi, Alexander, *Transsylvania et Bellum Boreo-Orientale: Acta et Documenta*, vol. II (Budapest: Magyar Tudományos Akadémia, 1891).

Szilágyi, Sándor (ed.), *Monumenta Comitialia Regni Transylvaniae*, vol. I-XXI (Budapest: Magyar Tudományos Akad. Könyvkiadó Hivatala, 1875–1898).

Tocilescu, Grigore G., Odobescu, Alexandru I., (eds.), *Documente privitoare la Istoria Românilor* (Hurmuzaki collection), vol. I/Supplement I (București: Ministerul Cultelor și Instrucțiunii Publice și Academia Română, 1886).

Ursuțiu, Liviu, *Domeniul Gurghiu (1652–1706): Urbarii, inventare și socoteli economice* (Cluj-Napoca: Argonaut, 2006).

Ursuțiu, Maria (ed.) *Rétyi Péter Naplója (1645–1674)* (București: Kriterion Könyvkiadó, 1983).

Veress, Andrei (ed.), *Documente privitoare la istoria Ardealului, Moldovei și Țării Românești, Acte și scrisori*, vol. XI (București, M.O. Imprimeria Națională, 1937).

Monographs and Articles

Andea, Susana, 'Evoluții politice în secolul al XVII-lea. De la Ștefan Bocskai la Mihail Apafi', in Ioan-Aurel Pop, Thomas Nägler, András Magyari (eds.), *The History of Transylvania*, vol. II (Cluj-Napoca: Centre for Transylvanian Studies. Romanian Cultural Institute, 2009).

Andea, Susana, *Transilvania, Țara Românească și Moldova. Legături politice (1656–1688)* (Cluj-Napoca: Presa Universitară Clujeană, 1996).

Anghel, Gheorghe, *Cetăți medievale din Transilvania* (București: Editura Meridiane, 1972).

Ardelean, Florin Nicolae, 'Evoluția funcției de căpitan general în Transilvania la sfârșitul secolului al XVI-lea și începutul secolului al XVII-lea', *Banatica*, 28 (2018), pp.561–582.

Ardelean, Florin Nicolae, 'Military Justice, Regulations and Discipline in Early Modern Transylvanian Armies (XVI-XVII centuries)', *Studia Universitas Cibiniensis, Series Historica* VIII/1 (2011), pp.183–189.

Ardelean, Florin Nicolae, *On the Borderlands of Great Empires: Transylvanian Armies (1541 1613)* (Warwick: Helion & Company, 2022).

Ardelean, Florin Nicolae, *Organizarea militară în Principatul Transilvaniei (1541–1691): Comitate și domenii fisclae* (Cluj-Napoca: Editura Academia Română. Centrul de Studii Transilvane, 2019).

Ardelean, Florin Nicolae, 'Piety, morality and discipline in the military regulations of the Transylvanian principality (1577–1683)', Ulrich A. Wien (ed.), *Common Man, Society and Religion in the 16th century/Gemeiner Mann, Gesellschaft und Religion im 16. Jahrhundert Piety, morality and discipline in the Carpathian Basin/Frömmigkeit, Moral und Sozialdisziplinierung im Karpatenbogen* (Göttingen: Vandenhoeck & Ruprecht, 2021), pp.263–275.

Ardelean, Florin Nicolae, 'Seimeni în slujba principilor Transilvaniei în a doua jumătate a secolului XVII', *Banatica* 22 (2012), pp.119–134.

Ardelean, Florin Nicolae, 'Steaguri de mercenari străini la curtea lui Mihail Apafi (1663–1684)', *Anuarul Institutului de Istorie «George Barițiu» din Cluj-Napoca*, LI (2012), pp.69–79.

Ardelean, Florin Nicolae, 'Political Boundaries and Territorial Identity in Early Modern Central Europe: The Western Frontier of Transylvania during the Sixteenth Century', *Territorial Identity and Development*, 6/1 (2021), pp.21–38.

Ardelean, Florin Nicolae, 'War and Social Conflicts in Early Modern Border Areas: Colonel Ludovicus de La Borde and Satu Mare (*Szatmár*) Frotress (1673–1677)', *Hiperboreea*, vol. 8, no.1 (2021), pp.16–38.

Ardelean, Florin Nicolae, Ciure, Florina, 'Guerra e diplomazia nella Transilvania dell'anno 1625. Da un documento dell'Archivio di Stato di Venezia', *Studia Historica Adriatica ac Danubiana*, X, 1–2 (2017), pp.68–93.

Ardelean, Livia, 'Gabriel Bethlen și politica economică și militară față de comitatul Maramureș', Veronka Dáné et al. (eds.), *Bethlen Erdélye, Erdély Bethlene: Bethlen Gábor trónra lépésének 400. évfordulóján rendezett konferencia tanulmányai: 24–25 október 2013, Kolozsvár* (Cluj-Napoca: Societatea Muzeului Ardelean, 2014), pp.509–516.

Balogh, Judith, *A székely nemesség kialakulásának folyamata a 17. század első felében* (Kolozsvár: Az Erdélyi Múzeum-Egyesület Kiadása, 2005).

Black, Jeremy, *European Warfare 1494–1660* (London: Routledge, 2002).

Borcea, Liviu, 'Contribuții la istoria campaniei militare turco-tătare în Transilvania (august-octombrie 1658)', *Crisia*, XV (1985), pp.97–118.

Borcea, Liviu, 'Contribuții la istoria cetății Săcuieni (comitatul Bihor) în secolele XV-XVII', Anuarul *Institutului de Istorie și Arheologie din Cluj-Napoca*, 26 (1983–1984), pp.319–332.

Borcea, Liviu, *Cronica de jale a lui Ioan Szalárdi: studiu critic* (Oradea: Arca, 2007).

Borosy, András, 'The Militia Portalis in Hungary before 1526', in János M. Bak, Béla K. Király (eds.), *From Hunyadi to Rakoczi. War and Society in Late Medieval and Early Modern Hungary* (New York: Columbia University Press, 1982), pp.63–80.

Bulboacă, Sorin, 'Acațiu Barcsai de Bârcea Mare, ultimul ban al Lugojului și Caransebeșului (24 decembrie 1644–14 septembrie 1658)', *Banatica*, 6 (2011), pp.105–114.

Bunta, Magdalena, 'Habanii în Transilvania', *Acta Musei Napocensis* VII (1970), pp.201–225.

Burai, Adalbert, 'Despre cetatea de tip italian din Satu Mare', *Studii și Comunicări. Satu Mare* I (1969), pp.143–160.

Cervioğlu, Mahmut Halef, 'Ottoman Foreign Policy during the Thirty Years' War', *Turcica*, 49 (2018), pp.195–235.

Cevrioğlu, Mahmut Halef, 'Sultan Murad IV's Polish Campaign (1634)', *Acta Poloniae Historica*, 122 (2020), pp.209–246.

Cîmpeanu, Liviu, 'The Transylvanian-Saxon University at War: Trabanten in John Sigismund Szapolyai's Campaigns at the North-Western Borders of Transylvania (1561–1567)', *Acta Musei Napocensis*, 58/II (2021), pp.11–29.

Cîmpeanu, Liviu, *Universitatea Saxonă din Transilvania și districtele românești aflate sub jurisdicția ei în evul mediu și epoca modernă* (Târgu Mureș: Editura Nico, 2014).

Constantinov, Valentin, *Țara Moldovei în cadrul relațiilor internaționale (1611–1634)* (Iași: Demiurg, 2014).

Costea, Ionuț, *Solam virtutem et nomen bonum: Nobilitate, Etnie, Regionalism în Transilvania Princiară* (Cluj-Napoca: Argonaut, 2005).

Crăciun, Ioachim, 'Răzvrătirea sașilor din Brașov la 1688', *Studii și Materiale de Istorie Medie*, I (1956), pp.199–211.

Czigány, István, 'The 1644–1645 Campaign of György Rákóczi I', Gábor Kármán (ed.), *The Princes of Transylvania in the Thirty Years' War* (Paderborn: Brill Schöningh, 2022), pp.86–112.

Cziráki, Zsuzsanna, 'Brassói és barcasági katonák Bethlen Gábor hadseregében,' *Belvedere Meridionale* XXII, 3–4, (2010), pp.86–102.

Dáné, Veronka, *"mennyi jobbágya és mennyi portiója." Torda vármegye birtokos társadalma a 17. Század első felében* (Cluj-Napoca: Societatea Muzeului Ardelean, 2016).

Demény, Lidia, Demény, Lajos, Stoicescu, Nicolae, *Răscoala seimenilor sau răscoală populară?* (București: Editura Științifică, 1968).

Demény, Ludovic, 'Registrele militare – izvoare de demografie istorică și de cercetare a structurii sociale la secuii din secolul al XVI-lea', *Sub semnul lui Clio. Omagiu Acad. Prof. Ștefan Pascu* (Cluj: Universitatea Babeș-Bolyai, 1974).

Derzsi, Julia, *Delict și pedeapsă: Justiție penală în orașele săsești din Transilvania în secolul al XVI-lea* (Cluj-Napoca: Egyetemi Műhely, 2022).

Domokos, György, 'A kassai királyi hadszertár fegyverzete és felszerelése a XVI-XVII. században az inventáriumok tükrében', *Hadtörténelmi Közlemények*,110/4 (1997), pp.667–749.

Duffy, Christopher, *Siege Warfare: The Fortress in the Early Modern World 1494–1660* (London: Routledge & Kegan Paul, 1979).

Feneșan, Cristina, 'Transilvania și Războiul de treizeci de ani,' *Anuarul Institutului de Istorie și Arheologie*, Cluj-Napoca, no. 26 (1983–1984), pp.119–141.

Feneșan-Bulgaru, Cristina, 'Problema instaurării dominației otomane asupra Banatului Lugojului și Caransebeșului', *Banatica*, IV (1977), pp.223–238.

Gálfi, Emőke, 'A gyulafehérvári udvarbírák és területi hatáskörük Bethlen Gábor uralkodásának első szakaszában', Veronka Dáné et al. (eds.), *Bethlen Erdélye, Erdély Bethlene: Bethlen Gábor trónra lépésének 400. évfordulóján rendezett konferencia tanulmányai: 24–25 október 2013, Kolozsvár* (Cluj-Napoca: Societatea Muzeului Ardelean, 2014), pp.319–327.

Gebei, Sándor, 'II. Rákóczi György lengyelországi hadjárata, 1657', *Hadtörténelmi Közlemények* 105/2 (1992), pp.30–64.

Glück, Eugen, 'Contribuții cu privire la istoricul cetății de la Ineu', *Ziridava*, XIII (1981), pp.131–147.

Gyulai, Paul, 'Inventarul cetății Oradea la 1632', *Acta Musei Napocensis*, X (1973), pp.665–673.

Harai, Dénes, *Gabriel Bethlen: Prince de Transylvanie et roi élu de Hongrie (1580–1629)* (Paris: L'Harmattan, 2013).

Hámori Nagy, Zsuzsanna, 'Transylvania and France in the Thirty Years' War: The Origins of a Treaty,' Gábor Kármán (ed.), *The Princes of Transylvania in the Thirty Years' War* (Paderborn: Brill Schöningh, 2022), pp.199–230.

Hausner, Gábor, 'Bethlen Gábor erdélyi fejedelem hadi edictuma,' *Hadtörténelmi Közlemények*, 124, 2–3 (2001), pp.469–485.

Horn, Ildikó, 'The Princely Council in the Age of Gábor Bethlen,' *Hungarian Historical Review* 2, no. 4, (2013), pp.824–855.

Hossu, Valer, *Nobilimea Chioarului* (Baia Mare: Biblioteca Județeană 'Petre Dulfu', 2003).

Izsán, Csaba, 'A zsoldos darabontok számadásai és a város védműveinek javítási költségei Kolozsvár 17. századi számadáskönyveiben', Áron Tőtős et al. (eds.) *Ezerarcú Erdély. Politika, társadalom, kultúra* (Kolozsvár: Erdélyi Múzeum-Egyesület, 2019), pp.337–352.

Izsán, Csaba, 'Between Soldier and Guard: the Roles of the Town Mercenaries in the Late Sixteenth–Early Seventeenth Century Cluj (Klausenburg/Kolozsvár), Sighișoara

(Schässburg/ Segesvár) and Brașov (Kronstadt/Brassó)', Florin Nicolae Ardelean et al. (eds.), *From Medieval Frontiers to Early Modern Borders in Central and South-East Europe* (Berlin: Peter Lang, 2022), pp.191–206.

Jármy, József, 'II. Rákóczy György szász-fenesi csatája, megsebesülésének és halálának körülményei. (Második és befejező közlemény.),' *Erdélyi Múzeum* 19/4 (1902), pp.221–235.

Jeney-Tóth, Annamária, „... *Urunk udvarnépe ...": Udvar és társadalma Báthory Gábor és Bethlen Gábor fejedelemsége idején a kolozsvári számadáskönyvek tükrében* (Debrecen: Debreceni Egyetemi Kiadó, 2012).

Jörgensen, Christer, Pavkovic, Michael F., Rice, Rob S., Schneid, Frederick C., Scott, Christopher L., *Fighting Techniques of the Early Modern World. AD 1500 ~ AD 1763: Equipment, Combat Skills, and Tactics* (New York: Thomas Dunne Books, St. Martin's Press, 2005).

Kármán, Gábor, *Confession and Politics in the Principality of Transylvania 1644–1657* (Göttingen: Vandenhoek&Ruprecht, 2020).

Kármán, Gábor, 'György Rákóczi II's Attempt to Establish a Local Power Base among the Tributaries of the Ottoman Empire 1653–1657', in ed. Maria Baramova et al. (eds.), Power *and Influence in South-Eastern Europe, 16th–19th Century* (Zürich: Lit, 2013), pp.229–244.

Kármán, Gábor, 'Külföldi diplomaták Bethlen Gábor szolgálatában,' Gábor Kármán, Kees Teszelszky (eds.), *Bethlen Gábor és Európa* (Budapest: ELTE BTK Középkori és Kora Újkori Magyar Történeti Tanszéke and the Transylvania Emlékeiért Tudományos Egyesület, 2013) pp.145–183.

Kármán, Gábor, 'The Thorny Path to an Uneasy Alliance: Transylvanian–Swedish Negotiations 1626–1643', Gábor Kármán (ed.), *The Princes of Transylvania in the Thirty Years' War* (Paderborn: Brill Schöningh, 2022), pp.154–199.

Kenyeres, István, 'The Fiscal Capacity and War Expenses of Transylvania and the Habsburg Monarchy during the Rules of Gábor Bethlen and Ferdinand II: A Comparison,' Gábor Kármán (ed.), *The Princes of Transylvania in the Thirty Years' War* (Paderborn: Brill Schöningh, 2022), pp.112–130.

Keul, István, *Early Modern Religious Communities in East-Central Europe: Ethnic Diversity, Denominational Plurality and Corporative Politics in the Principality of Transylvania (1526–1691)* (Leiden, Boston: Brill, 2009).

Kolçak, Özgür, 'A Transylvanian Ruler in the Talons of the 'Hawks': György Rákóczi II and Köprülü Mehmet Pasha,' Florentina Nițu et. al. (eds.) *Turkey & Romania: A History of Partnership and Collaboration in the Balkans* (Istanbul: Union of Turkish World Municipalities: Istanbul University, 2016), pp.341–359.

Kosáry, Dominic, 'Gabriel Bethlen: Transylvania in the XVIIth century,' *The Slavonic and East European Review*, vol. 17, no. 49 (1938), pp.162–173.

Kovács, András, 'Gábor Bethlen and the Construction of the New Seat of the Transylvanian Princedom,' *Hungarian Historical Review*, 2, no.4 (2013), pp.880–900.

Kovács, Klára, *Cetatea din Gherla. Răspândirea fortificației în sistem bastionar italian în Transilvania* (Cluj-Napoca: Phd. Thesis, Babeș-Bolyai University, 2009).

Kovács, Klára, 'Fortresses-Building in 16th Century Transylvania. The Recruitment of Labor Force,' *Transylvanian Review*, Vol. XXI, Supplement No. 2 (2012), pp.163–181.

Krcho, János, 'Standing watch in Kassa' City Walls and Watchtowers and their Phases of Construction,' *Periodica Polytechnica Ser. Architecture*, 36/1–4 (1992), pp.189–213.

Kropf, Lajos, 'Bethlen Gábor lovassága a fehérhegyi csatában, 1620', *Hadtörténelmi Közlemények*, XI (1910), pp.460–461.

Lázár, Miklós, 'Kolos-vármegye 1634-iki lustrája', *Magyar Történelmi tár*, 3/1 (1878), pp.198–204.

Lockhart, Paul Douglas, *Denmark, 1513–1660: the rise and decline of a Renaissance monarchy* (Oxford: Oxford University Press, 2007).

Lupescu, Radu, 'The medieval fortifications of Sibiu,' Olaf Wagener (ed.), „*vmbringt mit starcken turnen, murn ". Ortsbefestigungen im Mittelalter* (Frankfurt am Main: Peter Lang, 2010), pp.351–362.

Magina, Adrian, 'Conscripția și inventarul bunurilor cetății Ineu în anul 1605', *Banatica* 21 (2011), pp.90–104.

Magina, Adrian, 'Înnobilările din Lugoj în secolul al XVII-lea,' Ligia Boldea, Rudolf Gräf (eds.), *Vocația istoriei: Studii în memoria profesorului Nicolae Bocșan* (Cluj-Napoca: Mega, 2017), pp.81–90.

Magina, Livia, 'Cross-Border Mobility: War Refugees in early Modern Transylvania,' Florin Nicolae Ardelean et al. (eds.), *From Medieval Frontiers to Early Modern Borders in Central and South-East Europe* (Berlin: Peter Lang, 2022), pp.95–114.

Magina, Livia, 'Rezerve de alimente în cetățile Principatului Transilvaniei,' Zeno Karl Pinter, Anca Nițoi, Claudia Urduzia (eds.), *Relații interetnice în Transilvania: Militaria Medievalia în Europa Centrală și de Sud-Vest* (Sibiu: Astra Museum, 2018), pp.179–186.

Michels, Georg B., *The Habsburg Empire under siege: Ottoman expansion and Hungarian revolt in the age of Grand Vizier Ahmed Köprülü (1661-1676)* (Montreal: McGill-Queen's University Press, 2021).

Neagoe, Claudiu, *Seimenii în Țările Române: Contribuții la istoria organizării militare a românilor în secolele XVII–XVIII* (București: Ars Docendi, 2017).

Neagoe, Claudiu, Peligrad, Costin, 'Lupta de la Șoplea, pe Teleajen (16/27 iunie 1655)', *Revista de Istorie Militară*, 5–6 (2019), pp.1–16.

Németh, Michał, 'Remarks on the etymology of Hung. hajdú 'herdsman' and Tkc. haydamak 'brigand,' *Studia Turcologica Cracoviensia*, 10 (2005), pp.297–309.

Oborni, Teréz, 'Gábor Bethlen and the Treaty of Nagyszombat (1615)', *Hungarian Historical Review* 2, no. 4, (2013), pp.761–789.

Olchváry, Ödön, 'Bethlen Gábor hadseregének szervezete s hadviselési módszere a II. Ferdinánd ellen viselt háborúkban,' *Hadtörténelmi Közlemények*, I (1881), pp.601–616.

Olchváry, Ödön, 'Bethlen Gábor első támadása II. Ferdinánd,' *Hadtörténelmi Közlemények*, III (1890), pp.333–360, pp.528–562.

Ostapchuk, Victor, 'Cossack Ukrain in and out of the Ottoman Orbit, 1648-1681', in Gábor Kármán, Lovro Kunčević, (ed.), *The European Tributary States of the Ottoman Empire in the Sixteenth and Seventeenth Centuries* (Leiden and Boston: Brill, 2013), pp.123–152.

Pakucs-Willcocks, Mária, 'From "old" fashion to "new" fashion in pre-modern Transylvania,' in Constanța Vintilă et al. (eds.), *Luxury, Fashion and other Political Bagatelles in Southeastern Europe 16th–19th Century* (București: Humanitas, 2022), pp.357–365.

Pálffy, Géza, *Hungary between Two Empires (1526-1711)* (Bloomington: Indiana University Press, 2021).

Pálffy, Géza, 'The Kingdom of Hungary in the Thirty Years' War,' Gábor Kármán (ed.), *The Princes of Transylvania in the Thirty Years' War* (Paderborn: Brill Schöningh, 2022), pp.1–21.

Pálffy, Géza, 'The Origins and Development of the Border Defence System against the Ottoman Empire in Hungary (Up to the Early Eighteenth Century),' Géza Dávid, Pál Fodor (eds.), *Ottomans, Hungarians and Habsburgs in Central Europe: The Military Confines in the Era of Ottoman Conquest* (Leiden: Brill, 2000), pp.3–71.

Papp, Klára, 'Várad, Debrecen és Kassa szerepe Bethlen Gábor fejedelemsége idején,' Veronka Dáné et al. (eds.), *Bethlen Erdélye, Erdély Bethlene: Bethlen Gábor trónra lépésének 400. évfordulóján rendezett konferencia tanulmányai: 24–25 október 2013, Kolozsvár* (Cluj-Napoca: Societatea Muzeului Ardelean, 2014), pp.537–548.

Parker, Geoffrey, *The Thirty Years' War* (London: Routledge, 2006).

Pavelesco, Eugène, *Georges II Rákoczy Prince de Transylvanie (1648-1660). Essai sur sa politique extériure* (Iași: «Versuri și Proză», 1924).

Péter, Katalin, 'The Golden Age of the Principality (1606-1660)', in László Makkai, Zoltán Szász (eds.), *History of Transylvania*, vol. II (New York: Columbia University Press, 2002).

Péter, Katalin, 'Two Aspects of War and Society in the Age of Prince Gábor Bethlen of Transylvania,' János M. Bak, Béla K. Király (eds.) *From Hunyadi to Rákóczi. War and Society in Late Medieval and Early Modern Hungary* (New York: Columbia University Press, 1982), pp.297–315.

Prodan, David, 'Boieri şi vecini în Ţara Făgăraşului în sec. XVI-XVII,' *Din istoria Transilvaniei. Studii şi evocări* (Bucureşti: Editura Enciclopedică, 1991).

Prodan, David, *Iobăgia în secolul al XVII-lea*, vol. II (Bucureşti: Editura Ştiinţifică şi Enciclopedică, 1987).

Radvánszky, Béla, *Udvartartás és számadáskönyvek. I. Bethlen Gábor udvartartása* (Budapest: Atheneum, 1888).

Rezachevici, Constantin, 'Efectivele oştilor din Ţara Românească şi Moldova în veacul al XVII-lea,' *Studii şi Materiale de Muzeografie şi Istorie Militară*, nr. 6, (1973).

Rusu, Gabriel-Virgil, 'O mărturie documentară despre Cetatea Gherla la 1675,' *Studia Universitatis Babes-Bolyai – Historia*, 1–2 (2003), pp.65–94.

Seres, István, 'Bethlen Gábor hadainak szállás- és hadrendje 1621-ből: Újabb források az erdélyi hadsereg történetéhez,' *Hadtörténelmi Közlemények*, 126/4 (2013), pp.1,050–1,066.

Sima, Claudia, 'Arsenalul militar al cetăţii Făgăraş din secolul al XVII-lea,' *Acta Terrae Fogarasiensis*, VIII (2019), pp.73–81.

Stoicescu, Nicolae, *Curteni şi slujitori: Contribuţii la istoria armatei române* (Bucureşti: Editura Militară, 1968).

Stoicescu, Nicolae, *Matei Basarab* (Bucureşti: Editura Academiei Republicii Socialiste România, 1988).

Sudár, Balázs, 'Ottoman Auxiliary Troops in Gábor Bethlen's Armies 1619–1626,' Gábor Kármán (ed.), *The Princes of Transylvania in the Thirty Years' War* (Paderborn: Brill Schöningh, 2022), pp.130–154.

Szabó, András Péter, 'A besztercei levéltár jegyzékei az erdélyi fejedelmi udvarról (1636–1659),' *Lymbus* (2016), pp.67–122.

Szabó, János B., 'A székelyek katonai szerpe Erdélyben a mohácsi csatától a Habsburg uralom megszilárdulásáig (1526–1709),' in József Nagy (ed.), *A Határvédelem évszázadai Székelyföldön: Csíkszék és a Gyimesek vidéke. Szerkesztette és a jegyzékeket összeállította* (Szépvíz, 2018), pp.101–153.

Szabó, János B., 'Asedierea cetăţii Oradea de către tătari şi turci 1658, 1660,' Teréz Oborni (ed.), *"Oradea cum e ocrotită": Lupte pentru Oradea în epoca modernă timpurie. Studii despre istoria Ţării Bihorului* 7 (Oradea: Fundaţia Culturală Varadinum, 2020), pp.133–151.

Szabó, János B., 'Bethlen Gábor, az újjászervező. A kora újkori hadügyi fejlődés Kelet-Közép-Európában: az Erdélyi Fejedelemség példája a XVII. század első felében (1. rész),' *Hadtörténelmi Közlemények*, 126/4 (2013), pp.963–988.

Szabó, János B., 'Bethlen Gábor, az újjászervező. A kora újkori hadügyi fejlődés Kelet-Közép-Európában: az Erdélyi Fejedelemség példája a XVII. század első felében (2. rész),' Hadtörténelmi Közlemények, 127/1 (2014), pp.41–76.

Szabó, János B., *Erdély Tragédiája 1657–1662* (Budapest: Corvina, 2019).

Szabó, János B., 'Gábor Bethlen's Armies in the Thirty Years' War,' Gábor Kármán (ed.), *The Princes of Transylvania in the Thirty Years' War* (Paderborn: Brill Schöningh, 2022), pp.58–86.

Szabó, János B., '„Sors bona nihil aliud" Az 1657. évi erdélyi 'Blitzkrieg' kudarca Lengyelországban,' Ildikó Horn et al (eds.), *Művészet és mesterség: tisztelgő kötet R. Várkonyi Ágnes emlékére* (Budapest: L'Harmattan, 2016), pp.231–250.

Szabó, János B., 'Splendid Isolation? The Military Cooperation of the Principality of Transylvania with the Ottoman Empire (1571–1688) in the Mirror of the Hungarian Historiography's Dilemmas', in Gábor Kármán, Lovro Kunčević, (ed.), *The European Tributary States of the Ottoman Empire in the Sixteenth and Seventeenth Centuries* (Leiden and Boston: Brill, 2013), pp.301–339.

Szabó, János B., 'The Army of the Principality of Transylvania in the Period of the Thirty Years' War,' Gábor Kármán (ed.), *The Princes of Transylvania in the Thirty Years' War* (Paderborn: Brill Schöningh, 2022), pp.21–58.

Szalai, Ágnes, '"Aceasta fiind cetate de graniță în locul Oradiei...": Rolul guvernământului princiar în cadrul tratativelor referitoare la cetatea de graniță Săcueni,' Teréz Oborni (ed.), *"Oradea cum e ocrotită": Lupte pentru Oradea în epoca modernă timpurie. Studii despre istoria Țării Bihorului* 7 (Oradea: Fundația Culturală Varadinum, 2020), pp.151–184.

Szilágyi, Sándor, 'Az erdély 1681-ik hadjárat előkészületéinek történetéhez', *Hadtörténelmi Közlemények*, vol. IV, (1891), pp.415–420.

Várkonyi, Ágnes, 'Historical Personality, Crisis and Progress in 17th Century Hungary', Etudes Historiques, Budapest (1970), pp.265–299.

Volkmer, Gerald, *Siebenbürgen zwischen Habsburgermonarchie und Osmanischem Reich. Völkerrechtliche Stellung und Völkerrechtspraxis eines ostmitteleuropäischen Fürstentums 1541 – 1699* (München: De Gruyter Oldenburg, 2015).

Wittman, Tibor, *Bethlen Gábor* (Budapest: Magyar Történelmi Társulat, 1952).

Zahariuc, Petronel, *Țara Moldovei în vremea lui Gheorghe Ștefan voievod (1653–1658)* (Iași: Editura Universității Al. I. Cuza, 2003).

Other titles in the Century of the Soldier series

No 24 *The Last Army: The Battle of Stow-on-the-Wold and the End of the Civil War in the Welsh Marches, 1646*

No 25 *The Battle of the White Mountain 1620 and the Bohemian Revolt, 1618–22*

No 26 *The Swedish Army in the Great Northern War 1700–21: Organisation, Equipment, Campaigns and Uniforms*

No 27 *St. Ruth's Fatal Gamble: The Battle of Aughrim 1691 and the Fall Of Jacobite Ireland*

No 28 *Muscovy's Soldiers: The Emergence of the Russian Army 1462–1689*

No 29 *Home and Away: The British Experience of War 1618–1721*

No 30 *From Solebay to the Texel: The Third Anglo-Dutch War, 1672–1674*

No 31 *The Battle of Killiecrankie: The First Jacobite Campaign, 1689–1691*

No 32 *The Most Heavy Stroke: The Battle of Roundway Down 1643*

No 33 *The Cretan War (1645–1671): The Venetian-Ottoman Struggle in the Mediterranean*

No 34 *Peter the Great's Revenge: The Russian Siege of Narva in 1704*

No 35 *The Battle Of Glenshiel: The Jacobite Rising in 1719*

No 36 *Armies And Enemies Of Louis XIV: Volume 1 - Western Europe 1688–1714: France, Britain, Holland*

No 37 *William III's Italian Ally: Piedmont and the War of the League of Augsburg 1683–1697*

No 38 *Wars and Soldiers in the Early Reign of Louis XIV: Volume 1 - The Army of the United Provinces of the Netherlands, 1660–1687*

No 39 *In The Emperor's Service: Wallenstein's Army, 1625–1634*

No 40 *Charles XI's War: The Scanian War Between Sweden and Denmark, 1675–1679*

No 41 *The Armies and Wars of The Sun King 1643–1715: Volume 1: The Guard of Louis XIV*

No 42 *The Armies Of Philip IV Of Spain 1621–1665: The Fight For European Supremacy*

No 43 *Marlborough's Other Army: The British Army and the Campaigns of the First Peninsular War, 1702–1712*

No 44 *The Last Spanish Armada: Britain And The War Of The Quadruple Alliance, 1718–1720*

No 45 *Essential Agony: The Battle of Dunbar 1650*

No 46 *The Campaigns of Sir William Waller*

No 47 *Wars and Soldiers in the Early Reign of Louis XIV: Volume 2 - The Imperial Army, 1660–1689*

No 48 *The Saxon Mars and His Force: The Saxon Army During The Reign Of John George III 1680–1691*

No 49 *The King's Irish: The Royalist Anglo-Irish Foot of the English Civil War*

No 50 *The Armies and Wars of the Sun King 1643-1715: Volume 2: The Infantry of Louis XIV*

No 51 *More Like Lions Than Men: Sir William Brereton and the Cheshire Army of Parliament, 1642–46*

No 52 *I Am Minded to Rise: The Clothing, Weapons and Accoutrements of the Jacobites from 1689 to 1719*

No 53 *The Perfection of Military Discipline: The Plug Bayonet and the English Army 1660–1705*

No 54 *The Lion From the North: The Swedish Army During the Thirty Years War: Volume 1, 1618–1632*

No 55 *Wars and Soldiers in the Early Reign of Louis XIV: Volume 3 - The Armies of the Ottoman Empire 1645–1718*

No 56 *St. Ruth's Fatal Gamble: The Battle of Aughrim 1691 and the Fall Of Jacobite Ireland*

No 57 *Fighting for Liberty: Argyll & Monmouth's Military Campaigns against the Government of King James, 1685*

No 58 *The Armies and Wars of the Sun King 1643–1715: Volume 3: The Cavalry of Louis XIV*

No 59 *The Lion From the North: The Swedish Army During the Thirty Years War: Volume 2, 1632–1648*

No 60 *By Defeating My Enemies: Charles XII of Sweden and the Great Northern War 1682–1721*

No 61 *Despite Destruction, Misery and Privations..: The Polish Army in Prussia during the war against Sweden 1626–1629*

No 62 *The Armies of Sir Ralph Hopton: The Royalist Armies of the West 1642–46*

No 63 *Italy, Piedmont, and the War of the Spanish Succession 1701–1712*

No 64 *'Cannon played from the great fort': Sieges in the Severn Valley during the English Civil War 1642–1646*

No 65 *Carl Gustav Armfelt and the Struggle for Finland During the Great Northern War*

No 66 *In the Midst of the Kingdom: The Royalist War Effort in the North Midlands 1642–1646*

No 67 *The Anglo-Spanish War 1655–1660: Volume 1: The War in the West Indies*

No 68 *For a Parliament Freely Chosen: The Rebellion of Sir George Booth, 1659*

No 69 *The Bavarian Army During the Thirty Years War 1618–1648: The Backbone of the Catholic League (revised second edition)*

No 70 *The Armies and Wars of the Sun King 1643–1715: Volume 4: The War of the Spanish Succession, Artillery, Engineers and Militias*

No 71 *No Armour But Courage: Colonel Sir George Lisle, 1615–1648 (Paperback reprint)*

No 72 *The New Knights: The Development of Cavalry in Western Europe, 1562–1700*

No 73 *Cavalier Capital: Oxford in the English Civil War 1642–1646 (Paperback reprint)*

No 74 *The Anglo-Spanish War 1655–1660: Volume 2: War in Jamaica*

No 75 *The Perfect Militia: The Stuart Trained Bands of England and Wales 1603–1642*

No 76 *Wars and Soldiers in the Early Reign of Louis XIV: Volume 4 - The Armies of Spain 1659–1688*

No 77 *The Battle of Nördlingen 1634: The Bloody Fight Between Tercios and Brigades*

No 78 *Wars and Soldiers in the Early Reign of Louis XIV: Volume 5 - The Portuguese Army 1659–1690*

No 79 *We Came, We Saw, God Conquered: The Polish-Lithuanian Commonwealth's military effort in the relief of Vienna, 1683*

No 80 *Charles X's Wars: Volume 1 - Armies of the Swedish Deluge, 1655–1660*

No 81 *Cromwell's Buffoon: The Life and Career of the Regicide, Thomas Pride (Paperback reprint)*

No 82 *The Colonial Ironsides: English Expeditions under the Commonwealth and Protectorate, 1650–1660*

No 83 *The English Garrison of Tangier: Charles II's Colonial Venture in the Mediterranean, 1661–1684*

No 84 *The Second Battle of Preston, 1715: The Last Battle on English Soil*

No 85 *To Settle the Crown: Waging Civil War in Shropshire, 1642–1648 (Paperback reprint)*

No 86 *A Very Gallant Gentleman: Colonel Francis Thornhagh (1617–1648) and the Nottinghamshire Horse*

No 87 *Charles X's Wars: Volume 2 – The Wars in the East, 1655–1657*

No 88 *The Shōgun's Soldiers: The Daily Life of Samurai and Soldiers in Edo Period Japan, 1603–1721 Volume 1*

No 89 *Campaigns of the Eastern Association: The Rise of Oliver Cromwell, 1642–1645*

No 90 *The Army of Occupation in Ireland 1603–42: Defending the Protestant Hegemony*

No 91 *The Armies and Wars of the Sun King 1643–1715: Volume 5: Buccaneers and Soldiers in the Americas*

No 92 *New Worlds, Old Wars: The Anglo-American Indian Wars 1607–1678*

No 93 *Against the Deluge: Polish and Lithuanian Armies During the War Against Sweden 1655–1660*

No 94 *The Battle of Rocroi: The Battle, the Myth and the Success of Propaganda*

No 95 *The Shōgun's Soldiers: The Daily Life of Samurai and Soldiers in Edo Period Japan, 1603–1721 Volume 2*

No 96 *Science of Arms: the Art of War in the Century of the Soldier 1672–1699: Volume 1: Preparation for War and the Infantry*

No 97 *Charles X's Wars: Volume 3 – The Danish Wars 1657–1660*

No 98 *Wars and Soldiers in the Early Reign of Louis XIV: Volume 6 - Armies of the Italian States 1660–1690 Part 1*

No 99 *Dragoons and Dragoon Operations in the British Civil Wars, 1638–1653*

No 100 *Wars and Soldiers in the Early Reign of Louis XIV: Volume 6 - Armies of the Italian States 1660–1690 Part 2*

No 101 *1648 and All That: The Scottish Invasions of England, 1648 and 1651: Proceedings of the 2022 Helion and Company 'Century of the Soldier' Conference*

No 102 *John Hampden and the Battle of Chalgrove: The Political and Military Life of Hampden and his Legacy*

No 103 *The City Horse: London's militia cavalry during the English Civil War, 1642–1660*

No 104 *The Battle of Lützen 1632: A Reassessment*

No 105 *Monmouth's First Rebellion: The Later Covenanter Risings, 1660–1685*

No 106 *Raw Generals and Green Soldiers: Catholic Armies in Ireland 1641–1643 Polish, Lithuanian and Cossack armies versus the might of the Ottoman Empire*

No 108 *Soldiers and Civilians, Transport and Provisions: Early Modern Military Logistics and Supply Systems During The British Civil Wars, 1638-1653*

No 109 *Batter their walls, gates and Forts: The Proceedings of the 2022 English Civil War Fortress Symposium*

No 110 *The Town Well Fortified: The Fortresses of the Civil Wars in Britain, 1639-1660*

No 111 *Crucible of the Jacobite '15: The Battle of Sheriffmuir 1715*

No 112 *Charles XII's Karoliners Volume 2 - The Swedish Cavalry of the Great Northern War 1700-1721*

No 113 *Wars and Soldiers in the Early Reign of Louis XIV: Volume 7 - Armies of the German States 1655–1690 Part 1*

No 114 *The Army of Transylvania 1613-1690: War and military organization from the 'golden age' of the Principality to the Habsburg conquest*

SERIES SPECIALS:

No 1 *Charles XII's Karoliners: Volume 1: The Swedish Infantry & Artillery of the Great Northern War 1700–1721*

For the complete range of Century of the Soldier titles please go to
www.helion.co.uk/series/century-of-the-soldier-1618-1721.php